D1253677

The WRECKING *of the*
EIGHTEENTH AMENDMENT

The WRECKING *of the* EIGHTEENTH AMENDMENT

by
ERNEST GORDON

THE ALCOHOL INFORMATION PRESS
FRANCESTOWN, NEW HAMPSHIRE

CONTENTS

INTRODUCTION

The first two years of National Prohibition, together with the preceding two of near-Prohibition, vindicated it as the ideal method of treating social alcoholism. It was as when a door opens from a dark room and then closes. It has at least revealed the difference between darkness and light. Prof. Henry W. Farnam of Yale wrote of those early years, "We see that Prohibition has produced just the kind of effect that was desired. It would be difficult to find in all the history of social legislation a case where the effect of a law can be traced so quickly and so accurately. For we find uniformly, in spite of the many conflicting forces which affect all laws, that . . . Prohibition, when carried out in good faith . . . is capable of diminishing with a speed which would have seemed impossible twenty years ago, deaths from alcoholism, drunkenness, poverty due to liquor, and much crime" (1).

He gave us the evidence from his own state. Now every one of the five representatives from Connecticut in Congress voted against the Eighteenth Amendment and indeed the state never ratified it. A probable majority of its population was of recent foreign extraction, the law enforcement system inadequate, the press hopelessly prejudiced. Yet these brilliant results followed notwithstanding, which disposes of the theory that Prohibition won't work "until public opinion is educated up to it."

The number of prisoners in Connecticut jails charged with drunkenness fell from 7,314 in 1917 to 943 in 1920; arrests for assault and breach of peace, to less than one third. Jail commitments for vagrancy all but ceased. "The old-time hobo has nearly disappeared from our state. Seven eighths of them are leading orderly lives." Commitments for alcohol insanity in 1920 were less than one third the number of 1917; the death rate from alcoholism and cirrhosis, less than one half. Accidental deaths which, in 1917, were 10.7 to the 10,000, in 1920 were but 7.3, the automobile death rate falling 40%. Prof. Farnam's statistician tells us that almost no progress was made in combating tuberculosis in the last ten years before Prohibition. In 1917 the death rate in Connecticut was 15.3 per 10,000; but in 1921, 9.6 and in 1929, 6.3. Deaths from pneumonia, to which alcoholists are peculiarly liable, fell one half. The general death rate of the state during the last years of license showed no appreciable change. After Prohibition it maintained a level 25% lower (2).

"THE NOBLER MODES OF LIFE"

President Charles W. Eliot of Harvard had been a life-long opponent of Prohibition but the evidence was too strong to be questioned. To the Massachusetts legislature he wrote:

"Evidence has accumulated on every hand that Prohibition has promoted public health, public happiness and industrial efficiency. This evidence comes from manufacturers, physicians, nurses of all sorts (school, factory, hospital and district), and from social workers of many races and religions, laboring daily in a great variety of fields. This testimony also demonstrates beyond a doubt that Prohibition is actually sapping the terrible forces of disease, poverty, crime and vice. These results are obtained in spite of the imperfect enforcement, in some communities, of the Eighteenth Amendment to the Federal Constitution. . . . Let Massachusetts at once take her whole share in putting into execution these prohibitory measures which are sure to promote public health, public happiness, and industrial efficiency throughout the country, and to eliminate the chief causes of poverty, crime, and misery among our people" (3) (A).

MASSACHUSETTS EVIDENCE

A similar immediateness of improvement was observable in Massachusetts as in Connecticut.

The average yearly arrests for drunkenness in Boston in the seven wet years 1912–18 was 59,308; in the two first dry years 1920–21, 26,393. The commitments for drunkenness to the House of Correction, Deer Island, averaged in 1912–18, 4,281; in 1920–21, 1,023. The decrease of drunkenness among women was especially marked,—523 committed in 1916, one in 1920, and in 1921, *none*.

The Massachusetts prison population, which averaged in the seven wet years, 1912–18, 5,839, in the first two dry years sank to 2,819, a clean drop of 52%. In the Wayfarers' Lodge, the municipal lodging house of Boston, during the seven wet years 1912–18, the average yearly number of lodgers was 11,721; in 1920–21, 4,317. Mr. Kelso of the State Farm, "one of the most populous prison farms for drunkards and vagrants to be found in the United States," declared that "since the coming of Prohibition the inmate population has not afforded enough labor to keep the farm tilled and the state is already considering the wisdom of converting the immense plant to other uses."

The Family Welfare Society of Boston saw intemperance as a factor in poor relief fall from 27% in 1917 to 2.5% in 1920–21. The Boston Provident Association found that of the 7,775 dependent families aided within a period of eight years up to 1917, 1,400 showed intemperance as a factor. This was 18% of all. In 1920–21 the percentage had fallen to 2%.

The proportion of cases that were handled by the Massachusetts Society for the Prevention of Cruelty to Children, into which intemperance entered, dropped from 47.7% in 1916 to 16.8% in 1921. Mr. Carstens, the head of the Child Welfare League of America, said that the decrease of neglected children, removed through court action from drunken parents, was so marked that in certain cities drunkenness had ceased to be a factor (4).

THE AXE AT THE ROOT

"Thousands are hacking at the branches of evil to one who is striking at the root." This saying of Thoreau now had its application. The drink traffic was discovered to be a veritable taproot of social evils. When it was cut out these evils began to wither and lose strength. The U. S. Statistical Abstract (1926, p. 71) gives this picture of the shrinkage of the more vulgar forms of crime associated with alcohol.

Table I	Per 100,000	
	1910	1923
Prisoners in all penal institutions	121.2	99.7
Commitments for drunkenness	185.9	83.1
for disorderly conduct	99.9	48.5
for vagrancy	54	25.5
Paupers admitted to almshouses	91.5	71.5

Of the decline in vagabondage and drunken disorder one gets a good picture in Commander Evangeline Booth's testimony before the House Judiciary Hearings of Feb. 1930 (p. 891).

"In the pre-Prohibition raids of the Salvation Army on New York saloons a thousand wretched, ill-smelling drunks would be brought by a fleet of autobuses to some central hall on Thanksgiving Day and fed. On the first Thanksgiving Day after Prohibition they made another raid of the same sort.

"Our best endeavor produced only 400 men and these, although poor, were sober and entirely dissimilar to the type that, on the preceding Thanksgiving Day, had packed our hall. You could not assemble today at any place in New York a crowd of upward 1,000 men of the described type. The vast army of broken and debased men have emerged into a cleaner and nobler type" (B).

Also the army of broken and debased women. "The rapid decrease of prostitution since the Amendment" was commented on by the National Committee of Social Workers studying Prohibition. "Report after report says the disorderly houses are gone and there is practically no solicitation on the streets." "Is this due to Prohibition?" asks Mrs. Bruère. "Probably only in part, although some of the reports insist that it is the sole reason" (5) (C).

Miss Jane Addams wrote of "those halcyon days of the early Prohibition period. . . . During those first two years, beginning with 1919, we were all elated by the marked decrease in disorderly conduct. A large section of the Chicago House of Correction was closed; also the so-called tremens ward of the county hospital" (6).

VICTORIES NO LESS RENOWNED THAN WAR

Of the country at large Dr. Horatio M. Pollock, statistician for the N. Y. State Hospital Commission, wrote: "In its mental disease record, in its crime record, in its drunkenness record, the year 1920 stands without an equal in the recent history of this country" (7). Dr. Haven Emerson of Columbia University confirms this: "Wherever the records are obtained for the first admissions for alcoholic psychoses or for all admissions for alcoholic psychoses to mental hospitals, the evidence is very definite that in 1919, 1920, and in 1921 a lower level was reached than had ever occurred before" (8). Dr. Emerson shows how the curve struck bottom in New York City for deaths from nephritis and Bright's disease and pneumonia. For tuberculosis the death rate from 1911 to 1917 was constant. "Then it fell," he adds, "in the seven years of Prohibition (1920–26) at a faster rate than at any previous period in our history. This was the first practical evidence we have ever had of the astounding effect on the mortality of the country of making alcohol relatively inaccessible" (9).

In regard to the reaction on poverty there is no end of testimony. Judge Gary, President of the U. S. Steel Corporation, said of the 300,000 employees of that corporation: "In the last two or three years the improved conditions among these people is one of the most remarkable chapters ever written in the history of civilization." And Prof. Paul Douglas, foremost student of changes in American wage levels, after calling attention to the unprecedented increase in hourly real wages, continued: "It may not be without significance that the increase in real wages on any appreciable scale first began in 1917 when the Prohibition laws of the various states and the wartime restrictions of the national government greatly reduced the amount of liquor sold. The rise of real wages was particularly marked during the years 1919–1923 when the enforcement of the prohibitory amendment was probably more effective than immediately thereafter" (10). The years 1921–22 were years of sharp depression yet in a study of Prohibition in New Jersey the Hon. George S. Hobart reported: "At the end of 1922 there were thirty more savings banks and trust companies than at the end of 1917; 431 more building and loan associations; 357,572 more building and loan association members; 40,917 more depositors in savings banks; and an increase in five years of 92.5% in deposits, viz. $655,569,944" (11). It was this sort of thing under his very eyes that made the first citizen of New Jersey, the inventor Thomas A. Edison, say: "I feel that Prohibition is the greatest experiment yet made to benefit man" (12).

The old Shakespearean tag runs,

"to climb steep hills
Requires slow pace at first"

but it is amazing the pace that can be made with this policy providing conditions are reasonably favorable.

ENEMY TESTIMONY

Even those whose wet testimony was later most virulent recognized the success of early Prohibition. "Incredible as it may seem," wrote Mr. Elmer Davis, "there was a time when Prohibition really prohibited even in New York. For a year or two it was pretty generally observed and observed curiously enough because it did not occur to most people that it was possible to do anything else" (13). Mr. J. J. Forrester, consultant of the Wickersham Commission, says the same: "Paradoxically the first two or three years of National Prohibition witnessed a far greater degree of observance than has since been obtained. Enforcement was comparatively easy. People generally obeyed the law" (14). So Miss Ida Tarbell: "In the last year I have travelled some thousands of miles in this country, journeys which took me into at least fifteen different states. One sees liquor so rarely that you forget there is such a thing" (15). M. André Siegfried, scornful as he was concerning the law, had to acknowledge that "one can go through whole regions without seeing any liquor or meeting a single drunkard. The great mass of the people are undoubtedly benefiting in health, standard of living, working efficiency, and in increased wages" (16). "Prohibition is perhaps the most wonderful fact in the wonderful times in which we live," was the 1920 comment of the London *Daily Chronicle* (17) (D).

THE ZERO HOUR OF OPPOSITION

The saloon was fresh in memory and people were generally satisfied with the great change. The brewers had ever been the driving force on the anti-Prohibition side and the brewers had just received a terrific castigation from the Overman Senatorial Committee which had made public their correspondence and had pulled their crooked leaders out into daylight. This also probably tended to keep wet politicians quiescent for the time being. They well knew that the government had held back correspondence which implicated them also. Both elements had been driven to cover. Enforcement was in the hands of Mr. Carter Glass of the Treasury and Mr. Roper of the Internal Revenue, upright men in sympathy with the law. The people trusted the national government for honest enforcement. The brewers had generally abandoned hope of a reaction.

Andrew W. Mellon had hardly risen above the horizon. Few indeed outside of his home town, Pittsburgh, knew of this retiring, urbane, ruthless, Machiavellian master of high finance.

Mr. Merz has pointed out (18) how insignificant the opposition was at the time,—no petitions against the Amendment, no demonstrations of hostility, the press indifferent, no discussion of the matter in 1918 when Mr. A. E. Smith was running for governor of New York. In the first six months of 1920 Prohibition was referred to only six times, even briefly, in the two houses of Congress. The matter was considered settled. There is no doubt, for example, that Prohibition was at the bottom of the long deadlock in the Democratic Convention of 1924. The wet urban states were mobilized behind Gov. Smith against the dry South and West behind Mr. McAdoo. But the curious thing is that although this must have been well known it was not a matter of convention debate. Smith, Ritchie, and Edwards, violent wets, were present,—and silent. They did not care to risk offending the dry sentiment of the country by anti-Prohibition utterances. Nor was it different in the Republican convention. Dr. Nicholas M. Butler sat through the entire three days and never felt impelled to broach the matter. The exception was Mr. John W. Davis, the Democratic candidate from Wall Street, who indiscreetly, on billboard advertising, announced, "I stand for personal liberty" and "I stand against unlawful search and seizure." He has never been heard of since politically (19).

So strong was Prohibition sentiment even in 1924, three years after the wreckers of the Harding administration had been in control. Even the Association Against the Prohibition Amendment stated in its articles of incorporation, "It shall be the purpose of the society to favor and encourage obedience to the 18th Amendment and to all laws passed to carry into effect its provisions" (House Judiciary Hearings, Feb. 1930, p. 3913). This was not so, yet they felt it necessary so to affirm.

GOVERNOR PINCHOT'S BLUNT CHARGE

What was it that brought the revulsion of sentiment in later years? No man knows more about what Prohibition had to face in the way of underhanded treachery than Gov. Pinchot of Pennsylvania. Pennsylvania was the Penrose-Mellon state and in this state nullification was peculiarly flagrant until Mr. Pinchot took it in hand. In an address before Pennsylvania State College (Oct. 27, 1933) he said:

"In spite of the successful efforts which have been made to wreck it, Prohibition has not been a failure as its enemies claim. Both morally and economically Prohibition has been a success. Nothing like the success it would have been if it had been given something resembling a fair trial, but still a success.

"Moreover, I am equally convinced that *the violation of the 18th Amendment and the racketeering in liquor were both deliberately encouraged by the controlling Federal authorities* and by many minor authorities. They were encouraged for the purpose, which has been successfully accomplished, of breaking down the national confidence in Prohibition and of bringing liquor back.

"When the 18th Amendment went into effect there was immediate compliance with it on the part of the liquor interests. Years of honest enforcement of the excise law by the Federal Government had taught them to expect honest enforcement of the Prohibition law. They began by respecting it. But almost at once *they learned that the authorities at Washington did not respect it themselves and had no intention of enforcing respect from others.*

"The Treasury Department had at its command the highly-trained, highly-efficient, and thoroughly reliable corps of special agents which had made for itself so enviable a record in enforcing excise law. Authorities who intended to enforce the law would have retained it and would have been thankful for the chance. Instead of that, these men with their record, their reputation, and their experience, were dismissed. *That in itself was notice to every law-breaker that he was expected to break the law.*

"In the place of the invaluable corps of special agents the Treasury Department began installing the scum of the political underworld,—men who were totally incapable of enforcing any law, even if they had not been selected, as they were, for the express purpose of nullifying this one. In state after state the Federal Administrator of the Volstead Act was guilty of breaking the law he was appointed to enforce. In Pennsylvania incompetent after incompetent followed crook after crook. . . . These political nominees were all appointed for . . . the discrediting of the 18th Amendment by wet officials in Washington, many or most of them habitual violators of the law they were ostensibly appointed to enforce."

Let us see what evidence there is to support this charge.

REFERENCES TO CHAPTER I NOT IN THE TEXT

1. H. W. Farnam, "The Law of the Land and Our Moral Frontier" and "After Prohibition."
2. "Prohibition in Connecticut" by Ralph H. White.
3. From a letter sent Feb. 17, 1922, to Hearings of the Massachusetts Legislature.
4. Stoddard and Woods, "Wet and Dry Years in a Decade of Prohibition" and Hearings, Senate Judiciary Committee, April 1926, pages 921–923.
5. Bruère, "Does Prohibition Work?" page 301.
6. The Survey, October 1, 1929.
7. "Alcohol and Man," page 371.
8. Survey Graphic, December 1928, page 330.
9. Senate Judiciary Committee Hearings, April 1926, pages 787, 789, 792 and Survey Graphic, December 1928, page 292.
10. Quoted by H. F. Miller, "An Economist Looks at Prohibition," October 1930 and verified by letter from Professor Douglas.
11. Annals of the American Academy of Political and Social Science, September 1923.
12. National Prohibition Amendment Hearings, February 1930, page 568.
13. New York Tribune, December 17, 1933 (VIII), page 4.
14. Current History, No. 33, page 808.
15. Collier's, April 21, 1923.
16. Quoted in Clip Sheet of Methodist Board of Temperance, February 14, 1920.
17. André Siegfried, "America Comes of Age," page 89.
18. Charles Merz, "The Dry Decade," page 36.
19. Raymond Robins, "Prohibition. Why? How? Whither?"

NOTES TO CHAPTER I

A. Dr. Henry Smith Williams, after Prohibition had been destroyed, said (1937): "There were some of us who were active advocates of temperance in the old days but who could not persuade ourselves that Prohibition was, or could be, a means to the solution of the alcohol question (and whose open opposition to the Prohibition movement was vehemently criticized), who nevertheless became convinced in watching the events in the Prohibition period that the noble experiment (for such it truly was, whatever else) was working better than we had ever believed it could work" ("Drugs Against Men," Henry Smith Williams, M. D.).

B. After Repeal these derelicts of course reappeared. Mr. H. H. Curran, the leading executive for the Du Ponts' Association Against the Prohibition Amendment, is now a city magistrate in New York. In the Readers' Digest, Jan. 1940, he describes "the usual midnight platoon of bums from the Bowery," coming before his court. "Unshaved, dirty, drunken, down and out,—they went on their way to jail like a shadow parade of the hulks of sunken ships. Their collective smell fouled the air."

C. Dr. Parran does not mention Prohibition as the redemptive factor but he says: "Commercial prostitution did not again appear on the scale of big business until about the beginning of the depression." "Shadow on the Land," p. 215.

D.   Mr. Hearst's editor, Arthur Brisbane, was wet in all his associations but he knew, what everybody knows, that drink is a nuisance and a scourge.   Of Prohibition he wrote: "One hundred percent efficiency has been added at one stroke to the people of America, half of the misery of half of the people has been abolished.   Three hundred thousand traps have been closed into which a considerable portion of the youth of the country fell every year.   The suppression of the drink traffic is an expression of the highest morality upon which we are entering" (Carlson's "Brisbane," p. 250).

CHAPTER II

THE LAW'S BETRAYAL

Ill-enforcement was due in part to the promoters of the law. A provision had been written into the Volstead Act exempting positions under it from civil service classification. The excuse was that this concession to politicians in Congress was necessary in order to secure its passage. But no congressional group would have long dared to nullify the 18th Amendment by refusing to pass an enabling act. Mr. William Dudley Foulke of the National Civil Service Reform League ought not to have been able to say to the National Anti-Saloon League:

"If you could not get your bill through except by excluding appointments from the classified service, you could at least have declared that you were not cooperating with that part of the bill and did not approve it. Many years have passed since that time. . . . We have repeatedly sent our representatives to confer with enforcement officers and have drafted a bill providing for the classification and re-examination of all persons in this branch of the service, yet you have never lifted a finger to stay the abuses you created" (1).

Wayne Wheeler wrote later: "We have recently appealed to the President to put Prohibition agents under Civil Service by executive order" (2). But this neither Harding nor Coolidge did, although both must have known that such a step was essential to effective enforcement.

"THE VILLAINS MARCH WIDE BETWIXT THE LEGS AS
IF THEY HAD GYVES ON: FOR INDEED I HAD MOST
OF THEM OUT OF PRISON."

It was not long before the chickens came home to roost. Mrs. Willebrandt wrote that appointment of Prohibition agents was, until 1926, made as a result of political endorsement. "The frequent reward for polling precincts, getting out the votes on election days, marking and stealing ballots, slugging the opposition poll-watchers and generally being useful in operating the machin-

(11)

ery of politics, was appointment as a Prohibition Agent" (3). As late as March 1929, according to official report, there were still more than 600 Prohibition agents, inspectors, investigators, and chemists holding so-called temporary appointments without Civil Service examination. This was practically one third of the total of Prohibition employees.

In 1926 Congress finally passed the necessary civil-service legislation but, characteristically enough, neglected to make the appropriation needed to put it into effect. Wet senators, headed by Senator Bruce who stood very near to Mr. Mellon, fought this legislation, exhausting every parliamentary resource to prevent its coming to a vote. It was finally clotured and passed March 2, 1927. (The Senate had invoked cloture only four times in its history.) Not until 1930, ten years after the Volstead Act became law, was the process of placing the entire personnel of the Bureau of Prohibition in the classified civil service completed (4).

Major Chester P. Mills estimated that three-fourths of the 2,500 dry agents were of inferior type and declared that "the bosses never relaxed their interest in a henchman whether he was found guilty of negligence or of outright crookedness" (5). On Jan. 1, 1926, General L. C. Andrews reported that 875 members of his force had been discharged for malfeasance in office. This represented 25% of all. The offences were extortion, conspiracy, drunkenness, falsification of accounts, insubordination, and the like (6).

All of which proves, not the impracticability of Prohibition, but the enormous importance of civil service safeguards. To quote Mrs. Willebrandt once more, "The whole question of Prohibition enforcement resolves itself into one of getting the right persons in the right places."

PART I

THE OHIO GANG AND NULLIFICATION

Such was the situation in the lower ranges of the enforcement hierarchy. What was the situation at the top?

"YOUR WORDS AND PERFORMANCES ARE NO KIN"

President Harding was by nature a typical politician, easygoing, friendly, without sharply defined principles. When the tide went out he drifted out; when it crept in he crept in with it.

Fox, the Secretary of the U. S. Brewers' Association, reported a confidential agent as saying: "Mr. Warren G. Harding who is running for the United States Senate . . . is a strong license advocate and will vote and work against National Prohibition in case he is elected" (7). That was in 1914. Six years later the situation had changed and Harding with it. There was nothing reprehensible in this. I have no doubt he really meant it when he wrote:

"In every community men and women have had an opportunity now to know what Prohibition means. They know that debts are more promptly paid, that men take home their wages once wasted, that families are better clothed and fed, and (that) more money finds its way into the savings banks. . . . *In another generation I believe that liquor will have disappeared not only from our politics but from our memories"* (8).

It would have seemed that one who could thus pay tribute to the law would have shown personal respect for its observance. Not so! Mrs. Nicholas Longworth described as "shocking the way Harding disregarded the Constitution he was sworn to uphold" and gave an unedifying picture of the cocktailing which took place in the upper regions of the White House, "the study filled with cronies, Daugherty, Jess Smith, Alec Moore, and others, the air heavy with tobacco-smoke, trays containing every imaginable brand of whisky, cards, and poker chips" ("Crowded Hours," p. 324). This was the *milieu* of the Ohio gang and President Harding was at home in it. Yet in his message to Congress, Dec. 8, 1922, he could say: "There is a demand for every living being in the United States to respect and abide by the laws of the Republic. Let men who are rending the moral fibre of the Republic through easy contempt of the Prohibition law . . . remember that they set an example and breed contempt for law which will ultimately destroy the Republic."

THE ATTORNEY GENERAL'S ALTER EGO

In the center of President Harding's entourage was Jess Smith, a political roustabout and intimate of Attorney General Daugherty. Indeed the two lived together in the McLean house on H Street (9). It was understood that Smith had access to all the files of the Department of Justice and he was popularly supposed to be next in influence to the Attorney General, although not in government service. Smith, with Mannington, another of Daugherty's friends, was actively engaged in securing permits by which whisky in bond could be released "for medical purposes," and marketed by bootleggers. The case of George Remus is typical. This "bootlegger king of the Middle West" was finally caught in the government toils and in his extremity was defended by James M. Linton of Columbus, *Special Assistant Attorney General to Mr. Daugherty* (10). In the evidence it came out that Remus had had various rendezvous with Jess Smith in order to get permits. Regarding this the following dialogue spun itself out in the droning Senate Committee room.

REMUS AND BRER DAUGHERTY

Senator Wheeler. You had no other purpose for meeting Jess Smith?

Remus. Other than to do what he could from the viewpoint of holding a person harmless in the event of legal entanglements.

Wheeler. Exactly. So that you wanted him to hold you harmless in the event of any prosecutions (11)?

Remus. Yes. . . . He was pretty close to the Attorney-General. He said that for a consideration he would obtain permits if I would pay so much per case.

Wheeler. What did he say with reference to your being indicted in these matters or prosecuted?

Remus. That there never would be a conviction: maybe a prosecution but no ultimate conviction; that no one would have to go to the penitentiary.

Wheeler. How much did you pay (Jess Smith) in the aggregate?

Remus. Oh, between $250,000 and $300,000.

Wheeler. And that money was paid Jess Smith for protection, was it not?

Remus. Yes.

Wheeler. Do you know approximately how much you paid at Indianapolis?

Remus. Oh, possibly about $30,000.

Wheeler. Now you met him at this hotel. Who, if anybody, did you meet with him there? Anybody?

Remus. No one but him. I subsequently saw him again at the Union Station.

Wheeler.   And who was with him at the Union Station?

Remus.   Attorney-General Daugherty.

Wheeler.   After you were indicted did you have any conversa-
           tion with Jess Smith?

Remus.   I met him a number of times at the Commodore Hotel
           and the Plaza.

Wheeler.   And did you discuss with him anything with reference
           to your indictment?

Remus.   Yes. The Department of Justice would put up a
           vigorous battle but ultimately I would never see the
           penitentiary.

Smith told Remus after his conviction that he would not
have to serve a day. "He would get a suspension of sentence
through his (Smith's) influence with the Attorney-General (12).
The Attorney-General had assured him of that."

Remus.   Mr. James Clarke, the former district-attorney of Cin-
           cinnati, told me after my conviction that he had talked
           with the Attorney-General, at which time the Attorney-
           General had told him that he had to prosecute my case
           as there was some talk in Columbus that he (Daugh-
           erty) was one of my partners (13).

Senator Jones.   Did he tell you what the Attorney-General
           said (14)?

Remus.   He said the General would do everything he could in
           the premises.

A SEED OF EVIL-DOERS

Captain Scaife, a former special agent of the Department of
Justice, wrote a letter to Attorney-General Daugherty about this
time in which he said, "So far as the Department of Justice is concerned, it no longer functions except in the capacity of first-aid to
crooks" (15). The testimony taken by the Brookhart Committee
revealed a strange interlocking of bootleggers, politicians and government officials. Thus C. H. Kerns, convicted of conspiracy to
violate the Prohibition law, May 1922, was paroled out by the
Attorney-General on Feb. 26, 1924. His attorney was Mr. Todd,
the Attorney-General's law partner in Ohio, whom Kerns paid
$6,000 a year for services (16).

Senator Wheeler. Now the reason you employed Mr. Todd was because you thought he would have influence with the Attorney-General at Washington?

Kerns. Most certainly.

The clerk of the Ohio Senate, Mr. Haley, another intimate of the Attorney-General (17), was, with his partner Barnett, in close contact with Jess Smith.

Kerns. Mr. Barnett said that they were able to do business in securing permits in Ohio, that they had a (Prohibition) director appointed by their influence there named Russell. The Washington cooperation came through Mannington.

Wheeler. Now what did he say to you about Haley being Daugherty's right-hand man in Ohio politics?

Kerns. Well, that was mentioned by him and he said that they could absolutely guarantee that they could get the permit. He left the unmistakable inference that Mr. Russell, the director-general (of Prohibition), had been bought and paid for (abridged).

Kerns had 500 bbls. of whisky in the Hayner Distillery, Troy, O., which he wanted to sell. Abe Ungerleider was ready to buy, was in a position to get the permits (for withdrawal) in Washington; had influence, explaining that $50,000 had been contributed to the Republican campaign fund of 1920 (18) (A).

Wheeler. He told you that there was a tacit understanding that if he would contribute $50,000 he would be permitted to get the money back through whisky interests?

Kerns. That is correct.

ISRAEL IN EXILE

As an illustration of the general entanglement spoken of I may say here that Ungerleider's partner, Grossberg, had been indicted and had fled to Canada. His counsel, while he was a fugitive from justice, was Stuart R. Bolin, a special prosecutor of the Department of Justice under Attorney-General Daugherty (19). It is not surprising, then, that Grossberg "successfully resisted the proceedings." There were three Ungerleiders, Abe, Jake, and Sam, who before Prohibition ran "The Acorn" on the Ohio-West Virginia frontier, with its forty bartenders, reported to be the largest saloon in the world. Now they sold gin to bootleggers all over Ohio through the Columbus Physicians' and Druggists' Supply Co. (20).

Sen. Wheeler. Ungerleider is closely associated with Harry S. Daugherty the Attorney General?

Kerns.   It is so reported throughout the State of Ohio.

Sen. Brookhart. Now what is there about his (Remus') case that makes you think there was collusion between the Treasury Department and the Department of Justice (22)?

Kerns.   Well, he purchased . . . six or nine distilleries and sold openly to the bootleg trade. And at that time he had not been prosecuted.

Brookhart. How long did he keep that up?

Kerns.   About two years and a half.

Wheeler.   He kept it up until it got to be such an open and notorious thing down there that they had to force a prosecution. Isn't that correct?

Kerns.   Yes, that is correct. It is openly said he had on his payroll different officials who had charge of the Prohibition officials.

Wheeler.   Is it not a well-known fact that . . . unless the bootleggers bought from Remus they would be indicted?

Kerns.   Yes, sir.

Wheeler.   And if they bought from him they would not be indicted?

Kerns.   Yes, they were free from molestation if they dealt with him.

Sen. Chamberlain. Now who was giving him that immunity? Was it the Department of Justice or some investigating agency of the Prohibition Unit (i.e. in the Treasury) (23)?

Kerns.   *I think the agencies you speak of worked more or less in unison.*

DIVISION OF SPOILS

Kerns named Clem Herves, secretary to Remus, as the source of his information. Another witness was cross-examined by Senator Wheeler who asked:

Did he (Jess Smith) not tell you that he had made a

> division with the Attorney-General of the United States
> and the then Attorney-General would not return his
> part of it?
> He did? Everybody knew that Mannington and Jess
> Smith were working directly with the Attorney-General
> on the sale of the permits in New York City . . .
> everybody inside the whisky ring (24).

The relations between party funds and bootlegging comes
out again on pp. 2167–71 of the Brookhart Report. Witness
Kraffmiller had collected $12,000 to $15,000 campaign funds for
the Harding campaign, turning the money over to Mannington,
Daugherty's co-worker. When Kraffmiller went to Washington
to receive his reward he was able to secure a liquor permit for the
General Drug Co. of Chicago, for which $20,000 was paid him.
One third of this he retained; the other two thirds went to Mannington (A).

Wheeler.   You did know that Mr. Mannington had files from
the Department of Justice in his house there? (The
green house on K street.)

Kraffmiller.   Yes, these were political patronage files.

Wheeler.   And you did know that Mr. Mannington was helping Mr. Daugherty to select people for various offices from Ohio and New York and various places
about the country?

Kraffmiller.   Yes, sir.

Wheeler.   Now you did know that the Prohibition officer in
the state of Ohio was appointed because of the fact
that he was recommended by Mannington?

Kraffmiller.   Yes.

So much for the Department of Justice under President Harding's Attorney-General. Now let us examine the Department of
the Treasury under the Hon. A. W. Mellon during three ad-
ministrations.

PART II

THE GREAT FIRST CAUSE OF NON-ENFORCEMENT
AND HIS LIEUTENANT

"The reason Prohibition has not been successful is that they
have appointed as head of the Treasury and Prohibition Enforce-

ment a man who has been in the whisky business for the last forty years. I refer to Andrew W. Mellon." *Senator Wheeler of Montana.*

"So far as I know none of the friends of Prohibition feel that Secretary Mellon has made a serious attempt to enforce the law." *Senator Harris of Georgia.*

"The supreme power to enforce Prohibition does not believe in Prohibition. If we want Prohibition we must take it out of the hands of this great financier." *Congressman Blanton of Texas.*

Mr. Mellon's acceptance of the Treasuryship was in itself a violation of the law of the United States. That law provides that no one, directly or indirectly concerned or interested in carrying on the business of trade or commerce, or being owner in whole or part of any sea-vessel, shall be appointed to the office of Secretary of the Treasury (Sec. 243 Restrictions upon the Secretary of the Treasury).

Congressman Patman in his impeachment resolution filed a list of corporations owned by Mr. Mellon either wholly or in part. The resources of those corporations totalled $2,342,306,120. And as to shipping it was discovered that he owned, or had interest in, four Norwegian vessels, fourteen tankers, under the Venezuelan flag, and thirteen general cargo vessels of American register. Mr. Mellon was, as Secretary of the Treasury, chairman *ex officio* of the Federal Reserve Board. Now no member of that Board is allowed to hold stock in any bank, banking institution, or trust company. Mellon averred that he had disposed of all his bank stock. He did not say how this was done, but it was intimated by Mr. Patman that the Melbank Corporation was a holding company formed to take over Mellon bank stock. In other words it was as if money were simply transferred from one drawer to another.

In the economic sphere Mr. Mellon was comparable to that super-dinosaur, the *Diplodoccus carnegiei* of the Pittsburgh museum. The minority report of the May 1, 1929 Committee of the Judiciary on the Eligibility of Andrew W. Mellon, said of him: "In the financial world Mr. Mellon has perhaps more at stake in the carrying on of trade or commerce than any one citizen of the United States. He is one of the dominating influences in the business world." Then it added these significant words:

"The President of the United States is about to appoint a

Commission to study the subject (of law enforcement) with a view of bringing about better enforcement of our laws. Is it not true that the ordinary citizen will not have the same respect for law generally if he understands that a plain statute is being violated by those in control of the government itself? . . . The high official, the appointing power, must obey the same law for which he demands obedience of the citizens" (26).

The penalty for violation of this government restriction is a fine of $3,000, removal from office, and *incapacity forever thereafter to hold any office under the United States.* The House Judiciary Committee, it is quite certain, intended to offer a resolution impeaching Mr. Mellon. To avoid this, apparently, he was transferred by President Hoover to the diplomatic service and made Minister to England, a further indignity to the law and sorry commentary on Mr. Hoover's saying: "Law enforcement should begin at the top."

. . . THAT GOOD EARL
ONCE PRESIDENT OF ENGLAND'S COUNCIL AND HER TREASURY,
WHO LIVED IN BOTH UNSTAINED WITH GOLD OR FEE.

Milton

It is necessary to recall something of Mr. Mellon's past if we are to appraise properly his career in the Treasury Department. One of his great industrial holdings was the Standard Steel Car Co. of Hammond, Ind. Now the Hon. Wm. J. Graham of Illinois, Chairman of the Committee on War Frauds, said of this company, "Approximately $2,000,000 was paid to the Standard Steel Co. of Hammond, Ind., without justice or foundation. Civil and criminal proceedings might well be brought in this case" (27). The report of the same committee gives in detail what happened: "This company contracted to build 964 nine and a half inch howitzer carriages that we could use prior to the armistice. The War Department spent in this venture $18,582,426.88. After the Armistice the Ordnance Department had them finish 200 of these carriages. The company placed in the record a statement that the cost of production was about . . . $4,600,000. The balance of this vast sum, or about $14,000,000, was used in overhead and in building an immense plant filled with costly machinery. . . . The company was permitted to take buildings and machinery that cost $2,987,200 for $600,000 and materials that cost approximately

$5,558,999 for $300,000. . . . The company was charged with stealing a carload of small tools from this plant and removing them clandestinely to their own plant. The wonderful machines which they took from the government as junk they have since sent to their subsidiary factories for use" (28). The story of Mr. Mellon's Koppers Co. was—an investment by the government of $16,737,932, and no product delivered (28). (Graham Committee) ("None of the coke oven projects came into production prior to the Armistice," p. 58, House Report 1900, March 2, 1921.)

Certainly one who was unable to detect such operations going on in his own companies was hardly the man to be an effective watch-dog of the Treasury or to checkmate the ultra-crooks engaged in nullifying the National Prohibition Law. On the basis of these revelations concerning the Standard Steel Co. the Hon. Lamar Jeffers said bluntly on the floor of the House: "They were proven to be the worst type of the grafters who robbed this government on war contracts both during the war and in settling up the unfinished contracts after the war. Now this same Mellon of the Mellon affiliated interests is your (Republican) Secretary of the Treasury, prince of profiteers and greatest of grafters on this government" (29). The Graham Committee itself recommended that the U. S. Constitution be amended to make such unconscionable taking of the nation's resources in time of war, treason (p. 148, Report No. 816, April 10, 1920).

"HIS NAME BIDS FAIR TO STAND WITH THE GREATEST MASTERS OF FINANCE IN MODERN TIMES." PRESIDENT HIBBEN OF PRINCETON IN AWARDING THE DEGREE OF LL.D. TO MR. MELLON.

Congressman Frear of Wisconsin addressing the House (Nov. 25, 1922) on tax evasion made the following allusions to Mellon properties:

"Among other charges placed in my hands by well-informed witnesses that should be investigated are that the Aluminum Co. of America received from Treasury officials an amortization of $15,000,000 on about $30,000,000 valuation, although the property was then generally employed in production.

"That the Standard Steel Co. has an alleged $8,000,000 tax

due although the assessment letter has never been sent out but remains in the files of the income tax unit.

"That the tax unit of Gulf Oil has been made under questionable surroundings and methods that challenge full publicity. Secretary Mellon is alleged largely to own or control these companies.

"Is it true," asked Mr. Frear, "that due to legal evasion possible under existing law disclosed by the secret records of your office, Mr. Rockefeller, Mr. Morgan, Mr. Mellon and others of great wealth are not paying one fifth of the income tax they are popularly supposed to pay under the law" (30)?

The enormous tax refunds to great corporations and wealthy individuals, which were a special feature of Mr. Mellon's administration of the Treasury, are estimated to have approximated three billions (31) and it is surmised that the passage of this money to Wall Street was an important factor in the orgy of speculation and the resulting crash in 1929. In view of these things it is not surprising that neither Mr. Coolidge nor Mr. Hoover cared to send in Mr. Mellon's name as Secretary of the Treasury for confirmation by the Senate but preferred that he should be a hold-over from administration to administration.

"AND WERE'T NOT MADNESS TO MAKE THE FOX SURVEYOR OF THE FOLD?"

And there were special reasons why Mr. Mellon was unsuited to the task of enforcing dry legislation. Mr. Boyce stated the case in the *Saturday Blade* of Chicago, Nov. 5, 1921. "When President Harding selected A. W. Mellon, the Pittsburgh banker, brewer, distiller, street-railway and trust magnate as Secretary of the United States Treasury, the whole country was shocked and believed then, as it does now, that it was not a personal selection of the President but was forced upon him by the politicians. . . . The amount of his contribution to the Republican campaign fund has never been disclosed and no doubt never will be, because it would be put through different names and paid into the campaign fund by others than himself." Mr. McAdoo asserts that this Republican campaign fund of 1920 amounted to $7,000,000 (32). *Plain Talk* for Jan. 1932 (p. 46) thinks Mr. Mellon's contribution was $400,-000. Back of Mellon was Penrose (33) the evil genius of Pennsylvania politics, who represented in the Senate the triple alliance of railroads, steel and breweries. From his sickbed in Philadelphia he had by telephone cooperated in the nomination of Harding. It is extremely probable that he was also party to the appointment of Mellon to the Treasury, although this is attributed to Frick and Knox. (Frick was Old Overholt distiller as Mellon and a director of U. S. Steel; Knox, Senator from Pennsylvania by grace of a half-million fund coming from Frick and from Cassett of the Pennsylvania R.R. Penrose was in closest political relation with all four gentlemen.)

It was Penrose who devised the seven year time-limit when he saw that the 18th Amendment was going through Congress, and proposed it to Senator Sheppard (34). This to prevent ratification by the states. When this scheme failed the appointment of a distiller to the Treasury was obviously the plan for scuttling enforcement. The drink interest was Penrose's indispensable ally.

As far back as 1914 the *Public Ledger* (Nov. 1, 1914; also Feb. 20, 1914) spoke of abundant documentary evidence which showed Penrose to have collected an immense fund from the liquor-dealers of Pennsylvania, systematically assessing the saloons and breweries, and making no accounting as demanded by law. To protect this interest would be his first concern and for this protection they naturally paid. When he died a quarter million in cash was left by him in a safe deposit vault apart from his personal property (35). This was a Republican political fund which apparently came from permitted nullification of the 18th Amendment.

When protests against Mr. Mellon's appointment poured in Penrose quieted them by explaining that Prohibition enforcement was soon to be transferred to the Department of Justice and beyond Mellon's control. After the appointment the matter was dropped (36). Responsible observers have found here the root of the whole trouble. Thus Congressman Strong of Texas (Cong. Record, March 16, 1933, p. 527) speaks of "the unheard of and unprecedented act of placing the enforcement of a general law in the hands of the Secretary of the Treasury while it should have been the duty of the law department of this government to enforce it. *I feel I am stating the truth when I say the administration of the Volstead Act by the Secretary of the Treasury is largely responsible for all the outlawry to the nation for the past twelve years. . . . He was opposed to the 18th Amendment and practi-*

cally said to the bootlegger . . . The United States is open to you" (abridged).

UP THE STREET CAME THE REBEL TREAD
ANDREW MELLON RIDING AHEAD

Mr. Mellon's background was sympathetic to the wet side. There had been a distillery on the old Thomas Mellon farm (37). His second wife was daughter of an Irish distiller. By a curious coincidence his vintner in Bordeaux was named André Mellon. The Duquesne club in Pittsburgh, of which Mr. Mellon was the most influential member, was known as the wettest in the country (38). His daughter married the son of that super-wet, Senator Bruce of Maryland. At his little personal parties such wet leaders as Pierre S. Du Pont and General Atterbury were intimate guests (37). He lived in a wet belt. More whisky was stored in the Pittsburgh U. S. Revenue District than in any whole state save Kentucky. For many years he was business partner with Henry C. Frick in the celebrated Overholt Distillery in Western Pennsylvania. He categorically stated in a letter to Senator Caraway (*N. Y. Times,* Oct. 4, 1928, p. 4) that he had withdrawn from this interest several years prior to Prohibition. "The Overholt distillery in which I owned an interest absolutely ceased the manufacture of whisky and from doing any business. The entire property was conveyed to a trust by irrevocable deed with direction to dispose of the property. . . . My entire investment was only $25,000." But attention has been called to the fact that on Sept. 5, 1922, according to Prohibition Mimeograph 3005 of the Commissioner of Internal Revenue, A. Overholt and Co. was designated by the Treasury Department as a concentration internal revenue bonded warehouse (*N. Y. Times,* June 27, 1924, p. 1). On May 25, 1925, David Schulte, President of Park and Tilford, bought from Mr. Mellon's Union Trust Co. the Overholt distillery and grounds, together with 1,800,000 gallons of Overholt whisky. The price paid was $15,000,000 and it was alleged that Mr. A. W. Mellon owned a third interest in the property sold. As late as Oct. 14, 1933 a United Service despatch from Pittsburgh, under the heading, "Mellons sue United States for Liquor Taxes," read:

"Andrew W. Mellon, former Secretary of the Treasury, and his brother R. B. Mellon, banker, today sued for $390,289.41 in income taxes. They also asked interest from May 19, 1927. They allege that double taxation was imposed by the government in the liquidation of the A. Overholt and Co. and the West Overton distillery."

Senator Blaine in the Senate Judiciary Report, May 7, 1929, p. 106 (on the Eligibility of Andrew W. Mellon) called attention to the fact that the "whisky of the Overholt distillery was sold between March 4, 1921 and October 2, 1928. It is not in dispute that Mr. Mellon was beneficiary under such trust agreement and received his share of the proceeds and profits from the sale of the whisky while he was Secretary of the Treasury. The trustee acted in no other capacity than as an agent for Mr. Mellon and his co-partners." In 1924 Gov. Pinchot declared that Mr. Mellon was still owner of thousands of barrels of whisky and charged improper withdrawals from the Overholt distillery. Indictments against those concerned were quashed and the guilty parties never punished. Congressman O'Connor, who has an intimate knowledge of whisky operations, tells us that "about 1922 Mellon sold a few hundred thousand gallons of Overholt to the bootleggers at about $3 per gallon. Of course the Mellons knew that whisky was going into bootleg channels. They knew it was not going to be dispensed in Bellevue Hospital. Today the bootleggers have some of that whisky left, 77,000 gallons I understand, and National Distillers are negotiating to buy it back from them" (39).

The Mellons were charged with being in the retail as well as in the large sale of intoxicants during the Prohibition era. A witness before the Brookhart Committee (40) declared that the Motor Square Hotel, a roadhouse owned by Mellon interests, ran wide-open, protected by town, county, and Federal officials, "as outrageous a place as ever existed in the United States. It was the center of the whisky ring covering the state of Pennsylvania."

(Mr. Mellon called this "vicious piffle" but what seems verification has come to me from a trustworthy source. The Motor Square Hotel, now known as the Ritz American, is reported as "running a night club." It is owned by W. L. Mellon et al and is located across the street from the Motor Square Garden, a building used for political meetings, prize-fights, etc. The Garden is the property of E. P. Mellon, Mary Mellon, and McClung Mellon.)

"AND OFT 'TIS SEEN
THE WICKED PRIZE ITSELF BUYS OUT THE LAW"

According to testimony before the Brookhart Committee, Gaston Means with Capt. H. L. Scaife of the Department of Justice as assistant had been hired by President Harding to report on the Prohibition Enforcement situation. (Gutzon Borglum testified to seeing the Harding letter authorizing this investigation. *N. Y. Times,* June 27, 1924.) The President was evidently alarmed at the brazenness of official nullification. "There are conditions relating to enforcement which savor of nation-wide scandal," he had said to Congress in his message of Dec. 24, 1922. In pre-Prohibition days the banks had made great loans to distillers upon whisky stocks during the four or five years of its aging. These warehouse receipts were frozen credit which the banks wished to liquidate. Means, a one-time detective for Mr. Mellon, tells us that his investigation led up "to government officials that were taking graft and it led to the top (41). There is no question about that because these were frozen credits in the Mellon line of banks. And nobody is quite so familiar with the value of whisky as Mr. Mellon himself and his banking interests. The banking interests wanted to release those frozen credits in order that they could get their money where they had made tremendous advances on whisky certificates."

Senator Ashurst.	Do you mean to assert that they had bought warehouse certificates for liquor?
Means.	Yes, sir . . . They had advanced money on the whisky and could not get the money out until the whisky was released.
Senator Chamberlain.	What bank do you refer to?
Means.	Including Mr. Mellon's institutions and the Chatham-Phoenix Bank in New York City (42).

To release this whisky (for "medicinal purposes") permits were required. "Sixsmith, Mellon's right hand man," was the one who did it (43).

FINANCING THE REPUBLICAN PARTY

Now comes an interesting side-light. Capt. Scaife, of whom we shall hear later, had asked Secretary Mellon in a personal interview, whether he had ever endorsed a plan for the withdrawal of whisky, a plan submitted by a well-known bootlegger, according to which he and his confederates were to pay off the indebtedness of the Republican National Committee in return for permits issued by Mr. Mellon's office. "And did this powerful and notorious bootlegger have authority from you to write letters over his signature stating that you had agreed to such a plan" (B)?

To this, according to Mr. Scaife, Secretary Mellon made an affirmative reply (with unessential qualifications) (44). In written correspondence, however, Mr. Mellon withdrew this affirmation. Now it was testified before the Brookhart Committee that Jess Smith, Attorney-General Daugherty's intimate, had exhibited documents showing that Mellon had gone into arrangements with Rex Sheldon of the Republican Committee, to provide him with withdrawal permits in return for specified contributions to the Republican National Committee (45). After which Mr. Mellon was charged with trying to load the responsibility for the contract upon Senator Bursum's shoulders. The Senator, however, bluntly insisted that the Secretary of the Treasury was not telling the truth.

SHADOWING SCAIFE

And another interesting side-light here broke in. Captain Scaife wrote Mr. Mellon after this, accusing him of using espionage upon him with Treasury agents. This Mr. Mellon denied. But it appears that the Under-Secretary of the Treasury had been doing this very thing. "They did send him to every town he ever lived in and put men in front of his office" (46). Mr. Scaife printed affidavits from those visited. They affirmed that these agents obviously sought evidence which would blacken his character. Why was this done? Presumably because Scaife had threatened to expose the Treasury's operations and it was desirable to have material which would show Mr. Scaife to be untrustworthy. That the Harding-Daugherty-Mellon administration used these methods is suggested by the remark of Senator Ashurst (Brookhart Report, p. 485): "Mr. Chairman. The observation you made awhile ago that this Committee (of the Senate) *was being spied upon and its witnesses intimidated by the entire secret service of this government, is quite true.*"

This was the first method of defense. The second was described by Under-Secretary Gilbert: "He (Scaife) cannot get his situation into the newspapers. . . . We come mighty near controlling the metropolitan press and we will control it as long as we want to and Captain Scaife will not be able to get his stuff into the papers pertaining to this arrangement for the giving of permits for the withdrawal of whisky through Rex Sheldon" (47).

More side-light, this time from "The Washington Merry-Go-Round," p. 174 (confirmed by the Couzens Investigation, p. 263) : "It may be true but it is scarcely conceivable that Mr. Mellon was ignorant of the favoritism shown to certain newspapers which supported the administration. He may not have known, for instance, that whereas the excess profits tax for 45 representative newspapers was about 20%, some of them who had stood by the Grand Old Party had theirs scaled down to around 2%. He may not have known also that Hearst's Star Publishing Co., a staunch supporter of the administration, got reductions on tax liabilities for three years totalling $1,737,000."

Mr. Mellon, Scaife says, "stated that he later found, upon investigating the names submitted to whom the permits could be issued, that none of them were the type of people he felt could be trusted with permits, and that *the arrangement that had been started* was later stopped by him."

THE GREAT SCOFFLAW

"But the La Montagnes *were* satisfactory. . . . They were worth millions and the permits went to the La Montagnes" (48).

Dr. Nicholas Murray Butler objects to the term "wet" applied to himself as "insolent and vulgar" (49). Nevertheless his relationships are with the wettest of the wets. In 1907 he was married by Father McKinnon of the Jesuit Church of St. Ignatius Loyola to Miss Kate Montagne whose father E. La Montagne, was one of the largest liquor dealers in New York (at 45 Beaver Street). The only other guests at the wedding were Mr. James Speyer and wife. Mr. Speyer, a president of the Association Against the Prohibition Amendment, was said to be banker for European wine interests. When Prohibition came the Montagnes, polo and tennis players of the Racquet Club, became bootleggers and were finally caught. They pleaded guilty and served jail sentences for two years in Essex County jail, N. J.

They had been big operators. They controlled the Green River Distillery and the Eminence Distillery. It was estimated that they put on the market between three and five millions worth of illicit liquors. They were said to have kept $5,000,000 in cash in a lock-box of the Harriman Bank in connection with their withdrawals of Green River whisky (52).

The President of this bootleggers' bank ("infamous den of thieves" Senator Neely called it), Mr. Joseph Harriman, now safe-housed in a Federal penitentiary for robbing his depositors of $1,393,090, was a prominent member of the Association Against the Prohibition Amendment. On pp. 46, 74 of the Senatorial Investigation of the Harriman Bank are references to Dr. Nicholas Murray Butler's dealings with it.

How can this colossal and insolent violation of law by President Butler's relatives be explained? "The La Montagnes were very sore that they were indicted. They thought they were working under proper protection . . . They were constantly promised that they would not be indicted and then, when they were indicted, that the case would not be pushed" (53).

The information which led to the investigation and indictment of these "society-bootleggers" came to Mr. Hayward, the Federal Prosecutor, from a volunteer witness. Yet the Prohibition Director of New York "had most of the facts the Grand Jury and my office have worked so hard to get as early as last June but did not see fit to report the facts to me (Hayward)" (N. Y. Times, Dec. 30, 1922, p. 5).

THE TREASURY INTERVENES

Captain Scaife says "that it was to the Montagnes that the permits went" (which were to bring in contributions for the Republican machine). Means confirms this. "And that led up to the case where I was after Mr. Mellon,—when Mr. Mellon had allowed Sheldon to draw the whisky from the Green River Distillery." Senator Wheeler intimated that Means with his damaging evidence was dismissed from the Department of Justice "because of objections Mr. Mellon made to Mr. Daugherty." William J. Burns of the Secret Service verified this:

"Means was on some very important work and got very important information for the U. S. Attorney, which was true and I knew it was true. But the Attorney-General had directed me to stop my investigation because, as I understand it, the Treasury Department were kicking about us butting into their matters.

Wheeler.   Exactly. He was getting some evidence on the very
high-ups on the inside of the so-called whisky ring in
the city of New York. Is that not true?

Burns.   Well, the District Attorney told me he was getting
some very valuable evidence.

Burns explained that the Attorney-General "came back from a
cabinet meeting one day and was very angry. He asked me why
we persisted in butting into matters that were wholly connected
with the Treasury Department. I told him because we had been
requested to do so either by Mrs. Willebrandt or by one of the
U. S. Attorneys. Well, he stated that the Treasury Department
was not at all pleased with our butting into their matters and for
me to let them alone. Mrs. Willebrandt was very much upset,
very much put out . . ." (54).

Means and Scaife got the Montagnes indicted. "Then it suddenly stopped. Somebody double-crossed the President" who had
employed them (55). Scaife found himself obstructed by the
secret service of the Treasury. He complained to the Department
of Justice without results. "Government officers testified that their
hands were tied and they couldn't get anywhere. I undertook to
go forward and expose these conditions . . . and then immediately instead of assisting me, which they agreed to do, they began
to obstruct" (56).

EXPORTS BECOME IMPORTS

Another damaging episode centered about the Overholt distillery. The *Philadelphia North American* for Sept. 19, 1922,
said: "One of the scandalous phases of the enforcement situation
is that a considerable portion of the liquors captured from smugglers in American waters consists of domestic products released by
Commissioner Blair's department ostensibly for legitimate export
purposes. This fact has been withheld from the public. A still
more startling circumstance is that part of the contraband taken
originated in the Mellon distillery, the serial numbers showing
that within a short time after its release the stuff is in the hands of
rum-runners off the coast. It is said that negotiations undertaken
to induce foreign governments to cooperate in preventing violations of our laws, have been embarrassingly complicated by the
revelation that a substantial part of that smuggled booze is Ameri-

can liquor,—including consignments derived from the distillery owned by a Mellon bank."

"WITH FAR-HEARD WHISPER O'ER THE SEA OFF SHOT THE SPECTRE BARK."

Verification of this story can be found in the 1925 Investigation of the Bureau of Internal Revenue, p. 2164. One of the most experienced government investigators of the period tells me that in 1922 a hundred and sixty-four box-carloads of whisky in barrels were brought to Philadelphia. Of this, 21,000 bbls. (mostly Overholt) were loaded *on a government-owned vessel under federal export permit from the Prohibition Bureau.* Prior to this a close friend of Mr. Mellon, Col. Blank, is reported to have hired a warehouse in Havre, presumably for the storage of this whisky when it should reach France. But to France it did not go. For over a year this Flying Dutchman promenaded the Atlantic, directed by wireless messages, copies of which have been in the hands of this investigator. Whisky at sea ages very fast and this improved Overholt would be priceless for flavoring industrial alcohol concoctions. Some time later 2,500 bbls. of Overholt were seized in a little Pennsylvania town.

Who was responsible for these operations is difficult to understand in view of Mr. Mellon's point-blank statement, "Any inference that I or the Overholt Company connived in any way in the illegal withdrawal of whisky is false" (quoted by Bent, "Strange Bedfellows," p. 72).

HOMEOPATHIC DOSES OF OLD OVERHOLT

Between Sept. 3, 1920 and Jan. 6, 1921, a certain Goodman, a saloon keeper of Beadling, Pa., a hamlet with one hundred and forty-five people, withdrew 42,000 gallons of whisky from the Overholt distillery. This was allegedly for medical purposes!

"When the agents asked Fatkins, the Overholt superintendent, for these permits (for illegal release of whisky from the Overholt distillery) they were informed that Goodman took them back to deliver them to the distillery's main office in Frick Building, Pittsburgh. However, instead of finding them there the agents discovered (that) these faked permits, properly belonging in the files of the Overholt distillery, were in the Mellon Bank."

"Had the Federal Prosecuting Attorney in Western Pennsylvania done his duty he would have immediately indicted Mr. Andrew Mellon because they had no business there."

"The agents called at the Mellon National Bank and requested that the permits be turned over to them. They were referred to De Wald Hicks who at first asked the agents to return the next day. This they refused to do and insisted on immediate delivery. Hicks then turned them over.

"The evidence involving the removal of this whisky from the Overholt distillery was submitted to U. S. Attorney D. J. Driscoll, who promptly subpoenaed 32 witnesses before the Federal Grand Jury, resulting in the indictments referred to. These indictments were returned on March 9, 1921. At the same time other liquor indictments were returned involving prominent men and politicians.

"On March 19, 1921, Mr. Driscoll was very suddenly removed from office and Walter Lyons was appointed U. S. Attorney. On Dec. 29, 1921, the new U. S. Attorney, without consulting Prohibition agents Walker or Gregg who worked up the Fatman-Goodman case, dismissed all these indictments for insufficient evidence. He also dismissed other very important Prohibition cases. So the gentle hand of Andrew Mellon forced Harry W. Daugherty to come to his rescue" (57).

Means testified (p. 2949): "I do know of my own knowledge that Mr. Daugherty was called off from attempts to enforce the Prohibition law by the Treasury Department. . . . I think we were called off the Guckenheimer case itself. . . . Mr. Mellon went to the President and the President had to tell the Attorney-General that he did not want Mr. Daugherty interfering with his (Mellon's) department."

PITTSBURGH BREWERS ESCAPE

At the hearings of the Internal Revenue Investigation 1924, Mrs. Willebrandt recounted the results of interference in the case of Pittsburgh breweries under indictment. There is no evidence known to me that Mr. Mellon or Mellon companies were interested in breweries (among the universal Mellon investments) although his bank, the Union Trust of Pittsburgh, was at this time registrar for two brewery trusts, the Pittsburgh Brewing Co. and the Independent Brewing Co., controlling 31 breweries. (The Independent Brewery Co., one notices, received large tax abatements under Mr. Mellon's administration of the Treasury and in general one should remember the tie-up of Pennsylvania breweries with the Pennsylvania Republican machine.)

Mr. John A. Friday of the Independent Brewery and Morris Friedman of the Hazelwood Brewery were charged with organizing a large bribery fund for the protection of seven breweries.

When the matter came up Mr. Mellon requested that an employee of his own department, Mr. Littleton, be made special assistant to the Attorney General to try the cases (p. 2644 Couzens Report). Mrs. Willebrandt was cross-examined regarding this.

Mr. Manson. Was the appointment of this man as the prosecuting officer made with your approval?

Mrs. Willebrandt. It was not.

M.   What was the outcome of these cases?

W.   One case was tried. The Friedman case was tried and lost and the rest of them, at Mr. Littleton's request, were *nolle prossed*. When the motion to *nolle prosse* was presented to the judge he refused to grant it.

M.   Is it not a fact the judge refused to *nolle prosse* those cases upon the ground that the case had not been properly presented?

W.   It was so reported to me. Yes, sir.

Senator Couzens. I am interested to know why this man Littleton was appointed since counsel has raised the question. Just why was he appointed for the specific case?

W.   I do not know.

C.   Was the regular staff of the Department of Justice unable to handle the cases?

W.   I do not know of any disqualification.

C.   They had time?

W.   They always found time.

C.   So you know of no reason for having Mr. Littleton specially appointed in this particular case?

W.   I know of none.

M.   Did you protest the appointment of Mr. Littleton?

W.   I did.

"Morris Friedman was acquitted though we never believed

him innocent" was the laconic statement of Judge Britt. The other conspirators also escaped.

Which perhaps would make pertinent comment on Mrs. Willebrandt's statement, "Prohibition has been dealt its hardest blows by those *at the head,* or near the head, of enforcement organizations" (58). Also on Senator Brookhart's remark to the writer: "Always at the back of non-enforcement stood Mr. Mellon."

(Comment of Senator La Follette on this case: "If Mrs. Willebrandt were serving the people's interest and not those of the Republican party she would tell why a group of rich brewers, powerful politicians, crooked prohibition agents, and a dozen or more smaller fry involved in the famous fifteen brewery case in Pittsburgh, have never been brought to trial. She could explain why this case was taken out of her hands nearly two years ago over her protest and against the ruling of the Department of Justice at the special request of politicians high in government circles.")

THE ONLY MILLIONS MELLON EVER DECLINED

Mr. Merz' contention is that dry Congresses for a decade passed legislation but neglected to appropriate the funds needed to empower such legislation. This may be, but in 1929 by the Harris amendment to the first deficiency bill, Congress was prepared finally to give enforcement the needed financial backing, namely $25,000,000. The Senate Appropriation Committee asked Mr. Mellon whether "such a sum could be judiciously expended and if granted by Congress how such an amount would be allocated." Mr. Mellon quibbled. He did not think "such a large sum should be appropriated until surveys specified were made" and stigmatized the appropriation as "an extravagant use of public funds."

This from the man who was refunding billions of taxes to rich corporations and individuals.

In a letter to Mr. Mellon, Jan. 18, 1929, Bishop Cannon stated what is obvious enough: "It will be difficult for the average citizen to believe that there is much zeal or eagerness on the part of the Secretary of the Treasury to secure adequate enforcement if he refuses this opportunity to develop and carry out an adequate program." Mellon had acknowledged that enforcement was greatly hampered for Coast Guard, Customs Service, and Border Patrol because of inadequate equipment. "Why," asked Bishop Cannon, "has not the Treasury Department prepared and sent to Congress a statement of the requirements of these arms of its service and asked for the funds needed?" Congress was ready to turn over an adequate lump sum to the Treasury, leaving it apparently to Mr. Mellon to allocate it as he thought best, and to hold in the Treasury any balance which he did not think wise to use.

The Tammany wets in Congress had fought this appropriation tooth and nail, but no political considerations stood in its way. It was before Congress in January 1929, that is directly after the great dry victory which put Mr. Hoover in the Presidency. The natural inference is that Mr. Mellon did not want absolute enforcement (Lobby Investigation of 1930 Report, pp. 4,765 and 4,768). Nor did Mr. Mellon want investigation. Speaking in Springfield May 11, 1924, Gov. Pinchot said: "The Secretary of the Treasury opposes any investigation. I am sorry, for official opposition to being investigated is always unwise. He has publicly defended conditions which our people know to be scandalous in the extreme. He has publicly denounced the proposal to let in the light."

PRESIDENT COOLIDGE RUSHES TO THE RESCUE

The Couzens Committee had been studying the fiscal operations of the Internal Revenue Bureau and had asked for information regarding tax returns of Mellon corporations. Mellon complained to the President. He intimated that if the Committee continued its prying he, as a self-respecting man, could not continue in office. President Coolidge answered this letter by sending, on the day following, to Congress a special message which Senator Walsh of Montana called "the most arrogant message sent to a legislative body in the history of English-speaking peoples." Coolidge declared that the Committee's request for a list of the companies in which the Secretary of the Treasury was interested was dictated by hostile motives, that "under procedure of this kind the constitutional guarantees against unwarranted search and seizure would break down" (C). But according to Senator Robinson, the desired information had already been supplied by Mr. Mellon (N. Y. Times, April 11, 1924, p. 2). The real occasion for his panic fear appears to have lain elsewhere. Senator Couzens at the suggestion of Governor Pinchot had proposed to hire Francis J. Heney, an accomplished investigator, to study exhaustively Mr. Mellon's conduct of Prohibition enforcement. That this was the reason for invoking the President's interference appears from the speech of Senator Watson (bosom friend of Penrose) the next day (C).

"Mr. Mellon knew that if the Committee, inspired by Pinchot and engineered by Heney and sustained by two Democratic members of the Committee, should start an investigation there would be no end of it! . . . *Nobody expected that Prohibition would be rigidly enforced*. . . . From all parts of the country all the books could be brought here, all the witnesses could be haled before this committee, that every one of the activities of the Prohibition Unit could be brought before the committee *and everybody knows what that would mean*. . . .

"*Senators, when we voted for Prohibition, those of us who did knew that the law could not be enforced in five or ten years but voted for it only with the understanding that it would be progressively enforced*. . . . *There is no use in dragging in all that gossip and scandal and having a saturnalia of vituperation and aspersion unequalled hitherto in the political annals of America*" (abridged) (*N. Y. Times*, April 13, 1924, p. 1).

EARLY SABOTAGE

In the earlier years Secretary Mellon's enforcement commissioner was David H. Blair, a Southern Republican politician. He appears to have been an intimate of the Secretary. When Mr. Mellon was being prosecuted by the Federal Government for tax evasion "a memorandum listing nine methods of legally avoiding the payment of income taxes" was read by Mr. Robert H. Jackson, counsel for the government (59). This document had been prepared for the Secretary of the Treasury pursuant to his request by David H. Blair of the Internal Revenue. Tax refunds by which Mrs. Blair materially benefited are on record (60). Blair's rulings were of enormous aid to the nullifiers. The Constitution forbade the *manufacture* of intoxicating liquor. For the convenience of the brewers this was permitted in the case of beer with the understanding that the beer should later be de-alcoholized.

The method was in violation of the letter of the Constitution and became a chief instrument for brewery nullification.

Blair but mirrored the sympathies of his chief in the Treasury. On March 8, 1921 Attorney-General A. Mitchell Palmer had ruled that physicians could prescribe beer "as a medicine." He explained that this "may mean beer at the soda fountains but never again over the saloon bar." (O never!) The brewers were jubilant. Ruppert commented, "It is the most cheerful news in a business way I have heard in five years. We are ready on a moment's notice to put out real beer. All that is needed to start the movement of beer to the drug-stores is the issuance of permits." Congress took the matter up but because of filibustering, legislation blocking the proposed flooding of the country was not passed until November 21. *Meanwhile on Oct. 24, 1921, the Internal Revenue Department, with the approval of Secretary Mellon, issued regulations allowing the sale of beer as a medicine in the quantity of two and a half gallons at a time* (N. Y. Times Oct. 25, 1921, p. 1)!

Blair is charged with having hampered his enforcement officers, restricting them to one difficult method of obtaining evidence. They were not permitted to stop a truck and seize its contents, but were obliged to knock out a bung, take a sample, have it analyzed, and then only prepare the case. Blair's appointees were often notoriously hostile to the law; his intelligence agents feared by honest enforcers rather than by nullifiers. His administration was marked by illegal withdrawals and by great robberies of the whisky storehouses of which he was the responsible custodian (*Philadelphia North American,* Sept. 19, 1922) (D).

It is not conceivable that so consummate an administrator as Mr. Mellon could have been unaware of all this. Yet he said to a Committee of Congress: "I am quite sure that we conscientiously made every effort to carry out our responsibilities under the law" (61). So did he "wash his hands with invisible soap in imperceptible water." The Secretary was speaking for himself and his lieutenant, Dr. James M. Doran, issuer of permits.

THE CHAMELEONS

Dr. Doran, who had charge of enforcement in the middle period, passed after Repeal into the employ of the whisky men and one sees his photograph with these worthies in trade papers, and reads speeches made by him at distillers' conventions. Mellon went from distilling to enforcement of the prohibition of distilling; Doran from enforcement to a $30,000 position with distilling interests. It seems like opera bouffe. "I don't believe there was as much steady drinking during Prohibition as before," he is reported as recently saying. "It may take a year or two to bring the steady drinker back to his old level" (62). Evidently this appears to him a desirable objective. He calls for cheaper whisky. "There is nothing purer than good alcohol" (63). There seems to have been no wrench in this transformation from prosecutor to guide, philosopher, and friend.

Does this mean that he was lax in prosecution during his larval state and before he appeared as full-blown whisky butterfly? Senator Brookhart thought so, charged the enforcement personnel as being inefficient from top to bottom and demanded the immediate removal of Mellon and Doran as the first step in a general clean-up (64). Such incidents as that of Paul Eschner lend color to Brookhart's opinion. Eschner, a convicted bootlegger and moonshiner, was put by Doran into the very responsible position of first assistant in the Division of Plant Control with charge of the supervision of breweries and distilleries from coast to coast. His task was to prevent diversion of alcohol and to see that no beverages with more than one half percent of alcohol were manufactured or sold. Thanks to the efforts of the Civil Service Commission this ex-bootlegger was separated from the service May 21, 1929, after holding the position for fifteen months (65).

INSIDE STUFF COMES UP

Under the caption "Former Government Official Unmasked" an article in *Inside Stuff*, Feb. 1, 1935, has this to say about Dr. Doran's administration. After speaking of the suits which the Federal Government is now conducting against certain of the great industrial alcohol companies for the collection of thirty millions of taxes due on liquor diverted by them to bootleggers, it says:

"Nominally the defendants are the U. S. Industrial Alcohol Co. of Baltimore, the American Solvents and Chemical Corporation, now defunct, the Syrups Product Co. of Yonkers, and the Glidden Co. of Cleveland. Against these outfits, their susidiaries and surety companies, the government is pressing suits for the collection of nearly $30,000,000.

"In an entirely different sense, however, the case is against

Dr. James M. Doran, for had Doran prevented the diversion of industrial alcohol, as it was in his power to do, the cases for tax collection could never have arisen. The government now seeks to collect $6.40 proof gallon on all alcohol diverted for beverage uses. The fact that all such diversion was illicit is not now the primary concern of the Department of Justice.

"The reorganization of 1930 whereby the Prohibition Bureau was split and the Bureau of Industrial Alcohol created under the control of the Treasury, was a boon to the alcohol manufacturers and to the Secretary of the Treasury, owner of a controlling interest in the U. S. Industrial Alcohol Company. Mellon appointed Dr. Doran chief of this new bureau.

"It was then that diversion, long practised, took a new lease on life. Today the companies charged with using the mask of beauty clay and lacquer thinner, for getting alcohol into beverage channels, make no denial of the illicit practices but rest their case on the invalidity of action based upon a law that has been repealed.

"With the coming of Doran into the new office the allotments grew larger and larger and the formulas grew simpler.

RENATURING MADE EASY

"Opposed to the use of wood-alcohol as a denaturant, Doran allowed the companies to dictate what formulas should be used, formulas prepared by their own chemists, their chief virtue being, that subsequent 'cleaning' would be easy. 'Thirty-nine B' was the most popular because it was easy to clean and because it was odorless. Another popular fromula was 44A.

"Throughout these operations Doran maintained that the alcohol companies were straight, that diversions were done by the bootleggers without their knowledge. But today men who were afraid to speak two years ago are revealing Doran in another light. They reveal that Doran O.K.'d special formulas at the behest of the alcohol companies and that he transferred employes when he found they were becoming suspicious. They reveal that Doran's activities were confined to prosecuting the little fellows while he kept hands off the companies which were the source of the diversion."

THE SOURCES OF BOOTLEGGER SUPPLY

What shall we say of this? First that there is no question about these operations of the industrial alcohol companies. When the present Attorney-General went after them in criminal suits for releasing alcohol to bootleggers, they pleaded *nolo contendere* and paid their fines. Government counsel in the cases tell me that while almost all the industrial alcohol companies were in the racket, they were described by the Treasury Department as "responsible companies, cooperating with the Government, who would not think of breaking the law." Whenever the matter was referred to President Hoover this was the explanation given and as a consequence case after case, which could have been successfully prosecuted, was dropped. Of the largest of these companies, the U. S. Industrial Co. of Baltimore, now being sued for $8,140,-415.88 in back taxes on illegally released liquor, *Plain Talk* says (Jan. 1932, p. 6): "It is well known that Mr. Mellon openly owned and it is believed that he still secretly owns control of U. S. Industrial Alcohol" (E), and adds (p. 46), "Among the tax refunds to Mellon companies is one to U. S. Industrial Alcohol for $970,164." The defendants in the U. S. Industrial Alcohol case are charged (Plaintiff's Brief, p. 117) "by misrepresentation and by perjury (to) have both reaped enormous profits and (to) have paid no tax." Among its directors were W. Murray Crane, mentor and backer of President Coolidge, Jules Bache of Cuba Distilling, Sid Klein of National Distillers, and S. F. Pryor, a director of Chase National, the Rockefeller bank. One wonders whether such other directorial names as H. H. Rogers, Oliver G. Jennings, and F. T. Bedford, do not imply a Standard Oil background. At any rate at the present writing, U. S. Industrial Alcohol is (according to *Space and Time* quoted in *In Fact*, March 2, 1942) in the Rockefeller domain and interlocked with National Distillers.

Dr. Doran was always optimistic. In the *N. Y. Times*, Feb. 6, 1930, p. 3, he estimated that not three percent of the total production of industrial alcohol was being diverted. Then he published a list of reliable permittees, among them the U. S. Industrial Alcohol Co., the Syrups Products Co., and the American Solvents and Chemicals Co., all three of which Attorney-General Cummings is now suing. One big bootleg concern, buying continuously from U. S. Industrial Alcohol for nine years, was suddenly cut off from this privilege. They protested against this suspension and declared that they were remonstrating at Washington for being discriminated against. To whom in the Government would they have applied to iron out their difficulties with U. S. Industrial Alcohol except to the Commissioner of Permits, Dr. Doran?

WHAT THE COMMISSIONER OF PERMITS PERMITTED

Dr. Doran, according to government attorneys with whom I have talked, was on friendly terms with the Washington attorneys of industrial alcohol companies. The bootleggers, having better chemists than the government, submitted easily cleaned formulas to the industrial companies and they accepted them and recommended their acceptance by the Treasury. This the Treasury appears to have allowed "after trying them out with inferior apparatus" according to Mr. J. H. Hoffa, government prosecutor. The testimony of Mrs. Willebrandt is that *"the production of industrial alcohol had not the same safeguards against diversion that existed before Prohibition, the exceedingly efficacious old Internal Revenue statutes."* Why not? She affirms as a result of eight years experience that *"the greatest single source of liquor supply was alcohol diverted illegally by concerns bearing the stamp of respectability in the form of government permit. . . . The regulations promulgated by the Treasury Department for authorized withdrawals (were) wholly inadequate"* (66). Mr. Mellon's successor, Mr. Morgenthau, bluntly stated in a press release Aug. 6, 1934, that his administration of the Treasury was *"the first honest attempt to stop the illicit manufacture of liquor,"* and spoke of having "absolute proof" that the law was not enforced during Prohibition (67). Senator Borah, too, has commented on "the scandal of the Federal permit system under which industrial alcohol was released" (68).

Certainly Dr. Doran has the faculty of being all things to all men. During Prohibition he addressed W. C. T. U. and Anti-Saloon meetings and was delegated to an International Anti-Alcohol Congress in Europe. Today he speaks of "the group I represent," of "our industry" (69), and lectures to the Jesuits of Fordham University on the ageing of whisky. Congressman Fuller of Arkansas says of him: "He is the very man that the distillers who have a monopoly of the whisky business wanted, and the very man who gave them their permits to operate in the old Prohibition days. During his service in the Treasury Department, as Commissioner of Industrial Alcohol, he named practically all now in that department and it is generally known he still controls that service while serving the whisky trust as Director of the Distillers Spirits' Institute" (70). Today his relations with that trust are of such a nature that the wholesale liquor dealers of New York are asking for a senatorial investigation (71).

Major Wright who enforced the law so brilliantly in Pennsylvania says: "The Treasury Department *must* have known about the illicit permits. It simply did not want to enforce the law" (interview).

"AS KILLING AS THE CANKER TO THE ROSE, OR TAINTWORM"

Back of the long, dull row of Doric columns on the Treasury façade sat for eleven years the Pittsburgh banker and *entrepreneur*. I think of him as of a borer in an apple-tree,—quiet, unobserved, unobtrusive, apparently the most harmless of white worms, yet source and cause of the *malaise* which befell the 18th Amendment. The tree was of the best stock and bore fruit, much fruit, and of good quality. But one could see that it was pining, that the leaves were tinged with an unwholesome yellow. Senator Norris has given the explanation: "Prohibition did not have a fair trial. *Its enforcement was in the hands of its enemies*" (3). So, too, that very able political investigator, Mr. F. Lundberg, calls Mellon "the master collaborator in the obstruction of law enforcement," and says Prohibition could undoubtedly have been enforced but "was sabotaged by the inner circle of the Republican party" (America's Sixty Families, p. 474).

PART III

ILLUSTRATIONS OF PERMITTED NULLIFICATION

These, then, were the men in charge. To make clear their operations in further detail let us bring the camera into sharper focus and turn it upon Pennsylvania, the state of which Mr. Mellon was the most powerful citizen.

The Director of the Alcohol Control Board of Pennsylvania from 1924 to 1927 tells me this:

"There was more Prohibition in 1920 than ever afterwards.

The law was strict and competent. Prior to Prohibition the United States liquor laws were highly respected. If a distiller found that he was out a hundred gallons in his report to the government it gave him sleepless nights (F). Alcohol was high priced and hard to get. The number of formulae for denaturization of industrial alcohol was but six or seven, and stiff ones at that.

"In 1921 came in the new administration, with A. W. Mellon in the Treasury. The formulae were increased to forty-seven in number. Seven or eight of them were so simple that 'one had only to blow on them' to renature them. Those most commonly used were 39a, 39b, 40, 18 and 4. The first three were for hair tonics and faked lotions, No. 18 for green soap, No. 4 for spraying tobacco. Permits were granted freely and in large amounts, ninety-nine percent of the permittees being Russian Jews. They started with 200 gallons a month. This presently became 500. Later, 5,000 a month was a small permit. Applications for permits were filed by Jewish lawyers. Soon enormous amounts were being set free by the Government." It seemed as if the Federal Government had consciously gone to work to destroy National Prohibition (G).

"ANY NOSE MAY RAVAGE WITH IMPUNITY A ROSE"

A Federal Grand Jury in Philadelphia reported:

"We have called before us in the neighborhood of fifty of these permittees, have looked at them, examined them, noted their type, their character, their evasive replies, their irregular ways of doing business, their lack of experience. We have inspected a number of their so-called manufacturing plants, have seen their supposed equipment.

"All of which leaves no room for doubt as to the illegality of the whole business. Some of these permit-holders were erstwhile policemen, drivers of bread-wagons, plumbers, tailors, jewelers, newspaper vendors, salesmen who could not state definitely what they sold, manufacturers of clothing and other things which they could not state definitely where they previously manufactured. All are of just the type and character which would be drawn into this business because of the actual and reputed easy money made through diversion of alcohol.

"The Colgate Soap people, with a trade supplying the world, used less than 10,000 gallons a month. Yet a government permit to withdraw 15,000 gallons of industrial alcohol monthly was being granted to a pair of irresponsible Jews working in a cellar.

"The case of the cigar-makers Bobrow brothers of Philadelphia is typical. They had permits for 100,000 gallons a month for curing tobacco. Now one gallon to 1,100 pounds of tobacco would ruin the tobacco. Bobrow himself confessed that he actually used a glycerine compound for his tobacco and no alcohol at all.

"When the matter was brought up on complaint, Dr. James M. Doran, then government chemist for the Bureau of Prohibition, appeared for the continuance of the permit. It was finally compromised and cut down to 20,000 gallons a month."

O MONSTROUS . . . THIS INTOLERABLE DEAL OF SACK

In his message to the Pennsylvania legislature, Feb. 10, 1925, Gov. Pinchot pointed out that in the two years ending June 30, 1923, the amount of specially denatured alcohol removed and disposed of in the Philadelphia district increased from less than 900,000 gallons to more than five million.

"In the first Pennsylvania District there are eighteen distillers, denaturers, and bonded dealers authorized under Federal permit to sell denatured alcohol. They can sell specially denatured alcohol only to manufacturers holding federal permits. Such manufacturers authorized to make toilet water, hair tonics, and tobacco sprays by the use of specially denatured alcohol, numbered in Philadelphia one hundred and fifty-one on Nov. 30, 1924.

"These withdrew in the first ten months of 1923 more than 1,100,000 gallons of specially denatured alcohol, enough to make toilet water, hair tonic, and tobacco sprays for the whole world. Nearly everyone did his supposed business in a single small room or small building utterly inadequate in size or equipment. . . . Only twenty-one of the hundred and fifty-one manufacturers had filed incorporation papers in this state and fifty-seven were doing business in contravention of the law which requires the true owners of a concern to register their names in Harrisburg. None of these concerns kept regular books. Most of them were without published rating. Thirty-four were doing business under assumed names.

"This business from end to end has the unmistakable marks of fraud and crime. The absurdly large amounts of alcohol withdrawn for purposes for which they could not possibly be used, the almost complete absence of manufacturing facilities, the elaborate system of cover-houses, and the almost total lack of commercial respectability among the persons engaged in the business,—all these combine to show beyond question both the existence of widespread conspiracies to violate the law and its actual violation on a huge scale."

These permits were issued with the certain cognizance of Commissioner Roy A. Haynes and of the Hon. A. W. Mellon, Secretary of the Treasury. There is reason to believe that Mr. Mellon hated Prohibition and desired to see it liquidated. (Cf. "Mellon's Millions," p. 236, on his unpublished anti-prohibition statement for the *Saturday Evening Post*.)

When Gov. Pinchot in the fall of 1923 asked Mr. Mellon under the power granted by Federal law, to have regulations adopted which would stop this huge illegal business, he was refused. "The regulations then in force were ample for all purposes." The Grand Jury denounced Federal administrative inefficiency in this direction and declared the methods and systems employed by the Federal Prohibition Bureau to detect diversion to be "childish."

Penrose and Mellon were allies in Pennsylvania politics. The biographer of Senator Penrose has described how the Pennsylvania boss allowed a bootlegger to pay $100,000 for the privilege of a state monopoly over liquor in government warehouses. For others he cut up the state into bootlegging districts who should pay for their district rights with contributions to Republican campaign funds ("Power and Glory. The Life of Boies Penrose" by Walter Davenport, p. 175). Penrose, in making these commitments, evidently understood that the Treasury had no intention of really enforcing the law. To illustrate. Gov. Pinchot requested Mr. Mellon to authorize the Pennsylvania State Police "to have full access at any time day or night to any plant holding a Federal permit." Mr. Mellon said he would be glad to do this if it would help the Governor enforce the law. When it came to a showdown, however, inspection of breweries was allowed "during ordinary business hours only." Governor Pinchot's remarks on receiving this extraordinary permit read: "This is the first proposal in my experience for restraining officers of the law from apprehending criminals except during business hours. Neither my request nor

Secretary Mellon's promise contemplated any closed season for law-breakers. . . . Criminals work mainly at night. Sec'y Mellon's promise meant a real inspection or it meant nothing. . . . I refuse to accept as a fulfilment of that promise your permission to inspect breweries and distilleries with a string to it that will hobble the officers of the law."

"The main trouble," said Gov. Pinchot in his 1927 message to the Pennsylvania Legislature, "was with the Federal Government which insisted, against my vigorous protest, in continuing to issue permits to breweries we had caught violating the law. In some cases we caught them seven times before we could get them out of business." General Smedley Butler was actually notified that deputy U. S. marshals would shoot his police if they entered certain nullifying breweries (*Collier's*, Dec. 12, 1925, p. 36).

"WHERE THE BLINDEST BLUFF HOLDS GOOD"

When convicted breweries were permitted to continue their operations the fine which they were asked to pay became, as Gov. Pinchot said, "nothing more than a high license fee for law-breakers." Mrs. Willebrandt before the Couzens Committee described how the Treasury thwarted the Department of Justice. While the latter wanted to use injunctions to close breweries, the former insisted on putting them in charge of armed guards, "a mere gesture because of the frailty of the guards and unfair financial burden upon the Department of Justice." . . . Breweries under guard continued to run illegally. After the Roehm brewery had been under guard eight months it was necessary to get an injunction. . . . So with the Hazelwood brewery, Pittsburgh. The Atlantic brewery of Philadelphia ran night times *when under seizure* (*N. Y. Times*, April 1, 1925).

In 1922 Mrs. Willebrandt declared that in Pennsylvania "law enforcement, both state *and Federal,* was under political control. It's a case of political strangulation all down the line" (Letter to the Law Enforcement League, *N. Y. Times*, October 23, 1924). The strangulation seems to have come from the Treasury for Gov. Pinchot called Secretary Mellon's attention to the fact that certain members of the Alleghany delegation to the Pennsylvania legislature, *supposed to be under the orders of W. L. Mellon,* had opposed dry legislation in the last two sessions and are opposing it at the present extra session. Secretary Mellon called this "indefensible insinuation." Whereat Gov. Pinchot delivered this undercut:

"How a plain statement of a plain fact known to every one who knows the fundamentals of Pennsylvania politics can be called an insinuation is beyond my understanding. The men to whom I refer and their local leaders *not only acknowledge but openly assert and even glory in the fact of Mellon control.* These men voted wet in the last legislatures and are expected to vote wet in the present extra session."

"THOU CUTTEST MY HEAD OFF WITH A GOLDEN AXE"
(Romeo and Juliet)

The Federal Government during National Prohibition reduced fines to a minimum in many cases. The Report of the Internal Revenue Bureau Investigation mentions the Fleischmann case as having been settled for $75,000 though the tax assessed was $2,779,999. (Later the Fleischmanns sued the government for all but $5,000 of this balance.) Senator King asked the witness why the Fleischmann permit was not revoked when the fraudulent operations were uncovered. "Was it because of a $10,000 contribution made by Fleischmann to the Republican campaign fund" (p. 2416)? (So on p. 2729 of the same investigation: "Finally a report was made on June 27, 1922, by John D. Appleby, Prohibition agent in New York, who wrote to Mr. Yellowly of the Prohibition Unit in Washington to the effect that druggists there had obtained from the Bornheim Co. some 4,000 cases of whisky and that *they had nothing to fear because in part the profits went to make up a part of the Republican campaign fund.*") In the Gaines and Kentucky Distilling Warehouse Co. case, the reduction of fines was from $2,700,000 to $75,000. During 1924 there were prepared and sent out to the various collectors of the Prohibition Unit, assessments aggregating $16,909,855.21 (for illegal selling). Of this 12%, or $2,652,337, was actually assessed, and $704,696 was the final compromise. "These things," remarked Senator Couzens, "were done behind closed doors and settlements were made without a public record" (p. 2504).

The tender heart of Andrew Mellon seems to have tempered the wind to the shorn bootleggers even after they had paid their taxes. In Senate Reports, Private Vol. C., p. 144 (Investigation of the Bureau of Internal Revenue), are long lists of refunds of taxes to corporations. The second largest was a refund of $3,996,-000 to the Gulf Oil Corporation, a Mellon concern. *Similar listed refunds of taxes made to bootleggers in the period 1921–25 amounted to $2,097,371.79.*

Senator Brookhart spoke of other expressions of kindheartedness, this time to bonding companies. "My attention has been called to 350 cases of bonds issued in connection with violation of Prohibition which were forfeited. Mr. Mellon settled these cases over his signature for one cent or one dollar. These bonds were mostly given in such a way that their enforcement would have meant enforcement of the Prohibition laws" (*N. Y. Times,* April 9, 1930). The great bonding companies escaped collection on forfeitures almost uniformly in tens of thousands of cases and the Government was left holding the bag. This of course gave welcome help to bootlegging violators of permits, and enriched bonding companies by millions.

"SUGAR IS THE LIFE-BLOOD OF ILLICIT DISTILLING"
1941 Circular of the Tax Unit

"If the Federal Government had made it clear that it was sincere in its enforcement policy, many reputable firms would not have cooperated with bootleggers," remarked Mr. Bielaski of the Secret Service to me. We were speaking of a New York molasses syndicate which in 1931 shipped great consignments of its staple to a New Jersey bootleg ring. Most of the great sugar and molasses firms were, at one or another time, in the racket, supplying illicit distillers with low grade sugars and molasses, not directly of course, but by roundabout, concealed sales methods which they had devised. This 1941 circular of the Tax Unit says: "Sugar is the one absolute essential which an illegal distiller is dependent upon when operating in any thickly populated area. One one-hundred-pound bag can result in a tax loss to the government of $37.05." So the Tax Unit of today, in order to prevent sugar from getting into unlawful hands, arranges with all sugar refiners, importers, and brokers in the New York, New Jersey, and Philadelphia districts, to send out a warning circular to customers in their regular monthly bills. Mr. Mellon, on the contrary, never took the least trouble to supervise effectively the sugar and molasses sources of law violation.

Did the Treasury Department know about all these things?

If not, its incompetence must have been monumental. But incompetence was the last thing one would charge Mr. Mellon with.

As early as 1922 he came to the conclusion that the United States government could not enforce this law enshrined in the Constitution by forty-six of the forty-eight sovereign states. "It was a failure."

That, Mr. Mellon, was as if Chronos, after swallowing his own children alive, had blamed them for not making a success of life.

THE BRIGHTER SIDE

All this indeed is one side of the medal and should be made known. The reverse is more encouraging. It shows that in spite of official iniquity and all the handicaps which National Prohibition suffered at the hands of those in authority in Washington, it still could be and was creditably enforced, not only in the country at large but where the tests were severest. The case of Pennsylvania is decisive. This state was one of the leading states in brewing and distilling. It was surrounded with wet states,—New Jersey with its rum row off the coast, Maryland with its crooked industrial alcohol companies and old whisky warehouses, New York with wet governors and a repealed enforcement code.

Up to the time when Governor Pinchot took office in 1923 whisky was being illegally removed from warehouses in the Pittsburgh District and indictments against big bootleggers quashed. In the Middle District the U. S. District Attorney had spent eighteen months to close the single Keystone Brewery of Dunmore. In the Eastern District prior to 1923 not a single law-breaking place had been closed by inspection. Saloons licensed by local judges of the Common Pleas Court were running openly under a fraudulent state statute and the immense renaturing business permitted by Washington was flooding Philadelphia.

Enforcement machinery was ineffective. The governor of Pennsylvania was without power to remove elected officials for failure to do their duty. Only "after due notice and full hearing on the address of two thirds of the Senate" were such removals allowed. "Nor," as Major William Burnet Wright explains in "Four Years of Law Enforcement in Pennsylvania," "has the Governor of Pennsylvania, as that of New York, the power to call a special Grand Jury to investigate law-breaking anywhere in the state, or to designate the Attorney General or a deputy to present cases of lawlessness to such a Jury, or to designate a judge sympathetic with law enforcement to hold such a term of court."

The Brooks High License Law of Pennsylvania had for years given opportunity to corrupt wet politicians to influence the judiciary. Through dominating political machines the liquor interests nominated and elected judges, prosecuting attorneys, and jury commissioners. The liquor power had behind it great financial interests of a general sort. In his 1927 Farewell Address to the Pennsylvania Legislature Governor Pinchot said of these interests:

"They invest in politics as they do in mills and mines and banks, to make money. They buy votes with excessive expenditures for campaign funds and through politicians who steal votes. Any such machine must include a body of the lowest politicians as the Mellon machine in Pittsburgh and the Mitten machine in Philadelphia actually do control, men who depend for their living and their power on liquor, crime, and vice."

After three years of Governor Pinchot's administration the situation was wholly changed. The licensed saloon had been driven from Pennsylvania; the Snyder-Armstrong Act had been wrung from the legislature making it possible to close illegal places by injunction. It is true that no appropriations for the enforcement of the act were granted but the necessary funds were raised by patriotic women of the W. C. T. U.

The Pennsylvania Alcohol Permit Board was created to control the production, sale at wholesale, and transportation of alcohol in the state. This move checked the lawless operations of the Federal Treasury in Pennsylvania and largely stopped the fake toilet-water, hair-tonic, tobacco, and disinfectant consumption of alcohol.

Of the 156 breweries operating in January 1923, 95 had quit and of the balance all but 10 were operating under Federal permits. By 1926 high percent beer could no longer be bought in the state. This was brought about by the State Police with state search warrants, inspections, seizures of contraband liquor, and arrests of brewery owners and employees. Over 230 cities and towns were surveyed, some as many as eleven times, for re-checking saloons in connection with injunction and enforcement proceedings.

The conclusion of the matter has been stated by Major Wright who was at the very heart of this enforcement campaign during three whole years. "Our investigation proved that at any time during the past three and a half years the Federal Government, almost in the twinkling of an eye, could stop the crooked alcohol business if the United States Secretary of the Treasury and Attorney General had used the great powers given by the Federal statutes to prevent and stop such law-breaking.

"Contrast the results secured by our small personnel (never more than five men in the field, never more than two for court and office work, besides two stenographers) against all imaginable handicaps as outlined, and with less than $8,500 a year available, with the large Federal personnel, the unlimited powers of enforcement in the Federal statutes and the hundreds of thousands of dollars appropriated yearly in each state by the Federal government. It then becomes evident that the Federal Government could have enforced the 18th Amendment as the law was, and with the appropriations made, if there had been a will to do so.

"As soon as a President of the United States follows the command of the Federal Constitution to 'take care that the laws be faithfully executed,' and by compelling his Secretary of the Treasury and his Attorney General to use their enormous powers without fear or favor, all talk and propaganda throughout the country that the 18th Amendment cannot be enforced will cease because then the great sources of supply of illegal liquor will be closed and the big violators put out of business or in prison" (Wm. Burnet Wright, "Four Years of Law Enforcement in Pennsylvania").

REFERENCES TO CHAPTER II NOT IN THE TEXT

1. Hearings before House Committee on Civil Service, Feb. 2, 1926, page 8, and Current History, December 1923, page 374.
2. Current History, February 1924, pages 847–849.
3. Willebrandt, "Inside of Prohibition," pages 132, 136
4. Charles Merz, "The Dry Decade," page 190.
5. Collier's, Sept. 17, 1927, page 48.
6. Current History, April 1928, page 12.
7. Overman Report, page 1044.
8. Annals of the American Academy of Political and Social Sciences, September 1923.
9. Brookhart Report, page 2496.
10. Brookhart Report, page 2401.
11. Brookhart Report, page 2404.
12. Brookhart Report, pages 2410, 2413.
13. Brookhart Report, page 2418.
14. Brookhart Report, page 2422.
15. Brookhart Report, page 779.
16. Brookhart Report, page 1449.
17. Brookhart Report, page 1451.

18. Brookhart Report, page 1453.
19. Brookhart Report, page 1455.
20. Brookhart Report, page 1490.
21. Brookhart Report, page 2265.
22. Brookhart Report, page 1482.
23. Brookhart Report, page 1483.
24. Brookhart Report, pages 1554–1555.
25. Brookhart Report, pages 2171, 2208–2209, 486.
26. Hearings House Committee on Judiciary, January 1932, pages 39, 89, 103, 41.
27. Congressional Record, June 1, 1920, page 8148.
28. Select Committee on Expenditures in the War Department, House Report 1400, March 2, 1921, page 75.
29. Congressional Record, March 23, 1922, page 4385.
30. Congressional Record, November 25 and December 7, 1922, page 198; January 19, 1934, page 946.
31. "Washington-Merry-Go-Round," page 174.
32. "Washington-Merry-Go-Round," page 168; McAdoo, "The Challenge," page 233.
33. Current History, May 1923, page 238.
34. Congressional Record, September 14, 1929, pages 3613–3614.
35. Mrs. Willebrandt, "The Inside of Prohibition," page 95.
36. New York Times, February 14, 1921, page 3; Current History, May 1923, page 238.
37. Harvey O'Connor, "Mellon's Millions," page 234.
38. Philadelphia Public Ledger, September 29, 1923.
39. Harvey O'Connor, "Mellon's Millions," page 237, and Congressional Record, January 4, 1934, page 95.
40. H. L. Scaife, "The Government's Whited Sepulchre," page 38.
41. Brookhart Report, page 2859.
42. Brookhart Report, pages 2859 and 2860.
43. Brookhart Report, page 2862.
44. "The Government's Whited Sepulchre," pages 2, 4, 6 and Brookhart Report, page 2916.
45. Brookhart Report, pages 2866 and 2868.
46. Brookhart Report, page 2869.
47. Brookhart Report, page 2870.
48. Brookhart Report, page 2916.
49. N. Y. Times, June 15, 1924, viii, page 6.
50. Samuel Wilson, "The Scoffs of a Scofflaw."
51. Brookhart Report, pages 2871 and 2872.
52. Brookhart Report, page 2873.
53. Brookhart Report, page 2874.
54. Brookhart Report, pages 1556, 1027, 1030, 1031.
55. Brookhart Report, pages 2834, 2305.
56. Brookhart Report, pages 2304, 2309.
57. Brookhart Report, pages 2917, 2918.
58. Mrs. Willebrandt, "The Inside of Prohibition," page 119.
59. New York Times, April 3, 1935.
60. Congressional Record, November 25 and 28 and December 7, 1922.
61. Prohibition Unit Hearings, House of Representatives, 8574, 71st Congress, 2nd Session, page 4.
62. New York Times, August 19, 1934, page 3 (sec. VIII).
63. New York Times, January 7, 1934, page 5.
64. Current History, February 1930, page 991; New York Times, January 1, 1930.
65. Plain Talk, November 1931, page 33.
66. Willebrandt, "The Inside of Prohibition," pages 59, 41, 43.
67. New York Times, August 7, 1934, page 9; Washington Post, August 7, 1934, p. 4.
68. Johnson, "Borah of Idaho," page 459.
69. Mida's Criterion, November 1935, page 70.

70. Congressional Record, July 23, 1935, page 12,184.
71. Joint Hearings, Ways and Means and Senate Finance Committees, December 11, 1933, page 217.
72. Congressional Record, December 18, 1931, page 773.

NOTES TO CHAPTER II

A.   Finn and Carey contributed $40,000 to the Republican campaign fund of Kentucky for the privilege of taking out whisky from the Belle of Anderson distillery near Lawrenceburg, Ky., and for the immunity from prosecution which went therewith (Brookhart Report, p. 148). How small alcohol permittees were shaken down by Republican politicians appeared in the Couzens investigation of 1924. A list of 100 permittees and the amount of their contributions to party funds was presented. Thus Apex Products Company $100, Archo Chemical Company $100, American Witch Hazel Supply Company $50, and so down the alphabet.

B.   Other questions in the Scaife letter intimate what was going on:
7.   Are you aware that there is documentary evidence to show that meetings attended by owners of whisky, brewers, and sworn federal officials, are held for the purpose of dividing the territory in which individuals or corporations are to operate in defiance of the law?
9.   Are you aware that enormous quantities of whisky have been transferred from one bonded warehouse to another in furtherance of schemes to withdraw the whisky from barrels, substituting therefor water or a combination of water and alcohol with the necessary coloring matter and that there are now thousands of such barrels, from which the whisky contents have been withdrawn, in bonded warehouses under your control? Are you aware that large numbers of barrels alleged to contain whisky are exported when said barrels contain water or substitute?
13.   Are you interested in the documentary evidence showing the banks and trust companies involved in violating the prohibition laws?
18.   Will you give the list of the breweries, distilleries, and the whisky certificates in which you, members of your family, business associates, or financial institutions which you control, are directly or indirectly interested? Is it not a fact that you and your associates and the institutions you control, are today the owners of the largest stock of whisky in America?
.   "The Government's Whited Sepulchre," by H. L. Scaife, was copyrighted and by law two copies should be in the Congressional Library. The card catalogue does not list them. On search, however, the Library authorities have found one in pamphlet form in the Library's pamphlet section; also a copy in the University of Illinois. These alone, in the entire United States, escaped.

C.   Of the Coolidge Administration, Governor Pinchot said, "As long as Coolidge talks dry and acts wet we can never have Prohibition enforcement."
Philip Grossman, a rich German saloonkeeper in Chicago, persisted in defying the law. A federal injunction restraining him from selling

drink was issued. He ignored the writ, comfortably coiled up in his saloon on the corner of Wells and Madison Streets. Judge Landis sentenced him Jan. 7, 1921, to serve a year in the Chicago House of Correction and pay a fine of $1,000. He appealed and the U. S. Court of Appeals sustained sentence. The U. S. Marshal failed to carry out the court order, claiming that Grossman had returned to his Fatherland, which was untrue. Finally Grossman secured as his attorney a Mr. Behan, partner of Homer Galpin, the chairman of the Republican Central Committee. Then things began to happen. *Senator MacKinley arranged an interview for Galpin with President Coolidge and a pardon for Grossman followed without his ever having spent an hour in jail.* (Glavis in Hearst's Cosmopolitan, May 1924.)

D.   Major C. F. Mills gave an extreme illustration: "A huge chain of 'speaks' in the Harlem Black Belt was being run by *colored Federal dry agents.* Major Heise, who discovered it, was shot at in his home, chased by a powerful car in an attempt to crush him, and worst of all *dismissed by the Federal government for doing his duty"* (abridged).

E.   In answer to my request for the grounds of this statement the editor of *Plain Talk* wrote me, May 11, 1936: "I have never heard anyone before doubt that Andrew Mellon controlled the U. S. Industrial Alcohol Company. It is a matter of general knowledge in Washington . . . Our specific information was based on positive statements of a former attorney for the Bureau of Prohibition who was discharged by Doran for being honest. This man had access to the files of the Prohibition Unit. In fact when he complained about skulduggery in the Unit he was put down in the file-room as a measure of humiliation, in order to make him resign voluntarily. It was there he learned too much for Doran's and Mellon's good."

Plain Talk had stated, Aug. 1933, p. 27: "It is generally understood at the Prohibition Bureau that Doran has a standing offer of $25,000 a year from Mellon's U. S. Industrial Alcohol Corporation. . . . This offer, according to those on the inside of things in the Prohibition Bureau, was brought about by an order given Mellon's distillery by Doran for (release of) 6,250,000 gallons of medicinal whisky. . . . On these 6,250,000 gallons former Prohibition workers estimate Mellon made a profit of $15,000,000. This deal was given Mellon, it is further said, to wipe out a debt of $5,000,000 (or thereabouts) which the National Republican Committee had secretly incurred and which Mellon refused to consider a donation."

That indeed Mr. Mellon invested heavily in Republican political finance appears from a quotation from the *N. Y. Times* in "Mellon's Millions," p. 117. Of a Republican campaign debt of $1,600,000 it says: "In the form of loans this amount has been almost entirely underwritten by a number of banks in the large cities of the East and Middle West. The Mellon bank in Pittsburgh *is understood to have underwritten $1,500,000 of the deficit."*

F. When the Federal Government, among other things, required the submission of a complete plan of every distillery, including all fixed pipes and "every branch and every cock or joint thereof and every valve therein," the keeping of a daily record of the name, residence, and duties of every person employed, the restriction of distilling and shipping to certain fixed times, and permission to an inspection officer, who might be refused admittance, to break in by force.

G. One peculiarly flagrant case of permitted law violation is that of a New Jersey ring, undisturbed not only by local authorities but even by the Federal Government, which for years has been cognizant of its operations. It has been openly charged with defrauding the Government of up to a hundred million dollars. At one time, when an official refused the $11,500 a week offered the ring for protection, he was transferred by the Government to a distant point. (Major Campbell in his *N. Y. World* articles Sept. 9, 1930, was perhaps referring to this case, for Col. A. J. Hanlon, when trying to cut down certain releases in Newark, was suddenly transferred to Porto Rico. Hanlon had also refused to issue industrial alcohol permits to the National Grain Yeast Company of Belleville, N. J., whose attorney was David K. E. Bruce, son of Senator Bruce, and son-in-law of Secretary Mellon. According to the *N. Y. Times,* Dec. 5, 1930, p. 52, Judge Runyon refused an injunction applied for to restrain Prohibition agents from interfering with this Belleville plant, because its management would not divulge the names of those backing it.)

This New Jersey bootleg syndicate is charged not only with operating illicit distilleries but, since Repeal, with distributing untaxed liquor. A card index made from checks cashed at the Union National Bank, Newark, in payment for liquor sold, represented 8,700 people. The names and addresses of nearly five thousand of their customers in New York City alone have been filed. Bank deposits to their credit amounting to more than twenty-five million dollars were at one time audited and the names obtained of 161 corporations and local and foreign governments, in whose stocks and bonds the ring had invested its surplus.

What is the explanation of this amazing leniency of our Government towards the underworld? Did Major Campbell say the enlightening word when he declared, "The political game is to buy campaign contributions with bootleg concessions"? quoting Republican politician S. S. Koenig as having been offered an exceedingly large campaign contribution ($200,-000), if he would get enforcement officers out of certain breweries (*N. Y. World,* Sept. 9, 1930). This is certainly the proven *modus operandi* of the gamblers. Upton Sinclair, when running for Governor of California, was offered "anything in reason" if he would promise to let them alone after his election (Epic Plan for California, p. 11).

CHAPTER III

THE WICKERSHAM COMMISSION

In view of the situation outlined in the preceding chapter it is not difficult to understand why the promise of the earlier years was but partially fulfilled. Dean Roscoe Pound, who wrote the Report of the Wickersham Commission, missed the mark altogether. The Amendment was not, as he affirmed, *"enforced* in a decade of prosperity." It was purposely nullified during this decade. It was not "backed by an exceptional machinery for special enforcement" which during many years was either in quality or in size adequate. It was not "guarded by strong organizations" (1). Nothing could have been feebler than the official dry defense. These premises falling, the conclusion falls, namely, that "the law had the best chance it was likely to have of showing what it could achieve." When his Radcliffe colleague affirmed that "adequate enforcement is impossible without the support of a much larger proportion of our population than it now commands" she put her dog-cart before her pony (2). The reason why support for the law waned was because enforcement had been deliberately sabotaged (A). Judge Kenyon laid his finger on the inflamed spot when he said, "The evidence before us is sufficient to demonstrate that, at least up to the creation of a Bureau of Prohibition in the Department of Justice, the enforcibility of the Prohibition laws had never been subjected to any fair and convincing test" (3).

HOW KANSAS WAS BLED

One could give various illustrations of how far the Commission was from getting at the roots of things. Their report, for example, mentions the case of Kansas. "It had had prohibition for over fifty years, sentiment in the state was in its favor, the state legislation was drastic, an appropriation had been made in 1929 for special enforcement attorneys. Yet a survey in 1930 showed that conditions were bad in the cities, bootlegging persistent, and the death-rate from alcoholism rising" (4). The conclusion was intimated. Prohibition, even under the most favorable conditions, is a counsel of utopianism.

But the explanatory information, which the Commission ought to have dug up and did not, makes things clear enough. This has been published by Mr. John B. Madden, Prohibition Administrator for the Kansas-Nebraska-Oklahoma district, a man of widest experience and unimpeachable veracity. County attorneys tried to bribe him. *Heavy contributions were made by bootleggers and vice rings to the State Committees of both parties.* The state had indeed voted $40,000 for additional enforcement. But what happened? *The Prohibition official appointed under this appropriation was picked by two Italian bootleggers in conspiracy with the Attorney-General of Kansas and in touch with Jewish vice kings of Wichita.* Particulars are given of the secret meeting in Hotel Kansan at which the Attorney-General received $1,500 from these underworld vermin. *This special enforcement officer was paid $200 a month by the state of Kansas for enforcing the law: also $400 a month for protection of Green Gables and other vice joints.* Madden was double-crossed and thwarted by his own Federal superiors and finally, with his intrepid asistant Armstrong, suspended because he went after the big shots instead of contenting himself "with gathering in half-pints, bell-hops, colored porters, and taxi-drivers" (5).

"WHERE MORE IS MEANT THAN MEETS THE EAR"

The trouble with the Wickersham Commission was primarily one of method. Its testimony was given behind closed doors and afterwards the vital facts were neither published nor made accessible to investigators. The public was offered conclusions without a chance to test them. As Judge Kenyon wrote: *"If the evidence produced before us could have been made public* I think it would have given to the country a true picture of why reasonable enforcement of the Prohibition laws could not have been expected" (6).

On the 20th of December 1929 (C. R., p. 999), the matter was debated in Congress. Senator Harris demanded that no more money should be appropriated until the Star Chamber method was abandoned. Evidence was withheld from the Senators themselves so that the reason therefor was proposed for investigation. The preamble to the resolution read in part (March 17, '30):

"Whereas the Commissioner of the Bureau of Prohibition has refused to furnish members of the Senate with copies of reports made by investigators in his department, either to prove or disprove the charges (of corruption) and

"Whereas the Commission appointed by President Hoover to study Prohibition enforcement has refused to hold public hearings so that the Congress or the people may know upon what evidence, if any, to base their conclusions. . . ." (7)

To this committee investigating the Commission Mr. Wickersham said, after speaking of the "immense amount of material (26 volumes) to be digested and analyzed," "I think when we finish our investigation we will have about as complete a picture of the workings of the Prohibition law as could well be assembled" (8). But of this the nation got practically nothing. The N. Y. Times (Jan. 23, '31, p. 7) made this statement: "Efforts to have the Commission open up the evidence of experts who prepared the data for it were ineffective today. Officials of the Commission refused to permit a perusal of printed volumes containing reports of the experts. At least two such volumes are known to exist and it is reported that there are more of them." The evidence, now in the White House, is guarded as carefully as ever treasure city by gilded dragon. Dean Pound seemed inclined at one time to let me into his copy but finally backed water. "It was too confidential." But he did tell me that it was "full of material relating to the interrelations of politics and bootlegging." President Wilson quietly suppressed matters in the correspondence of the U. S. Brewers' Association which implicated men high in public life. One wonders if the Wickersham Commission did not follow a similarly politic course. Judge Kenyon resigned from the Commission and withdrew his resignation only on the insistent pleading of the President. I am told by one of his life-long friends what the reason was. "Whenever the trails led to the higher-ups they were abandoned" (B).

"I have always," said Senator Norris, "believed that the evidence ought to have been published, so that anyone who wanted to pass on the judgment of the Commission in any conclusion it reached would have had the opportunity" (9). Senator Couzens suggested a Senate resolution making the evidence of the Wickersham Commission public records but unfortunately nothing has yet been done about it.

CARICATURE EVIDENCE

Instead of the real thing we were given five volumes of substitute evidence, much of which had no relation to the Commission's inquiries. Thus Volume 5 of the official records of the Commission has 675 pages and all but 132 are taken up with reprints of the literature of the Association Against the Prohibition Amendment and of the Moderation League,—worthless *ex parte* propaganda. There is also a long memorandum from Edward Landsberg, of Blatz brewery, known chiefly for having called a boycott on the Blackstone Hotel because it obeyed the Illinois Sunday closing law (Overman Report, p. 289); and an ancient anti-Prohibition essay by the Rev. S. H. Cobb printed in the *Princeton Review,* July 1887 (p. 175). Much space is given to the liquor systems of Canada, Finland, and Sweden. The Swedish material is of little value. I had it from the Swedish premier himself that U. S. Minister Morehead, who prepared the contribution on the Bratt System, never even once applied to the Swedish government for information on the subject. In any case these essays were not really germane to the purpose of the Commission. What would have been appropriate would have been a study of the activities of the European alcohol capital to break down our internal legislation. Nothing of this sort was made. The crux of the matter is the alcohol capital at home and abroad now organized internationally. Years ago Henry George wrote of the brewers as "an active, energetic, tireless factor in our practical politics, a corrupt and debauching element standing in the way of all reforms and progress" (10). The Commission left them uninvestigated and undisturbed (C).

But instead what trivialities! Volume 3 of the Records is chiefly given over to American Federation of Labor officials. These witnesses recall the rustics of the Midsummer Night.

Snug: Have you the lion's part written?

Quince: You may do it extempore for me. *It is nothing but roaring.*

That the able jurists of the Commission should have listened to 56 of these labor hacks and then reprint their foolish utterances in a whole volume of "evidence" is an amazing thing.

"The old reactionary Furuseth" (Sparks, *Struggles of the Marine Workers,* p. 15) of the Seamen's Union told them that "before Prohibition hard liquor was a curiosity to sailors"! Tobin of the Teamsters averred that conditions in Indianapolis were so bad that honest men feared to enter their own homes in the dark (p. 274). Burke of the Plumbers and Steamfitters estimated "the conditions to be about 10% as efficient today as seeing the men are all right that take hold of these jobs than we were formerly and the reason that we find for that is because of the bad booze." (Translated this means, if it means anything, that labor is only 10% efficient under Prohibition because of illegal liquor) (p. 162). McDonald of the Plasterers said that as many men cashed checks in speaks as formerly in saloons. He also said that in the good old saloon days a wife could easily find her drunken husband in the saloon he was known to frequent. Now she has to make the round of ten to fifteen speaks (p. 47). Mr. Frey declared it a common thing for children to be kept out of school because of their drunkenness and that the suburb of Cincinnati in which he lived never had a house of ill-fame until Prohibition (p .18).

This was the only cross-examination published. It is noticeable that although Mr. Forrester, the Commission's "Consultant," mustered 56 labor men, no dry labor leaders, men like Cooper or Keating or Stone, were presented. The ungrammatical Woll said (in German idiom), "Then I become resentment. What is law? It is merely a legislative victim. Law must have the popular desire behind it" (p. 159). After which definition the Dean of the Harvard Law School remarked with gentle irony, "We appreciate that very much. We are very much indebted to you" (11).

Contrast this deference with the indifference shown towards a really important witness. Mr. Maurice Campbell, Prohibition Administrator in New York City, was suggested in Congress as a desirable witness but the suggestion was smothered, "nor did the Wickersham Commission show the slightest curiosity in the matter" (12). He would have taken up the relations between illegal sale and Republican party politics and that was dealt with as the cat goes round hot porridge. Dr. Clarence True Wilson tells me that the very effective research department of the Methodist Board of Temperance was never able to get testimony in or before the Commission. Major William Burnet Wright did appear before it three times and gave them inside information but it was unused.

"They did not dare tell the truth! There would have been an explosion if they had" (personal interview)!

THE CONSULTANT

Apart from Col. Woodcock's statement the only really valuable study issued by the Commission was that of Mr. Albert D. Sawyer, a research man from the University of Michigan. This, in my opinion, far outsizes the Wickersham Commission Report in insight and value. Mr. Sawyer was hired by a Massachusetts manufacturer, Mr. Henry Dennison, who apparently sought to supplement the work of the Commission (13). The official "Consultant" of the Commission, Mr. J. J. Forrester, a railway clerk and labor official, appears to have had no training for this type of work. How wild and uncritical was his testimony appears from an article in *Current History* (33, p. 811) where he speaks of rum-runners going "from farm to farm, gathering up the product of home stills in five gallon containers much as milk is collected in the country."

There was little ground for criticism of the personnel of the Committee itself. They constituted on the whole a reasonably unprejudiced group whose attitude towards Prohibition could perhaps be best described in the phrase of Burke as one of "friendly hostility." Two of the eleven were drys. Mr. Newton D. Baker, when mayor of Cleveland, had allowed the saloons of the city to run wide-open in defiance of the Ohio Sunday law (C). There was at least a negative appropriateness in his presence on a Commission to study law enforcement. One wonders how many, if any, of the Commissioners had previously concerned themselves with the alcohol question in its endless ramifications. Certainly none were specialists.

President Hoover's first impulse always is "to get the facts" and on this principle rested his brilliant organization of the Department of Commerce. If all the facts assembled, or five per cent of them, had been released it would unquestionably have strengthened Prohibition sentiment and helped enforcement, for it would have uncovered the causes and preeminently the men responsible for defective enforcement. But instead of these indispensable data we got general discussion as to whether Prohibition was a good thing after all. This confused and discouraged enforcement officers and the public. It gave time for wet propaganda. It closed dry lips until the report should be forthcoming, a delay of eighteen months. Mr. Hoover himself could hardly have taken the lead until he had the Commission's statement.

MR. WICKERSHAM'S OPINION

In the light of what has happened since Repeal, Mr. Wickersham's conclusion seems to be about as near the truth as one could get. If one ventured to guess one might easily have believed that his experience as Attorney-General in the Taft administration had given him insight into brewery politics and the dangers to the Republic that inhere in them. This personal statement, appended to the main Report, runs as follows (abridged):

"I am in entire accord with the conclusions that 'enforcement of the National Prohibition Act made a bad start which has affected enforcement ever since,' that 'it was not until after the Senatorial investigation of 1926 had opened people's eyes to the extent of law-breaking and corruption that serious efforts were made' to coordinate 'the federal services directly and indirectly engaged in enforcing Prohibition,' and that not until after the Act of 1927 had extended the Civil Service Law over the enforcement agents, were there the beginnings of such an organization as might have been expected to command the respect of other services, the courts, and the public, and thus secure reasonable observance of the law and enforcement of its provisions as well as other laws are enforced. Until then, too, enforcement largely had expended itself upon a multitude of prosecutions of petty offenders. It measured success in enforcement by the number of cases, most of which were trivial and in few of which were substantial penalties imposed. I cannot believe that an experiment of such far-reaching and momentous consequence as this of National Prohibition should be abandoned after seven years of such imperfect enforcement and only three years of reorganization and effort to repair the mistakes of the earlier period. The older generation very largely has forgotten, and the younger never knew, the evils of the saloon and the corroding influence upon politics, both local and national, of the organized liquor interests. But the tradition of that rottenness still lingers even in the minds of the bitterest opponents of the Prohibition law, substantially all of whom assert that the licensed saloon must never again be restored. It is because I see no escape from its return in any of the practical alternatives to Prohibition that I unite with my colleagues in agreement that the 18th Amendment must not be repealed, and differing from some of them, I have been forced to conclude that a further trial should be made of the enforcibility of the 18th Amendment under the present organization with the help of the recommended improvements. . . .

"The whole subject is one of great difficulty. There is room for difference of opinion on most of the elements involved. Therefore, despite the well-financed, active propaganda of opposition to Prohibition and the development of an increasingly hostile public opinion, I am not convinced that the present system may not be the best attainable and that any substitute for it would not lead to the unrestricted flow of intoxicating liquor, with the attendant evils that in the past always were a blight upon our social organization" (14).

THE WITNESS OF THE SAVINGS BANKS

"The Wickersham Report is, I think, favorable to the theory of National Prohibition, critical of the methods and results of enforcement of the existing law, and hopeful of improvement of these methods and results in future" (15). This was Col. Woodcock's conclusion. There are, however, various points where the Report appears to minimize the good results from the law and to fall in with certain wet exaggerations.

Regarding the exceptional increase in savings deposits which marked the Prohibition Era the Report says: "It cannot be said that anything (!) is clearly established on this point," and partitions the credit among other causes,—general prosperity, the influence of thrift campaigns, and the fact of the growing employment of wives and daughters of wage-earners (16). The last fact was perhaps balanced by the tendency of employed women to return to the home when the drain of the saloon on family finance ceased. Thrift campaigns would be a very minor factor. Prosperity is of course a condition precedent to large savings; also to large alcohol expenditure which defeats savings. It should be noticed, too, that after the crash of 1929 and while Prohibition continued, the increase of savings still went on. The N. Y. Times pointed out (Jan. 29, 1931, p. 35) that in 1930, a panic year, savings in one hundred largest savings banks *increased* a clean billion,—a record advance. *New* depositors in New York savings banks numbered, in 1930, 239,780; in Massachusetts, 120,855. Clearly the momentum of Prohibition was still felt in spite of the financial collapse.

Wherever Prohibition has been introduced there has been an immediate and enormous rise in deposits in savings banks and in number of depositors. This was preeminently so in Russia; also in Finland, in Iceland, in Sweden during the famous "dry strike." Also when Theodore Roosevelt enforced the Sunday closing law in New York City. Also in Maine under state Prohibition, where accumulations of capital and savings-bank deposits were ever singularly high. One can almost speak of this phase of Prohibition as an economic law.

We are therefore entitled to assume *a priori* that the similar increase under National Prohibition in the United States was chiefly due to Prohibition. Certainly the increase was extraordinary. Thus in the eight pre-Prohibition years, 1911–1918, the advance in total savings deposits was $3,571,741,000; in the first eight Prohibition years 1919–1926 (1919 having been, by state and federal legislative prohibition, largely a Prohibition year),— $11,555,799,000, more than three times as much (Savings Deposits and Depositors, Compiled by the American Bankers' Ass'n, p. 3).

Trebling of deposits was accompanied by a similarly vast increase in depositors:

1918, 10,632,938.
1919, 18,221,453.
1928, 53,188,348.

Never since has the number of depositors reached that of 1928. In 1940 a year of enormous war wages, it was seven million less. This amazing increase in depositors certainly shows the influence of Prohibition, and invalidates the wet theory that the increased savings were deposits transferred by large corporations to savings banks, and not true savings.

Again the Report minimizes the effect of Prohibition on public health. "The steady development of medical science precludes any just comparison of the statistical data available" (17). *No evidence is cited.* The *clôture* is moved and we are supposed to accept this unsupported assertion. Yet as we have briefly noted one of the most striking features of Prohibition was the immediateness of its reaction on public health. The curves dropped with amazing responsiveness. It was as when the magnetic needle swings in answer to magnetic pull. Why, for example, as set forth in the annual statement of the Spectator Company (for 77 life insurance companies) did the average actual death-rate, compared with the expected, drop from 68.66 in 1914 to 65.21 in 1919 (the preliminary Prohibition year) and then to 51.73 in 1921 (18). One grants indeed "the continual advance of medical science" but this was something different, some sudden thing like de Vries' mutations.

THE WITNESS OF CONTAINERS

In the absolutely crucial matter of consumption during the Prohibition era the Wickersham Commission appears to have made no original studies but contented itself with reproducing old material, the extravagant estimates of Mr. Fox, Secretary of the U. S. Brewers' Ass'n and of Mr. Gebhart of the Ass'n Against the Prohibition Amendment (Vol. 1 of the official records). That these estimates, based on raw materials (and by Warburton and Gebhart even on such *imponderabilia* as alcohol sickness), were little trustworthy appears when we study the machinery of the business,—its barrelage, bottleage, transport, etc.

Thus Mr. Verdi of the Associated Cooperage Industries gave testimony before a committee of Congress (in 1932) which was absolutely devastating to the theory of great sales of beer in the Prohibition period. "In 1916, 1917, 1918," he said, "an average of 2,500,000 various-sized beer barrels was sold annually by American barrel manufacturers to breweries in this country. This represents replacements only. The average life of a beer barrel is seven years. This indicates an average, in all, of 17 to 19 million various sized beer barrels in circulation annually before 1919."

Then he continues:

"A careful survey conducted by our Association has shown less than 200,000 various sized barrels in the hands of all the brewers of the United States at the present time (1932)" (19).

This might well have been required for the legitimate near-beer trade leaving few kegs at all for the illegal traffic. The Ehret brewery alone before Prohibition sold a million barrels of beer annually in the New York City area. How could the entire American beer production in any Prohibition year approximate that?

Mr. Horn, Secretary of the Associated Cooperage Industries, testified at the Bingham Hearing and outdid Mr. Verdi. He said: "Prior to Prohibition 7,250,000 tight barrels were manufactured for the brewing industry annually." That makes the argument against large beer consumption during Prohibition three times as strong. As to the truth of the statistics we must leave it to these two experts to settle between themselves (20).

Further it must always be remembered that the business in containers for intoxicating liquors, whether of barrels or bottles, was outlawed. By the Supreme Court decision Danovitz vs. U. S. "barrels and containers were forfeitable when offered for sale in such mode as to disclose intent to sell for manufacture of liquors."

A FAMINE OF KEGS

Certainly immediately after the relegalization of 3.2% beer there was an unparalleled rush for beer kegs. I happened to be in Europe at the time and clipped from the papers such despatches as these:

"Price of beer kegs gone up fourfold since beer was legalized. American brewers sending to all lands for kegs. Brewery industry needs not less than 17 million beer kegs, the total circulation before Prohibition. A St. Louis brewery sends to Germany a whole army of agents to make agreements with German coopers, paid in advance. Practically the whole of Germany's cooperage industry at work for this St. Louis firm. Other American brewers send their agents to France, Italy, and Spain."

The Wooden Barrel (Nov. 1933) reported: "April first to September fifteen the importation of European barrels into the United States cost the American cooperage industry a cool four million dollars,—685,066 bbls., casks and hogsheads, valued at $4,073,813. During the month of March, before manufacture and sale of beer was legalized, only 29 barrels valued at $92 were imported into the United States."

THE RUSH FOR WHISKY BARRELS

There was a parallel rush for wine and whisky barrels. The same trade paper, The Wooden Barrel, March '34, p. 21, wrote: "Repeal of the 18th Amendment has turned despair into prosperity in the wine producing industry in California and has already proven an important market for the cooperage industry. During the last three months of 1933 it is estimated that . . . well over eight million gallons in new cooperage was contracted for. This does not include the barrels for shipping. . . . The Pekin Cooperage Co., one of the most widely known companies in the whisky business prior to Prohibition, has resumed whisky barrel operations in Pekin, Ill. (April 1934, p. 19). . . . Chess and Wymon, Inc., Louisville, have been steadily enlarging capacity in the whisky barrel division which is now up to about 1,300 packages a day" (p. 21).

The National Coopers' Journal, Sept. 1933, tells the same story: "Federal increase in permits for medicinal whisky will call for more cooperage during 1933 than at any previous time in many years. . . . Requirements for medicinal whisky will mean increase from 41,000 bbls. to 143,000. The whisky barrel makers are not going to be caught flat-footed as the beer barrel people were. They will be ready to provide whisky barrels when the distillers are ready to use them." Of wine cooperage we have this testimony from Congressman Buck of California, speaking for the wine-growers (Tax on Intoxicating Liquor Hearings, p. 261 and 267): "The taste for the dry wine or the table wine, the wine we growers think should be rehabilitated, has *entirely disappeared during the period of Prohibition* and it is going to be a very hard thing to re-educate the public. . . . *During Prohibition cooperage (for wine) has been destroyed or diverted to other uses.* . . . Some eight million gallons of cooperage was constructed this year (1934) and more will be constructed next so that eventually California can easily supply 60,000,000 gallons. . . ."

BOTTLES ALSO

The Glass Containers Association of America makes 90% of the bottles used in America. Its representatives appeared at the Bingham Beer Hearings to plead for the breweries. "At no time since 1919 when the National Prohibition Law went into effect have the bottle factories of the country, capable of immediate and economic production, operated at more than 75% of their aggregate capacity. Very excellent and modern properties are idle and without hope of early resumption of operation in Glassboro, N. J., Newark, O., Clarksburg, W. Va., Terre Haute, Ind., Evansville, Ind., Okmulgee, Okla.

"There has been in recent years some growth in consumption of soft drink beverages, the distribution of which is in bottles, but this has only in a very limited way made up for the loss of beer bottle business occasioned by the legal ban upon the manufacture and sale of beer" (21).

Business Week, July 22, 1932, p. 20, in an article with the significant title, "Booze Travels in Bottles," described the effect which relegalization of beer had on the shares of the Owens-Illinois Glass Co. "They rose from 31 to 95." Mr. J. P. Curran of this company testified before the Bingham Hearing (p. 208): "Since 1919 over 23 bottle plants variously located, have discontinued business and some of these operated very largely, and a few exclusively, on beer bottles. The only brewery business being done at present is for near beer and the consumption of (bottles) is only a small percentage of what would be required for beer.

Congressman Ragon.   Where do the bootleggers get their bottles?

Mr. Curran.   The bootleggers are not making beer to any extent and most of them are using second-hand bottles.

Mr. Ragon.   In other words the volume of business is so small that they can handle it with second-hand bottles. . . . The illicit beer business must not be extensive, Mr. Curran, if a man in your business does not know anything about the volume of it" (22) (D).

Contrast this with conditions since Repeal. In the Congressional Record for Aug. 13, 1935, p. 13,406 one reads: "The President of Owens-Glass was one of those very few fortunate souls in the United States who paid an income tax on more than a million dollars of income. This was entirely derived from the business of manufacturing and selling bottles."

FURTHER EVIDENCE

Mr. John A. Voll, President of the Glass Bottle Blowers of the U. S. and Canada, quoted a report of the U. S. Tariff Commission which confirms the above. In 1918 about 5,672,632 gross of beer and liquor bottles were manufactured. *"This has been practically wiped out.* The membership of the workmen's organization is less than one third of that of 1918" (23).

Again, the Glass Containers Ass'n of America figures that the train movement of new bottles (not kegs) annually required for beer production at the rate registered in 1914, together with transportation of raw materials, would amount to 60,000 carloads annually (24). The wildest wet statistician would never contend that there was any beer bottle business on that scale in the Prohibition days and the logic is merciless,—without bottles and kegs relatively little beer.

Corroborating evidence comes from another quarter. The Barry-Wehmiller Machinery Co. makes bottle-cleaning machinery. Their testimony before the Bingham Committee was, "Since Prohibition and up to 1931, we have operated our plant at approximately 15% of pre-Prohibition capacity and that principally for export. Since 1931 we have operated at a loss" (25).

After Repeal the brewers acknowledged this effectiveness of Prohibition as far as their own industry was concerned. The U. S. Brewers' Ass'n Members' Bulletin (*Brewers' Journal*, July 1935, p. 68) wrote: "The new generation that has grown up during Prohibition (has) little or no knowledge of beer."

Oh, but, some say, there may have been little commercial beer handled but there was a tremendous amount of home brew. Did not Mr. Codman of the A. A. P. A. say that "home-brewing has its millions of votaries" (26), and Mr. Stuyvesant Fish of the same organization that "fifty thousand bales of hops are cut up into small packages in a year, indicating a production by the home brewer of ten million barrels" (27)? Did not Mr. Callan of the Maryland legislature explain to the assembled Congressmen that "before Prohibition children would go out and play after school, who now have to stay in and wash home-brew bottles" (28) these children of the "millions of homes" which as Matt Woll told us "were turned into breweries" (29)?

The best answer came from Mr. Fox of the U. S. Brewers' Ass'n. In a letter dated Jan. 28, 1924 he declared "the home-brew business negligible." Mr. Corradini found only 43 hop and malt stores in Greater New York and their stock insignificant (30). When this legend was tested it was found to be legend only. Mr. Beatty of the Madison Square Church House, N. Y., testified at the 1926 Congressional Hearing that in his section, between 28th and 40th Streets on Lexington Ave., there were before Prohibition 13 saloons doing a land-office business. He was told that this business had passed into the homes and that every house in a certain block was making home-brew. He visited 93 and found not a single one so doing (31).

Any argument from the sale of malt is countered by a prominent figure in the malting industry. Mr. G. Hafer testified:

"As an indication of the devastating effect of the Prohibition enactment on the malting interests *in New York state alone* I can point to the discontinuance and abandonment of malt houses situated in Syracuse, Geneva, Jordan, Weedsport, Clyde, and Palmyra" (32).

THE ARGUMENT FROM TRANSPORTATION

Mr. John R. Mauff, former Secretary of the Chicago Board of Trade, estimated that in 1918 it required 613,785 freight cars to handle the national beer production of that year (33). Mr. Owen Cull of the Milwaukee testified that that railroad alone, not to speak of the Northwestern, Wisconsin Central, and Soo lines, which had a larger volume of traffic out of Milwaukee, handled 31,000 cars of beer, or about 100 cars a day (34). For every car of beer shipped a car of empties returned. This entire traffic was wiped out by Prohibition. Gone the time when three long trains of fifty cars each steamed out nightly from Milwaukee, loaded with the product of Milwaukee breweries. Save in sporadic cases, and that only in the early years of Prohibition, the railways loyally observed the law. The railways being out of account whatever illegal liquor was transported must have been carried on autos. But Mr. D. C. Fenner, of the Mack-International Motor Truck Corporation, estimated that the number of trucks required in the first year after Repeal to handle the beer manufactured (35) would equal the entire purchase of heavy trucks in other lines by the country. In an article on "Beer as a *New* Factor in Transportation" in the *Brewers' Journal,* Aug. 1935, p. 38, we are told: "The total beer consumed in Indiana or shipped out of the state would, if placed in cases, put into service 134,998 motor trucks." How much of a wholesale business could have been carried on during Prohibition in passenger cars (not trucks) pursued by vigilant patrols and always liable to confiscation? Certainly not the four billion dollar expenditure for bootleg liquor, "the twenty-fivefold increase over pre-Prohibition liquor expenditure" which Mr. Pierre S. Du Pont on a national broadcast actually told the country it was making (36).

THE BIG WADS

To assist the movement of the huge phantom traffic of wet imagination we were told that bills of high figure were issued by the government. Thus Mr. La Guardia at the 1926 Senate Judiciary Hearings (p. 651) said: "The government even goes to the trouble to facilitate the financing end of the bootlegging industry. In 1925 $286,950,000 more in $10,000 bills were issued than in 1920 and $25,000,000 more in $5,000 bills. What honest business deals in $10,000 bills? The bootlegging industry has created a demand for bills of large denominations and the Treasury Department (has) accommodated them."

Mr. La Guardia was mistaken. It will be seen from the following table taken from the Annual Reports of the Treasurer of the United States that the number of $5,000 bills in circulation in 1925 fell to hardly 63% of the circulation in 1920; the number of $10,000 bills was practically stationary during these years.

June 30	In $5,000 denominations	In $10,000
1920	$141,960,000	$606,380,000
1921	71,025,000	413,990,000
1922	93,705,000	614,280,000
1923	92,990,000	612,110,000
1924	86,000,000	606,420,000
1925	88,900,000	611,130,000

THE TESTIMONY OF THE SOCIAL WORKERS

When the Wickersham Commission Report acknowledges success in certain directions we may be sure that here at least success is indisputable. But in the nature of the case this success would not have been confined to these phases. It would have its repercussions also in the statistics of crime, prisons, savings, home-building, mortality, legitimate expenditure, up through the whole social gamut.

We were assured that "there has been real and substantial improvement in the life of those with whom social workers come into contact" (37). This means that the extreme alcohol misery of slum and mean street disappeared. Miss Mary McDowell of the packing-house district, Chicago, is one of the Commission's witnesses to this effect: "Better homes, children better fed and clothed, less lawless rioting and shooting up in alleys. There were hundreds of saloons in that neighborhood prior to Prohibition. Now there may be some speakeasies but no open places to entice the workingman and relieve him of his pay-check" (38).

HUNGER-BITTEN CHILDREN FED

Miss Booth's letter addressed to 55 social service institutions of the Salvation Army brought back unanimously favorable testimony. In the Bowery Hotel of the Army where once they often had to burn the mattresses and bed-clothing because of the vileness of drink "we are housing 4,800 men every week and do not average more than 4 or 5 cases of drunkenness per week or about one in a thousand" (39). Dr. Katherine Richardson of the Mercy Hospital, Kansas City, Mo., testified before the Ways and Means Committee:

"When we built that hospital we found that we had built a receiving station for the children of the saloon, the spawn of drunkards. In the winter the children of drunkards froze. The parents were not low and depraved; they were drunk and forgot their children. I remember an Oklahoma laborer who brought his three children to Kansas City, put them in a cheap hotel room for the night and got drunk. Three days later we received the child that was alive.

"My nurses can walk down the street at night now. I remember when they couldn't. Beasts slept and loitered and watched on vacant lots. I remember when virtually all our cases were of children maltreated by drunken fathers and mothers,—frozen, starving, abused unspeakably" (40).

This enables us to understand what Joy Elmer Morgan, of the National Education Association, with 220,000 teachers behind him, meant when he stated in a Congressional Hearing: "As a result of my study of conditions among the children I have come to the conviction that, excepting only the founding of the Christian Church and the establishment of the common school, the 18th Amendment is the greatest child-welfare measure of all history. . . . The school people have under their charge the entire juvenile population of the country, some thirty millions. Children who formerly came to school without shoes or overcoats are now provided for in spite of the difficulties of the depression. The enrollment in the high schools of the United States was approximately two millions in 1920; today five millions" (abridged) (41). And Mr. Whiting Williams adds: "Librarians in the great industrial cities tell me that they have noticed a very great improvement in the clothing of the children that come to public libraries" (42).

ON THE EAST SIDE OF NEW YORK

Miss Lillian Wald, of the Henry St. Settlement, is perhaps the most experienced social worker in the United States. She was never identified with the movement against alcohol. She says:

"The Henry St. visiting nurses go out every day into some of the worst sections of New York to respond to calls for help. In the early days alcoholic cases were a common occurrence. Today they are so rare as to be a cause of general comment and this is true not of one district of the city but in all our twenty centres. Last year among the 60,000 patients cared for there was but one diagnosis of alcoholism. That record would have been impossible before the 18th Amendment.

"The evils of the speakeasy are usually compared with those of the saloon. To us who knew the saloon in its heyday there is no comparison possible. Nothing can equal the brazen way in which the saloons flaunted their power throughout the years of their privilege or their farcical evasion of the numerous efforts to regulate and control them by legislative enactment and by moral pressure. On Saturday nights their influence was most obvious and most sinister. The trucks gathered round the curbs while the men went inside with their pay envelopes. The scene has disappeared from one end of the country to the other and with it has gone the tragic Monday morning when tearful women came to beg for advances on their husband's wages.

"The world-wide depression has cast its shadow over our nation today and nowhere are its effects more acutely felt than in the neighborhoods served by settlements and social organizations. But there is one ray of light in the gloom. No longer do we see the hideous alcoholic wrecks who a few years ago patronized the breadlines. The majority of unemployed men along the Bowery and at the municipal lodging houses today give no token that it is drink that has brought them to the waiting-line. An even more significant change is reflected in the statistics of family welfare organizations. When the saloon was in flower, the records of the New York Charity Organizations' Society showed that one out of every four families who applied for relief registered drink as a factor in dependence. In 1928–9 the figures show only one out of eleven families so handicapped. Could there be any more eloquent testimony to the efficiency of Prohibition? One of my settlement colleagues put it well when she said recently, 'Drunkenness twenty years ago and drunkenness today are as small-pox before and since men learned vaccination.'

"To expect complete success for the Prohibition experiment in ten or twelve years would be to expect a miracle. Is it too much to ask for honest and sincere support for our adventure for at least a generation" (43)?

ON THE WEST SIDE

Mr. John L. Elliot, another experienced social worker in the Chelsea district of New York, testifying before the same committee, confirmed Miss Wald. His opinion was based on thirty-eight years' residence in the tenement districts.

"The closing of the saloons has been of inestimable benefit. . . . There is now nothing like the amount of drinking, either of beer or hard liquor, in the homes that there was formerly. . . . Neither on the street nor in the homes does one find anything like a fraction of the drunkenness which could be found up to the time of the introduction of Prohibition.

"In the earlier days practically all saloons opened before working hours and there were very many who never went to work without first getting their drink. It was a custom, too well-known to need proof, that vast numbers of workingmen stopped in at saloons to get a drink before going home. . . . Present intermittent drinking has nothing like the habit-forming power that the old daily and steady drinking had. . . . Among the many hundred young workmen whom I know there is not a single one who has formed the drink habit although a good many of them do drink on occasion. This change has been one of the greatest and most beneficent of the changes brought by Prohibition. . . . The problems of liquor at the present time among the unemployed are negligible" (44).

THE TESTIMONY OF MANUFACTURERS

The Commission Report agreed that "the greater number of large employers (found) a notable increase in production, elimination of blue Mondays and decrease in industrial accidents. . . . With all deductions we are satisfied that a real and significant gain following National Prohibition has been established" (45). Why, O why, then, did the Commission not give space to this evidence as well as to the senseless chatter of the A. F. L. witnesses? Mr. H. S. Dennison of the Dennison Mfg. Co., informally associated with the Commission, declared that "every factory manager with whom he had talked save one has spoken in unqualified certainty of the superior powers of quantity and quality product among his men since Prohibition" (46). Judge Kenyon quoted the president of a great coal company:

"The old days of the pay-day whoopee are gone. What drinking there is is under cover. The practice of drinking a whole month's pay and challenging the world to mortal combat has passed. A drunken miner in public is so rare a sight that when it happens one would think a dancing-bear had come to town and even his chance acquaintances rally to get him out of sight.

"I have seen pay-days when it was not safe to ride on the branch line train going to and from mining towns. I have seen at Christmas season the station platforms jammed with a swearing, fighting, vomiting mob with cheap Christmas toys thrown away, trampled on and lost. I have lain awake listening to the crack of revolvers as miners staggered up and down the railroad tracks. I have fought with crazy drunks at the pay window. . . .

"No matter how much mine operators may talk wet and drink wet, in the great convention cities, they do not want any modification at their mines."

"There are many other statements of similar import and only a few of different view," adds Judge Kenyon (47).

Men like Mr. Buffington of the Illinois Steel Corporation, Mr. Verity of the American Rolling Mills and Mr. Pietz of the Link Belt Co. said their employees were spending practically nothing for drink (48). Mr. McClary, President of the Yoland Coal and Coke Co., Birmingham, declared the 18th Amendment "the greatest forward step industrially that ever has been taken" and the President of the National Cast Iron Pipe Co. of the same city: "There is absolutely no argument against Prohibition." Mr. Cather, editor of the *Southern Labor Review,* contrasted the time "when the saloons used to fill as soon as the five o'clock whistle blew, with the present when thousands from shops, mines, and railroads go straight home and most of them in their own cars" (49). A highly intelligent labor group, the Law Printers' Division of the United Typothetae (Chicago), sent this to a Congressional Hearing: "We believe that Prohibition has already proven of inestimable benefit to all skilled industries and (ours) in particular. We therefore call on Congress and all law-enforcing officials to redouble their efforts to suppress the inefficiency-breeding liquor traffic" (50).

ENTER THE PROFITEERS

I have introduced these extracts to show how, in spite of the way enforcement was betrayed behind the *coulisses* in the Treasury Department, consumption must have sunk enormously and with it the ordinary consequences of social alcoholism. As this was never advertised by the press it seems to have been little realized by multitudes of the unreflecting and uninformed. "A great people should not deal with a deliberately adopted social policy like a fickle child throwing away a new toy," said Prof. Frankfurter of the Harvard Law School concerning the turn which things now began to take (51). True enough. But why did they? Why did the nation "feebly cease ere it had well begun"?

Because a factor hitherto uninterested had now begun its sinister operations. The dry movement was up against Wall Street.

REFERENCES TO CHAPTER III NOT IN THE TEXT

1. House Documents 722, 71st Congress, 3rd Series, page 160.
2. House Document 722, 71st Congress, page 113.
3. House Document 722, 71st Congress, page 117.
4. House Document 722, 71st Congress, page 41.
5. John B. Madden, "Stabbing Prohibition in Kansas."
6. House Document 722, page 117.
7. Investigation of Prohibition Enforcement, Senate Judiciary Committee, 71st Congress, March 17, 1930.
8. Investigation of Prohibition Enforcement, Senate Judiciary Committee, 71st Congress, March 17, 1930, page 7.
9. Congressional Record, January 26, 1931, page 3120.
10. "The Arena," Vol. 1, No. 1.
11. Official Records of the National Commission on Law Observance, etc. Vol. 3, pages 12, 274, 162, 47, 18, 157.
12. New York World, September 8, 1930.
13. Letter from Mr. Dennison's Secretary.
14. House Document 722, page 161.
15. Current History, April 1931, page 7.
16. House Document 722, page 72.
17. House Document 722, page 73.
18. Reported by Hon. J. J. Lenz, Nat'l President American Insurance Union at Hearings February 1930, House Judiciary Committee, pages 1001–05.
19. Hearings on Modification of Volstead Act, Ways and Means Committee, December 1932, page 197.
20. Hearings Committee on Manufacturers, 1932, page 294.
21. Hearings Committee on Manufactures, 72nd Congress 1932, page 249.
22. Hearings on Modification of Volstead Act, Ways and Means Committee, December 1932, page 208.

23. House Hearings on Proposed Modification, April and May 1924, page 53.
24. Tillitt, "The Price of Prohibition," pages 96–97.
25. Hearings on Modification of Volstead Act, Ways and Means Committee, December 7, 1932, page 118.
26. Hearings Senate Judiciary Committee, April 1926, page 40.
27. Current History, June 1922, page 381.
28. Hearings Senate Judiciary Committee, April 1926, page 607.
29. Hearings Senate Judiciary Committee, April 1926, page 278.
30. Current History, September 1923, pages 1006–1007.
31. Hearings Senate Judiciary Committee, April 1926, page 771.
32. Hearings Committee on Manufactures, February 1932, 72nd Congress, page 445.
33. Tillitt, "The Price of Prohibition," page 96.
34. Hearings Modification of Volstead Act, Ways and Means Committee, December 1932, pages 113–114.
35. Hearings Modification of Volstead Act, Ways and Means Committee, December 1932, pages 202 and 197.
36. New York Times, June 10, 1932.
37. House Document 722, page 73.
38. House Document 722, page 130.
39. Hearings on Prohibition Amendment, House Judiciary Committee, February 1930, page 891 and New York Times, May 11, 1930.
40. Modification of Volstead Act Hearings, Ways and Means Committee, December 1932, page 420.
41. Hearings Committee on Manufactures, January 1932, page 368.
42. Hearings Committee on Manufactures, January 1932, page 428–429.
43. Quoted in Senate Committee on Judiciary Hearings, April 1932, page 109.
44. Committee on Manufactures Hearings, January 1932, pages 1500 and 399.
45. House Documents 722, page 71.
46. Congressional Record, January 16, 1930, page 1714.
47. House Document 722, page 128–129.
48. Hearings on Prohibition Amendment, House Judiciary Committee 1930, page 550.
49. Hearings Alcoholic Liquor Committee, 65th Congress, 1924–5, page 103.
50. Hearings Senate Judiciary Committee, April 1926, pages 1241–2.
51. Annals of American Academy of Political and Social Sciences, September 1923, page 193.

NOTES TO CHAPTER III

A.   Dean Pound writes: "We expect legislation to conform to public opinion not public opinion to yield to legislation" (p. 48). We expect both. The 18th Amendment was adopted by a larger proportion of the states than any other in the Constitution. Was not public opinion favorable by that test? Mr. Baker of the Commission wrote to Col. Callahan, March 17, 1932: "In my opinion the people of the United States are dry overwhelmingly." Doubtless true if one counts those who want Prohibition *providing adequate enforcement can be assured.*

B.   Dr. Clarence True Wilson made an address in Portland, Me., in which he treated the just published Wickersham Commission Report to scathing criticism. "On my way back to Boston a tall, handsome gentleman (who proved to be Judge Kenyon) came to my seat in the train, and said, 'I drove sixty miles yesterday to hear your address. You did not exaggerate a single point.' He then told me that he resigned from the Commission and that Mr. Hoover asked him to remain and try to save something out of the wreck. I was thoroughly confirmed in my adverse statements by the testimony of Judge Kenyon" (abridged from Ms.). Judge Kenyon's copy of the Commission evidence ("vast in amount" according to Miss Awe, his secretary) was destroyed by her after his death!

C. A church group in Cleveland found that 95% of the 1,630 saloons in that city were running Sundays. They placed the facts before the mayor, Mr. Baker, and were told that they had as little right to interfere in the affairs of the city as the city in their church affairs. Mr. Kohler, Mr. Baker's Chief of Police, when asked why he allowed this violation of law said that "the laws are like drugs and should be kept on the shelves just as a doctor keeps medicines to be used only when necessary." "Prohibition" by Lamar Beaman, p. 50.

D. But Mr. Taber of the National Grange testified, "Government reports and declarations of manufacturers show that America is now using more than twelve million bottles of soft drink annually." The increased manufacture of milk bottles under Prohibition must have been very large. Hearings of House Judic. Com. 1930, pp. 676–8.

The great "leak" was industrial alcohol and industrial alcohol was shipped in five gallon tin cans but before it could be sold in renatured form it too had to be bottled. These bottles appear to have been secondhand ones. The largest dealers, I am told, were Glickstein and Terner, Brooklyn and Pittsburgh. The turnover of this firm of "bottle-leggers" does not appear to have been excessive. The N. Y. Times of July 12, 1931 reported that the U. S. Circuit Court of Appeals ordered the return to Glickstein and Terner of 1,014 crates of empty whisky bottles and several hundred crates of other liquor bottles seized five years before when their warehouses were padlocked. Shortly before, a meeting of representatives of 28 glass bottle manufacturers bitterly denounced the 18th Amendment "for destroying one fifth of the bottle business" (N. Y. Times, Feb. 20, 1926).

Since Repeal New York "bottle-leggers" with warehouses filled to the very roof with whisky bottles operate undisturbed, even in bottles with the blown-in warning, "Federal law forbids sale or re-use of this bottle." The labels of the standard whiskies are cleaned and retained with the bottles. This traffic runs into the millions of bottles.

CHAPTER IV

WALL STREET AND REPEAL

"The controlling reason . . . is to transfer the income tax from organized wealth to the backs of the beer-drinkers of this country, those who have little means. . . . Who have brought this about? I say it is a group of not to exceed seventy-five millionaires" (Senator Robinson of Indiana, Cong. Record, Feb. 16, 1933, p. 4217).

"This same group of big bankers and their allied interests look at every proposition from their own cold-blooded standpoint and never fail to do what they believe will help them accumulate more money and secure more political power regardless of the consequences to the average citizen. *This is why most of them favor the return of the open saloon. It will enable them to make more money and will become a powerful additional political agency in their hands to be used by them in their further efforts to get complete control of all local, state, and federal government*" (Congressman Lankford of Georgia, Cong. Record, Feb. 27, 1933, p. 5155).

The American movement against alcohol has had in the past to contend with the drink interest alone, certainly a sufficiently powerful enemy. But the fight for Repeal has been the affair of Wall Street in collusion with the press controlled by Wall Street, a power without equal. Its major organization, the Association Against the Prohibition Amendment, came from the innermost circles of high finance. The parallel Women's Organization for (anti) Prohibition Reform was captained by the wife of the president of the Guaranty Trust, a great Morgan bank. The Crusaders were cubs of the Du Pont, Sabin, Wadsworth, Mather, and other rich families of the A. A. P. A. The Congressional Districts' Modification League, according to its secretary, was "in contact with big business and bankers in New York." Members of rich clubs, taking a number for a name, bound themselves together with men of other clubs to fight Prohibition (1). "The Association

(79)

Against the Prohibition Amendment is recognized as leader of the opposition to National Prohibition," said their tract. "Who? How? Why?" It was a leadership not of knowledge or social idealism but of crass and overpowering wealth (A).

THE WET INTELLECTUALS

These were not formidable. One has but to examine their writings to realize how little fearsome, because little competent, the alcohol theoreticians of the A. A. P. A. were.

Prof. Raymond Pearl was first heard of when, at the University of Maine, he discovered that resistance and length of life were greater in the young of alcoholized hens than of "dry" ones. Rare news for Maine farmers, so long hoodwinked by Neal Dow! When he got to Johns Hopkins he extended his bigger and better chick theory to man, publishing it jointly in the volume of the English physiologist, Starling, "commissioned" by the drink interest. In his contention that the "moderate" drinker shows up better than the abstainer in length of days he stands in Athanasian solitude over against all the actuaries and statisticians (B).

Dr. Stewart Paton, also of Johns Hopkins, in "The Prohibiting Mind" railed at this thing, Prohibition, which had come between the wind and his nobility. He described the prohibitionist as being as much shocked at wine-drinking "as angered when anyone tried to improve the condition of the insane" (3). Does Dr. Paton not know that leading psychiatrists of our time have been prohibitionists,—Forel and Kraepelin and Aschaffenburg and Bleuler and Legrain and Frey Svensson? He says, "Prohibition produces conditions favorable for . . . insanity" (4). All the downward curves of 1920 showed the exact contrary (Dr. H. M. Pollock, *Mental Hygiene,* Jan. 1921).

SCIENTIA ALCOHOLICA

Then there was the late Dr. Harlow Brooks, convinced of the danger of pure water under certain conditions, who averred that alcohol "almost without exception" supplied essential elements in food. The example given was "the essential vitamin furnished the Mexican in his pulque." In a footnote, however, Dr. Brooks refuted himself by explaining that this vitamin is existent only in the unfermented stage of pulque manufacture. "It largely disappears when fermentation has developed the usually desired alcohol content" (5). Dr. Brooks was attached to Bellevue Hospital where the alcohol-sick admissions during the first Prohibition years broke and ran to one-fifth of the maximum of preceding years (6).

Dr. Samuel Lambert thought alcohol necessary in pneumonia and the fevers of infectious diseases. His brother Dr. Alexander Lambert pronounced himself in hearty disagreement and explained that, in his experience, the death-rate was lowered ten percent by not using it (7). Emeritus Prof. Osborne of the Yale School of Medicine repeated the old charge that Prohibition was accompanied with an increase in the use of narcotics and declared diabetes to be on the increase because of the sugary soda-fountain mixtures which took the place of beer (8). There was no truth in the first statement; doubtless as little in the second.

A QUICK REVERSAL

Dr. Samuel Harden Church, President of the Carnegie Institute of Technology, Pittsburgh, before a Senatorial Committee, 1926, described "liquor as one of the greatest blessings that God has given to men out of the teeming bosom of Mother Earth." At the same hearing he also asserted in horror that "it had become the fixed habit in the whole student body of Pittsburgh to carry a hip flask." Given his premise this would seem not at all reprehensible. The student council of the Carnegie Institute, however, together with the deans of both men and women, indignantly denied any truth in President Church's charge. On his return home, when summoned before the students he swiftly retracted. "All the statements attributed to me which reflect upon our student body I withdraw. . . . I ask that you grant me your full and free forgiveness." The press, however, which had blazoned the false testimony from coast to coast, suppressed the recantation. At the Senate Hearing when Senator Walsh of Montana asked Mr. Baird if he could think of any reason for President Church's slander the reply came: "The cause might have been the seizure of one of his autos coming from Canada with a load of contraband liquor, an incident which cost him $1,000 in fines" (9).

WET NON-SEQUITURS

Mr. Fabian Franklin, of Hungarian birth, had borrowed an Anglo-Saxon surname little appropriate in view of the great Franklin's well-known aversion to beer. He took the lofty American line, " May the day be not far distant when we shall once more be a nation of freemen, upstanding Americans." He was wroth with the spiritual descendants of Hampden and Otis for breaking the power of the monstrous alcohol capital. The weight of Mr. Franklin's argumentation can be gauged by the following: "What does the law do to prevent the crime of forgery? Does it prohibit the manufacture, sale, and transport of pens and ink? Not at all" (10). So Mr. Channing Pollock, also member of the A. A. P. A., "We who have been forbidden a glass of beer today may be forbidden beef-steak because immoderate meat-eating creates uric acid." In this same hearing Mr. Pollock declared: "If these men in the Federal Council of Churches are not careful they will bring about the abolishment of the Church" (11).

Such was the nature and extent of the scientific trimming of the A. A. P. A., certainly not an imposing showing. When the financiers themselves attempted to state their case it was no better. Mr. Pierre S. Du Pont's "The Eighteenth Amendment not a Remedy for the Drink-Evil" is the utterance of a confused mind. Although the Repeal of the 18th Amendment was due as much to him as to any one person, he had to admit no first-hand knowledge of the matter. Congressman Bachmann drew out the following confession:

Mr. Bachmann.   I assume that your study and investigation has taken you all over the United States and has put you in touch with almost every state in the United States in order to enable you to reach your conclusions.

Mr. Du Pont.   No, I cannot fairly say that, because I have very little opportunity to make practical personal observation.

Mr. Bachmann.   Have you covered a considerable portion of the United States?

Mr. Du Pont.   Only in reading such articles as I have been able to get. . . . (12).

ATTORNEYS FOR LIQUOR AND LUCRE

Others in the Association were in the direct line of the alcohol tradition. Mr. J. H. Choate, Jr., who in 1937 became adviser to the New York Liquor Board of Trade, was son of J. H. Choate, brewers' attorney in the famous Mugler v. Kansas case. The elder

Choate's greatest feat in his long career as corporation lawyer was to secure the decision against the income tax law (Pollock v. Farmers' Loan and Trust Co.) which made the 16th Amendment necessary. This Choate was related to Rufus Choate who also appeared before the Supreme Court as whisky attorney in a famous case which was to become a corner-stone for Prohibition legislation. He, too, was a defender to the uttermost of property rights, including property in human flesh. Mr. Edgar Allen Poe of Baltimore bore a name which is the synonym for the misery of alcoholism. The A. A. P. A. should have barred that name above all others from their roster. In the common schools the great Poe is contrasted as typical drunkard with men like Lindbergh and Peary in temperance instruction (*Alabama School Journal,* Jan. 1932). Another member, Norman Mack, was owner of the *National Monthly.* Pages 108–9 of the Overman Report are taken up with receipts of money paid him by the U. S. Brewers' Association for the publication of editorials and articles.

"PROPUTTY, PROPUTTY, PROPUTTY"

But the real backbone and ribs of the Association Against the Prohibition Amendment were of beaten gold. A correspondent in the *Madison Capitol Times* calls this organization of Croesuses "a reactionary catspaw of big business" (13). Rather was it the hand guiding many catspaws. Its directors were chiefly bankers, capitalists, corporation lawyers with one gentleman farmer, ex-Senator Wadsworth, and Matt Woll to represent labor. The original little ring of high-powered multimills drew to itself an imposing list of rich men.

Nicholas Brady, capitalist
R. Agassiz, Chairman of Calumet and Hecla
General Atterbury, President of the Pennsylvania R. R.
M. C. Brush, President of the International Corporation
R. K. Cassett, banker
H. B. Joy, President of Packard Motors
Percy R. Pyne, banker
Samuel Sloan, City Bank Farmer's Trust Co.
Charles Hayden of Hayden, Stone and Co.

H. M. Sears of N. E. Trust Co.

G. E. Roosevelt, banker

and many more (C).

"HIS WAY HE WENDS

AN INCARNATION OF FAT DIVIDENDS"

The inner council consisted of Mr. Arthur Curtis James, owner of railroads and yachtsman, Mr. E. S. Harkness, oil capitalist, Mr. Charles A. Sabin, President of the Guaranty Trust, Mr. Grayson M. P. Murphy, banker with Morgan connections, and preeminently the Du Ponts with their shrewd business associate, Mr. J. J. Raskob.

The public now knows much about the Du Ponts, thanks to the Arms Inquiry. These revelations make clear how a small group, such as this, was able to rip an amendment out of the United States Constitution for the first time in the history of the country. Their potent wealth, source of their political power, came largely from war profiteering.

In the period 1915–18 Du Pont dividends are said to have amounted to 458% on the par value of original stock. "It is difficult to imagine a more satisfactory result" was the comment of their company report. Yet when the government in 1916, year of 100% profits, imposed a heavy profits tax they declared themselves "victimized."

These vast profits enabled them at the war's close to put $50,000,000 into the captured German dye industry and $47,000,000 into General Motors; also to obtain partial or entire control of twenty-six other corporations (16). They were closely allied to giant groups abroad, notably Imperial Chemical Industries. Their intimacies with War and Navy Departments, their influence in and about Congress, their influence on the press as great advertisers, their relationships with the House of Morgan and other banks, made them a power of the first magnitude. "This is our country and not the country of Congress," was the boast of their sales director, Major Casey (17).

When the Lobby Investigation of 1930 laid bare their dubious anti-Prohibition activities, Mr. Walter Lippmann rushed to their defense in the *Forum* (84, p. 130) demanding that "the never-ending audacity of elected persons (a Committee of the United States Senate!) be stopped." Four years later the Du Ponts were again on the carpet, this time the crimson carpet of Senator Nye's Committee room with its gray fluted columns. The flashes of the reporters' cameras were no more revealing than the merciless questioning of the investigators. Du Ponts were found ready to sell munitions to combatants on both sides (18), and to other lands, more cheaply than to their own "if the fact could be kept secret."

They were shown to be engaged in various of the irregularities of which they complained in connection with Prohibition. Thus as late as June 1934 they were in a consortium organized in Holland for trans-shipping war materials which could not *legally* go direct to China (19). Their attitude regarding attempts at Washington and Geneva to block export of arms to belligerents may be fairly estimated from the words of one of their agents: "About the agitation for an embargo . . . We immediately got busy. We reached some mighty high officials in the government and feel confident that nothing will prevent the execution of any business we can get" (20).

"Had you gentlemen no pity for these war-torn people of China?" asked Senator Clark of the Du Pont trio before his Committee. Apparently not. The military misery of nations does not trouble them. Why, then, should the alcohol misery of families (21)?

THE ALCOHOL PACTOLUS

The later literature of the Du Pont subsidized Association Against the Prohibition Amendment explained and defended the motives of the Association. One of its directors, Prof. E. R. A. Seligman, a former economist for the U. S. Brewers' Association, said (*Prohibition and the Deficit*), "The United States has voluntarily abandoned the greatest fiscal resource of virtually every country in the world." This is the alcohol tax. Now 90% of the alcohol consumption in the United States was beer and according to Mr. Fox, of the U. S. Brewers' Association, 90% of the consumers of this beer were wage workers (Overman Report, p. 85). The incidence of this taxation, then, fell chiefly on the day-waged. The 18th Amendment was a great emancipating measure. By it we broke away from the class taxation which prevailed in "virtually every country in the world" and substituted a juster type of taxation. According to Mr. Clark Warburton, investigator for

the A. A. P. A., "a hundred thousand wealthy persons would undoubtedly receive most of the benefits of tax change resulting
from Repeal (The Economic Results of Prohibition, p. 255).

"THE LUST OF GAIN IN THE SPIRIT OF CAIN"

Taxes on the super-rich have been evaded in various ways.
Mr. Mellon had his "shadow-sales" with his children, Paul and
Ailsa, which brought him fictitious losses. Mr. Mitchell of the
National City Bank observed a similar technique for writing off
taxable income. So Otto Kahn, Lamont, Morgan, Raskob and
Du Pont (N. Y. Times, May 6, 1937). Many were the devices,—
"Tax avoidance by sale of securities through foreign corporations,
tax avoidance in connection with short sales, by dissolutions of
partnerships at propitious intervals" (Senate Report No. 1455.
Stock Exchange Practises, pp. 321–331). The Association Against
the Prohibition Amendment planned a more cowardly method. It
meant placing again the heavy load of alcohol charges on poor
families. "This liquor tax," wrote Mr. Pierre S. Du Pont, "would
be sufficient to pay off the entire debt of the United States, interest
and principal, in a little less than fifteen years" (22). A desirable
consummation if it did not mean wringing blood out of the needi-
est in the community. "This steady and dependable source of revenue" had, during the Prohibition years, flowed through corner gro-
ceries, shoe stores, milk farms, butcher shops, clothing stores, into
kitchens and homes, with notable results. "The improvement in
mortality since 1920 has been chiefly among women and children,"
wrote Dr. Haven Emerson. "The presumption is, therefore, that
they have been the ones chiefly to benefit from the diversion of
drink-money to better housing, clothing, and food." But it also,
to use the interesting phrase of Morgan-partner Dwight W. Morrow, "transferred the habit of spending from those who had long
experience of spending to those who have no experience," a dangerous tendency in Wall St. eyes (Nicholson, Morrow, p. 394).

Let us digress a moment. Mr. Henry M. Leland, manufacturer of Cadillac and Lincoln Motors, described the propaganda
of the A. A. P. A. as "having more wealth behind it than any
propaganda ever inaugurated." Mr. Leland, known as Detroit's
best citizen, having refused to join the Association, was stigma-
tized by Mr. H. B. Joy, the ultra-rich Packard manufacturer, as a
fanatic. I do not envy Mr. Joy the answer which this conventional

wet insult called forth. Mr. Leland spoke of the poverty of his own early life as contrasted with Mr. Joy's childhood in a rich home. His father, a teamster who drove between Boston and Montreal, died of exposure and the mother had a bitter struggle to raise her children on a Vermont farm. They occupied the house with a related family, the head of which was a drunkard.

AND THE VITRIOL MADNESS FLUSHES UP IN THE RUFFIAN'S HEAD

"The most pitiable sight that ever came to my attention was to see his five children in the road nearly every day, watching for his return from the tavern. Each was tense and eager. When they saw him appear over the top of the hill this tensity was greatly increased. They looked to see if he staggered. If he did they would cry out, 'He staggers' and run to hide until the mother got him to bed. Then she would go to the barn or to the woods to bring home these children who were as afraid of their intoxicated father as they would be of a hungry wolf."

Mr. Leland then described the family struggles, the mother trying to hold body and soul together in factory towns by keeping boarders, the meagre income and twelve hours' work in mills for the children. "The tavern was everywhere in evidence. The bar-keepers, to ensure permanent business, enticed the boys with sweets." At fifteen he went from his village to Springfield to work in the government armory. Returning home after ten years he was amazed to find how many of his boyhood friends had drunk themselves into their graves. In his business life later, numbers of his foremen, managers, and employees went down as drunkards. He would hunt them out of saloons and take them home in spite of insults and threats from the saloon-keepers.

"I would ten thousand times rather be a fanatic," concluded Mr. Leland, "than to be arrayed with the galaxy of brilliants whom Mr. Joy mentions in his letter" (i.e. members of the A. A. P. A.).

In Colonial days, when nails were hand-wrought, there were miscreants who would set fire to buildings in order to get the nails out of the ashes, a true picture of those capitalists who, to lighten their taxes, destroyed the 18th Amendment and thereby brought back conditions such as Mr. Leland pictures. They have indeed proved to be "makers of bitter things for bitter living."

(Note, Dec. 25, 1941. A letter just received from *post-Repeal Vermont* has this sentence, "The little girl came, but her two brothers had to stay home to protect their mother from their drunken father." Merry Christmas from the A. A. P. A.!)

A TRANSFER OF LEADERSHIP

The opposition in the early years of National Prohibition was ineffective and desultory. With the passage of the 18th Amendment the liquor machine had been largely smashed. The brewers "yelled, gasped, and were abolished," at least most of them. Some committed suicide (Tosetti, the Lemps). Others, as Liebmann and Ehret, disposed of the enormous corner properties in New York which constituted their grip on the metropolis. Many went into honest business. The Association Against the Prohibition Amendment struggled along without making any particular impression on the country.

The distillers, too, capitulated. When the 18th Amendment was finally ratified National Distillers' Securities (the whisky trust) amended its charter (April 5, 1919) and became the U. S. Food Products Corporation, to manufacture food and cattle feed products, buying at the same time the entire capital stock of certain great molasses and sugar corporations. But evidently the turn of events, which the distiller-financier in the Treasury Department was effecting, switched distiller hopes back from food to drink again, for in 1924 (April 18) U. S. Foods Products Corp. became National Distillers' Products, controlling plants in Louisiana, Kentucky, Peoria, and Baltimore. National Distillers' Products also acquired, on a 50–50 basis with the Du Ponts, the entire capital stock of the Eastern Alcohol Corporation (organized in 1925). The Distilling Company of America, a subsidiary of National Distillers, is reported to have guaranteed dividends on the preferred stock of U. S. Industrial Alcohol Co., allegedly under Mellon control and certainly supplying the bootleg trade.

The plan was evidently to market beverage alcohol as "medicine." On the first of July, 1927, American Medicinal Spirits, Inc., Seton Porter, Chairman, was organized in close relations with National Distillers and its subsidiary, the Distilling Company of America. Its principal offices in 1928 were in New York, Louisville, and Baltimore, *with 122 branch warehouses throughout the United States!* In 1929 it was given by Mr. Mellon permits to manufacture 900,000 gallons of Bourbon whisky for "medicinal" uses, a move calculated to cut the very throat of Prohibition. ("There are no present-day physiologists to maintain the old theses. Alcohol has no necessary place in the equipment of the practical physician." Dr. Henry Smith Williams, *Drugs Against Men*, p. 41.)

(See Moody's Analyses of Investments 1924, p. 2475: 1925, pp. 2032 and 2147: 1927, p. 2505: 1928, pp. 1373, 2739, 446: 1930, p. 2490.)

With these interlockings in mind one is not surprised that about 1926 things began to pick up with the A. A. P. A. Into it had come a powerful Wall Street cavalcade led by Mr. Pierre S. Du Pont. Experienced politicians and newspaper men began work in Washington, in the state legislatures, in the Congressional districts. Various able men appeared one by one in key positions.

THE WET CHRYSOSTOM
(A mouth of gold for men of gold)

Thus in 1927 the Hon. James M. Beck, who had been Solicitor-General and Attorney-General of the United States, abandoned his lucrative practise of law in Washington to run for Congress. Mr. Beck had defended Vare when Congress investigated the election frauds which brought that outstanding wet crook to the door of the Senate. Vare's brother-in-law, Hazlett, resigned his seat in the House when it was felt desirable that Mr. Beck should represent this Philadelphia district. After his election a Citizens' Committee attempted to prevent his seating on the ground that his real residence was in Washington. The evidence produced was contradictory but Beck was finally allowed to take the seat. A minority report of the Committee on Elections declared this action "a frontal attack on the Constitution." Then it continued:

"In a day when a political machine can select any individual it chooses to put into the House there are multiplied dangers. . . . It is clear that if his contention is to prevail, an all-powerful, though it be unscrupulous, combine in control of a district machine can select any one to represent it."

Mr. Beck was a former corporation lawyer with office at 53 Wall Street. It was he who prosecuted Gompers, Mitchell, and Morrison in the famous Buck Stove and Range case, one of the severest defeats that American labor ever had. This Cincinnatus answering his country's call could no doubt be depended on to defend the general interests of big business in Congress but his present aim was undoubtedly Repeal. To this he dedicated his patrician eloquence, embroidered with quotation from Shakespere and Sophocles. Back in the rotten Philadelphia district, however, at the close of his more plebeian speeches, the heelers sang "Hail! de gang's all here."

MR. RASKOB MAKES A CHANGE

In Mr. Beck the wets had acquired a powerful mouthpiece in the House of Representatives. Next year found the Republican, Mr. Raskob, chairman of the Democratic National Committee. "I went into politics to fight Prohibition at the suggestion of Al Smith," said Mr. Raskob when it was all over (23). Smith was Tammany Sachem: Raskob, Wall Street operator. Their alliance symbolized the *entente* between Tammany and Wall Street which has existed from the days when Jay Gould put up a million to bail out Tweed, and J. J. Astor with six other capitalists gave the arch-thief a published certificate of good character. Raskob was member of the old-time Republican Union League Club and heavy contributor to the A. A. P. A. which was busy electing wet Republicans to Congress. He soon acquired a first mortgage on the Democratic party management by his large loans and contributions. "He underwrote the expenses of the Democratic headquarters in Washington," wrote Mr. Frank Kent, political annalist of the *Baltimore Sun* (Jan. 6, 1931), "(He) reduced the party debt from one million to $628,000 and took the responsibility for this large balance." Raskob is also reported to have made personal campaign contributions to Democratic Congressional and Senatorial candidates. He selected Mr. Shouse as executive chairman of the Democratic National Committee. What Shouse was there for can be surmised from the fact that he was later President of the A. A. P. A. Evidently this Association had the inside track in the Democratic party counsels, for its secretary, Mr. Stayton, wrote: "We are keeping in touch with the Democratic National Committee so that *we know what work they are doing and we are merely trying to supplement it*" (24).

"Raskob was detailed by the Wall Street crowd to run the Democratic party," said Senator Brookhart (25). He was at their disposition according to his own statement. As recipient of financial favors from the firm of J. P. Morgan and Company he wrote Mr. Whitney of that firm: "I appreciate deeply the many courtesies shown me by you and your partners and *sincerely hope the future holds opportunities for me to reciprocate"* (26).

MR. MORROW TURNS HIS COAT

The appearance of Mr. Morrow on the political scene was a parallel to that of Mr. Raskob. Morrow was member of the House of Morgan. Business associations had brought him into close contacts with the General Motors of Raskob and Du Pont. As wet Republican in the Senate he would have been in a position to serve the cause of Repeal in innumerable ways and would have given it a quality and prestige which the Binghams and Edwardses and Tydingses were without. But the thing would not stop there. Mr. Alexander Simpson, his opponent in the Senatorial race, publicly averred that he was being groomed for the Presidency in 1932 by Wall Street. If for any reason Mr. Hoover had declined to run Morrow would have made the most formidable candidate conceivable, with his huge Senatorial majority of 191,125 in the close state of New Jersey. When President Hibben of Princeton and ex-Gov. Stokes of New Jersey acclaimed him as Presidential timber he was content to smile and be silent (27). An untimely death closed his political career. If he had lived, that political career would have unquestionably run along with the strategy of the great wet financiers. Mr. Frelinghuysen made this clear: "Mr. Morrow is candidate of a group of bosses directly under the influence of the Public Service Corporation of New Jersey. The fact that the Public Service Corporation is a prospective link in the gigantic national light and power-trust now in formation, makes the question a national one" (28). He further alleged that the machine politicians back of Morrow were responsible for corrupt conditions in many counties of the state.

SHOCKED AT THE WRONG THING

Morrow was Presbyterian, trustee of Union Theological Seminary, and friend of Presidents. The unexpected defection of such a respectable was an ominous blow. On May 15, 1930 he made his peace with the brewers in brewer Krueger's Auditorium, Newark. His phraseology was almost the duplicate of that used by Gov. Smith when the latter betrayed his party platform in 1928 (E). "Is it well," he asked, "to have as a result of Prohibition a lawless, unregulated liquor traffic?" Someone has described to me his keynote speech in Jersey City. He was nervous and his hand shook as he read the written statement. The body of the house had been packed with the *élite* of the Jersey City underworld. In that Jersey City, before Prohibition, there were "one thousand saloons, all law-breakers, open seven days in the week and twenty-four hours in the day, crowded every Sabbath with scofflaws who laughed at regulation" (29). The worst and wettest hole in the United States, this Jersey City under Prohibition still counted, according to police census, 175 places doing a furtive business. This was, as Morrow said, "shocking" (F), but 825 places were gone. There was no reason to capitulate to the dwindling balance and still less on their account to abandon the nation's bulwark against drink. "I bring you no panacea for this deplorable condition," cried "the little wonder-worker." He might have bethought him of the prosaic formula of rigid law enforcement for this ragtail wet remnant.

"I do not understand Mr. Morrow," said honest Mr. Edison, and went on to narrate how on paydays before Prohibition hundreds of pale-faced women, shabbily-dressed, some with faded shawls over their heads, could be seen at his factory in West Orange, N. J. They were waiting to get some of their husbands' money before the husbands got to a saloon. "Within a year after the Amendment not a single woman appeared. Surely we Americans do not want a return of this state of affairs." But the fate of millions of such women is no concern of the House of Morgan or of the Morrows for that matter. The first steamer which came from England after Repeal brought to Mrs. Morrow's cellar thirty-nine cases of wine racing with one from Scotland which carried a consignment of twenty-five cases of whisky to J. J. Raskob (30).

"Repeal will not come as a victory of the liquor interests," was Mr. Morrow's confident assertion (31). A poor prophet! He "looked forward to the time when the moral leaders of the country would take up again the old system of experimenting in forty-eight laboratories rather than in one" (32). A bankrupt theorist! When he got to the Senate he showed himself unvarying friend of the power trust and of the brewers. "Morrow voted as Blaine voted on wet-dry questions, as Blaine was the wettest man in the Senate, since he aspired to a wringing wet leadership in New Jersey. When the bell rings for a vote Senator Hastings, Republican reactionary, looks at Senator Morrow. Senator Morrow knows what that means. When the roll-call is checked up his name is found on the side of reaction everytime" ("Washington Merry-Go-Round," pp. 289 and 292).

A PHILADELPHIA LAWYER

The Judiciary Committee of the House dealt with amendments to the Constitution and it was desirable that its chairman be a dependable wet, ready to influence both legislation and hearings. As it happened Mr. Volstead himself was chairman. In a Congressional election he was defeated by Mr. Kvale who, though dry as Volstead, was said to have had the unsolicited support of the wets. The elimination of Volstead from the House was played up all over the country as an indication that the nation was turning away from Prohibition. The successor to Mr. Volstead in the chairmanship of the Judiciary Committee was Mr. George S. Graham, wet politician from Philadelphia and, by a happy coincidence, former attorney for Mr. Pierre Du Pont. When the 1930 Hearings before this Committee were initiated by the A. A. P. A. Mr. Du Pont was present, though out of sight, to direct witnesses, with his former attorney in the chair (33). (These Hearings were announced by Graham without consultation with other members of the Judiciary Committee and in spite of the fact that the resolutions upon which they were called had not the slightest chance of passing. Graham said in so many words that they were pure propaganda. They "open the door for the spread of the views of those who have been conservative (i.e. Wall Street wets) and that is the object and main purpose of these meetings.")

The presence of Mr. Ogden Mills in President Hoover's entourage first as Assistant Secretary, then as Secretary of the Treasury, may have been only an accident from the point of view of wet politics. Yet it was a fortunate one for it placed at Mr. Hoover's elbow one who was certainly willing to promote wet strategy in every way possible. The diarist of the White House said of him: "The President (Mr. Hoover) had grown to lean upon the youthful secretary to an extent I had never seen before. Never did I know a President so dependent on a cabinet officer" (34). The President of the Pennsylvania Railroad, Gen. W. W. Atterbury, active member of the A. A. P. A., should perhaps also be mentioned in this connection. "I want to call attention," said Senator Brookhart, "to the fact that Mr. Mellon from the Treasury through Mr. Atterbury, *his Republican Committeeman from the state of Pennsylvania* and through his club, the Union League of New York, is at this time conducting a campaign against Prohibition in the United States. Mr. Raskob and Mr. Mellon are the Amos and Andy of the situation" (*N. Y. Times,* April 8, 1930, p. 21).

THE NATIONAL CIVIC FEDERATION

It is sometimes protested that organized labor is wet and that, if high finance were really ranged against Prohibition, the American Federation of Labor would not have been found fighting in the same trenches with it. But there is much to indicate that Wall Street has influence upon official labor leadership. Some years ago the National Civic Federation had a solemn meeting in joint memory of August Belmont and Samuel Gompers, deceased president and vice-president respectively of the Federation. This was the Belmont who testified before the Industrial Relations Committee "that the majority of the companies he represented opposed the right to organize, and maintained spy systems" (35). Gompers' intimacies with the $900,000,000 U. S. Brewers' Association are too well known to dwell on. Dr. Stires, rector of the ultra-fashionable St. Thomas' Church, closed his speech which closed the meeting with the quotation:

> "O God, to us may grace be given
> To follow in their train."

To the Red Ridinghoods it may seem strange to see the wolf of capitalism in the grandmotherly trimmings of the American Federation of Labor. Shrewd old Mark Hanna, who organized the National Civic Federation, knew what he was about in thus "bringing labor and capital together." The plan was to domesticate rather than to smash labor. Just now the acting president of the National Civic Federation is Matthew Woll of whom Mr. Foster says ("Misleaders of Labor," p. 151), "He is a brazen agent of the bosses. He has behind him the most corrupt influences in the labor movement. . . . The poisonous effects of the National Civic Federation upon labor leadership are," he continues, "incalculable." The Federation is financed wholly by rich wets, Morgan, Du Ponts, Ogden Mills, Nicholas Brady. It is significant that the constitution of the United Mine Workers provides that "persons engaged in the sale of intoxicating liquors and members of the National Civic Federation shall not be eligible for membership" (36) (H).

Mr. Adamic tells us that "some of the A. F. L. leaders are perhaps the worst enemies that organized labor has and are recognized as such by groups in the unions, but it is nigh impossible to remove them from their commanding, high-salaried positions." "The American Federation of Labor is recognized by the big industrialists and conservative politicians as the best obstacle to the emergence of a militant and formidable labor movement" (37).

WALL STREET'S MARIONETTES

All this helps to explain why labor officialdom was so useful to Wall Street wets in pulling their chestnuts from the fire. They constantly barked for beer before Congress, presumably at the suggestion of wet capitalism (E). In the Senate Judiciary Hearings of 1926 one of the most extravagant witnesses was Mr. Henry J. Hilfers, secretary of the A. F. L. of New Jersey (38). Mr. Hilfers went so far as to testify that in 1927 there was a still in practically every home (in New Jersey) (38). Next year he was reported short in his accounts and to the investigating committee he explained that 50% of the expenses of the State Federation were paid by the affiliated local unions. The rest, amounting to $100,-000 in a given period, was contributed by employers through the medium of advertising and donations to the Federation's Yearbook. Contributions came from such rabidly anti-union concerns as the U. S. Metal Refining Co., Durant Motors, U. S. Trust Co., United Lead and the Du Ponts. "To secure these contributions," says Foster, "Hilfers and his crowd manoeuvred aggressively against every attempt to organize the unorganized masses in New Jersey industries, a case in point being the flagrant betrayal of the Passaic 1926 strike" (39).

When Mr. Morrow started on his wet Senatorial campaign Hilfers spoke for him and told his hearers that this arm of the

Morgan octopus was "the fearless type of man needed in public life" (40). Morrow was attorney for Coleman Du Pont, described as "one of the greatest labor-crushing capitalists of the world" (Foster, "Misleaders of Labor," p. 113; "They Told Barron," p. 276).

A JANUS-FACED COMBINATION

At the First National Conference of Labor's National Committee for the Modification of the Volstead Act the two star speakers were Mrs. Sabin, wife of the President of the Guaranty Trust, N. Y. (assets $1,847,433,862) (G), and James M. Beck, the aforesaid prosecutor of Gompers, Mitchell and Morrison. Beck told these labor wets (Woll, Feeney, Colpoys) to send 200 men to the House of Representatives who would promise to vote no money for enforcement of the 18th Amendment. When the Women's Organization for National (anti) Prohibition Reform had its second national conference in Washington, the Vice-President of the A. F. L., Mr. Woll, spoke at the gala banquet and pledged to Mrs. Sabin the cooperation of 300,000 local unions. Mr. Woll appeared again with Wall Street bankers and attorneys, Paul Abbott, Clarence H. Low, G. G. Battle, as promoter of the Anti-Prohibition Battle Fund, Inc., to raise five million for Repeal (41).

The A. A. P. A. apparently inherited the grip on labor officialdom (which the U. S. Brewers' Association earlier had) through the Joint Committee of the A. F. L. and the A. A. P. A. (Duncan of the A. F. L., President, and Maguire of the Haffenreffer Brewery, Secretary); also through the above-mentioned Labor's National Committee for the Modification of the Volstead Act. Mr. Julian Codman of Boston, who represented the Joint Committee, was attorney for the A. F. L. and all-round Boston aristocrat. At the House Hearings in 1924 Gompers was introduced by Codman (42). He denied representing brewery interests. "No man representing them ought to have the effrontery to appear before a Committee of Congress of the United States. No such man ought to be permitted to associate with decent men and women." Strange statement to come from Gompers! The brewers' confidential correspondence revealed him constantly as their speaker and political worker (Overman Report, pp. 833 and 838, for example). At House Hearings (April 1924, p. 25)

Gompers boasted of his successful interference in New Zealand, Australia, Canada, and Sweden, at the time of Prohibition plebiscites. The famous Beer Special with eight Pullmans, which took him and his wet labor cronies to Washington for the beer demonstration on the Capitol steps, was paid for by brewers.

When Theodore Roosevelt wrote to Mr. Stelzle, "There are few things more important to our social advancement than the loosening of the grip of the liquor interests on the labor movement" (44), it is not to be supposed that he was referring to the rank and file alone (H).

A WET ALLY OF WET LABOR

The National Association of Manufacturers asked for strong beer as "an indispensable revenue measure" (45) and its Secretary, Mr. James A. Emery, appeared to plead the cause of beer at the Congressional beer-hearings of 1932 (46). This association is the bitterest anti-labor organization in the country. It has stood for the open shop, against the Seamen's Act, against restriction of immigration, against "excessive agitation under the guise of moral crusade, such as for child labor, railway, and similar reforms." This statement appeared in 1908 and, as originally framed, included Prohibition, which item, however, was later withdrawn, evidently for tactical reasons. (Bonnett, "Employers Associations in the United States," p. 341.) In writing to a brewers' association in this year Mr. Van Cleave, President of the National Association of Manufacturers, claimed to have defeated all the attempts of the labor lobby at Washington to pass an eight hour law, an anti-injunction law and the Hepburn Amendment. In a second letter, Mr. Van Cleave boasts of successes at the 1908 Republican Convention. In those days the Association supported Nagel, Bartholdt, Taft, and Cannon, the then representatives *par excellence* of beer and reaction (47) (I).

The O'Mahoney Investigation (Monograph, No. 26, Economic Power and Political Pressure) states that in close cooperation with the Nat'l Ass'n of Manufacturers are the Am. Bar Ass'n, the Chambers of Commerce, and the American Newspaper Publishers Ass'n. On p. 196 the Special Conference Committee of New York is described as an organization of high executives of twelve of the country's largest corporations. It works through the Nat'l Ass'n of Manufacturers. Three of the twelve are the Du Pont corporations,—Gen'l Motors, U. S. Rubber, and Du Pont de Nemours.

THE SOAK-THE-POOR PROGRAM

As would be expected, the National Association of Manufacturers advocated alongside a beer tax a sales tax. These two taxes, it was estimated, would make superfluous excess-profit taxes and income surtaxes. To avoid tax-paying, corporations had engaged in unnecessary building and in costly advertising programs. These evasions being exhausted, they financed propaganda, in which a large section of the press abetted them, for sales, or consumption, taxes. Mr. Jules S. Bache, a banker interested deeply in Cuba Distilling and U. S. Industrial Alcohol, appeared before Congress in behalf of this tax and remarked that "the poor could escape the tax by refraining from consumption" (when consumption was the crying economic need of the time). Congressman Frear remarked that this brilliant suggestion should be placed beside Marie Antoinette's, "If they have no bread let them eat cake" (48).

Mr. W. R. Hearst denounced the income tax and called for repeal of the 16th Amendment (the income tax amendment) and for the imposition of a sales tax (49). Senator Reed of Pennsylvania, of Reed, Smith, Shaw and McCoy, Mellon attorneys, was the protagonist of this tax in the Senate.

THE NATIONAL SECURITY LEAGUE ATTACKS PROHIBITION

The National Security League solemnly opposed Prohibition because "it foments and facilitates the easy commission of crime" (50). Here we find again the old crowd of rich wets, tax-shifters, and corporation lawyers. An investigation of this League by Congress (68th Congress, Report 1173) disclosed the fact that it was financed by Messrs. Morgan, Brady, James, Du Pont, Rockefeller, and Guggenheim, and that among its officials and members were Messrs. Haley Fiske, Root, Choate, Beck, Feigenspan, Coudert, and President Hibben of Princeton University, all militant wets. We may note, in passing, that President Hibben was killed on Lincoln Highway May 1933 by a beer truck. National security on the highways was not brought in by "Modification."

The purpose of this League was divulged by its founder, Mr.

Stanley Menken, who declared that "he wished to see the income tax lessened at the upper end and enlarged at the lower." He even went so far as to say that he thought an income tax should be imposed on every one's income, even down to those who worked for a dollar a day. The Security League sought systematically to elect members of Congress and to intimidate those in Congress. The Congressional investigation declared that "the League cared nothing for a candidate's party affiliations. What chiefly concerned them was how his attitude would affect certain interests that would be the subject of legislation by Congress during the reconstruction period." The League's political chart disclosed the fact that out of 435 members of the House "full patriotism" was allowed to only 47. Of these 45 represented Congressional districts along the Atlantic Seaboard where the income tax gathers its largest revenue.

WETS AND VETS

The Grand Army of the Republic for a generation buttressed the Republican party and the great financial interests back of that party. There have been obvious attempts of these interests to use the American Legion in the same way. Major-General Smedley D. Butler says of its leadership: "I have not known one that has not sold them out. . . . They (the bankers) have been using these dumb soldiers to break strikes. That is the reason they have all these big club-houses and that is the reason I pulled out." Resolutions passed at Legion conventions reflect Wall Street influence. Thus it was discovered by the Dickstein Committee that $91,000 was turned over to Legion leaders to put a sound money resolution through the Chicago Convention, and it is charged that Commander Stevens' speech was written for him by John W. Davis, personal attorney of J. P. Morgan. Col. John Thomas Taylor is the Legion's legislative agent in Washington; also treasurer of a national chemical defense organization. It was he who is said to have led the opposition to proposed treaties banning the use of poison gas in war, indeed secured from the Legion itself in convention a resolution against such treaties. Of this Mr. Hamilton Fish said in Congress:

"I deplore that this great body of civilians, who were veterans of the World War, have been imposed upon by outside and selfish forces. . . . (These) were able to railroad through a resolution putting the Legion on record against the pending treaty.

. . . The big interests, the chemical interests, working silently through skilful management, were able to manipulate it so that the resolution was adopted after a one-sided debate" (51).

DICKERING FOR BEER

Mr. Belgrano, a later commander of the American Legion, is president of one of the largest banks in America. Through his efforts adjusted compensation for the soldiers was long blocked. Back of the "Ex-Service Men's Anti-Bonus League" were familiar wet names, Mellon, Raskob, Sabin. The Detroit Convention of 1931 (Sept. 25) turned down the adjusted compensation resolution but passed a resolution for a referendum on the 18th Amendment (Cries of "We want beer" and pandemonium). Wall Street wets had apparently been seeking this twofold result. Thus in a letter soliciting financial aid with the date of March 3, 1931, Mr. Charles A. Sabin, Col. Grayson M-P. Murphy, E. S. Harkness, G. G. Battle, Phelps Phelps, and Pierre S. Du Pont are alleged to have "underwritten a substantial part of our budget of $128,265" (52). The American Veterans Association for the Repeal of the 18th Amendment, which sent out this letter, declared that they were organizing voters in every precinct of the country. It had been formed to control opinion in the American Legion. Congressman Patman was told by numbers present at the Detroit Convention that President Hoover's "flying squadron"—three administration office-holders who arrived in airplanes some days before the President—promised various delegations that Mr. Hoover would give the boys beer if they would lay off the bonus at this session (53). It is hard to think that Mr. Hoover would make any such proposition; also hard to understand how the veterans could veto their own bonus bill, but it is not hard to believe that the rich tax-shifters in the background would have been delighted to exchange a beer tax for a squelched bonus. They would have had it coming and going.

CHESSMEN IN THE WALL STREET WET GAME

It is obvious that the wet capitalists sought to use the American Legion as well as the American Federation of Labor as pawns. In Tennessee, wet meetings were held jointly by the A. A. P. A., the American Legion and the labor organizations, and the American Legion and the A. F. L. are classed together in wet publications as wet (Root, "Women and Repeal," p. 105). Plans were even laid to organize a wet party for Repeal of which the American Legion and the A. F. L. should be jointly the driving force. General Hartnett, Chairman of the Veterans Clearing House in Washington, and Matthew Woll of the A. F. L. were named as promoters (54). One can see how things were timed.

Sept. 24, 1931.   The American Legion voted for a referendum on the 18th Amendment.

Sept. 29, 1931.   The American Federation of Labor's Committee for the Modification of the Volstead Act declared that it was impossible to over-emphasize the action in protest taken by the American Legion.

Oct.   8, 1931.   The President of the A. A. P. A., supporting the demands of these two associations, called on both major parties to include submission resolutions in their platforms.

A FRESH AVATAR

But the Association Against the Prohibition Amendment, which was so ready to use the soldier for its own ends, was no friend to him when in need. As soon as the 18th Amendment was repealed the A. A. P. A. dissolved and its one-time President and Vice-President, Messrs. Curran and Gebhart, appeared as officials of a new organization, the National Economy League, a specific purpose of which was to prevent passage of bonus legislation. So was the little boy who turned the grindstone jeered off to school when the axe was sharp.

This organization was described by Congressman Tarver. "They had in charge of their propaganda one H. H. Curran, head of the A. A. P. A., whom these great financial powers have now hired to enter on a campaign against the veterans of the World War, humiliating them as grafters and blood-suckers." "They are trying to get members all over the nation," added Congressman Patman, "and are telling (them) that they will never be called upon to pay one penny, that they have some one else footing the bill. Committees are to be formed in 455 Congressional districts to push for veteran and other governmental economies" (55).

It is obvious that, as the main purpose of the A. A. P. A. was to save Wall Street from taxation, the National Economy League merely continued that program. The child was doubtless as wet as its parent.

THE AMERICAN LIBERTY LEAGUE

A later shuffling of the old pack was the American Liberty League. A letter from Mr. Raskob to Mr. Carpenter of the Du Pont organization bears, as Senator Nye said of it when read in his Senate Committee Room, "all the earmarks of having been the birthplace and birthtime of the Liberty League." Raskob called on Carpetner to take "the lead in trying to induce the Du Ponts and General Motors group, followed by other big industrials, definitely to organize to protect society from the suffering which it is bound to endure if we allow Communistic elements to lead the people to believe that all business men are crooks . . . and that no one should be allowed to get rich.

"Pierre (Du Pont) as a citizen," continued Mr. Raskob, "has set us a fine example (i.e. in his wet activities) and I think you and Irenée . . . will find tremendous support and will be able to do one of the finest jobs that could be done for the nation. . . ."

OLD FACES REAPPEAR

This organization was formed to counter New Deals and taxation for Federal relief. The president, Mr. Jouett Shouse, was former president of the A. A. P. A. The League's roster was mottled with familiar wet names, Stayton, Wadsworth, John W. Davis, Al Smith, Mrs. Sabin, H. B. Joy, S. H. Church, G. E. Roosevelt, J. M. Beck, Pierre Du Pont, A. C. James, Mrs. Robert W. Lovett, G. M-P. Murphy, T. W. Phillips, J. J. Raskob, Elihu Root, and Wm. Gammell. The ladies of the anti-Prohibition Reform were also enlisted. Mrs. Sabin is reported to have said that "75 out of 84 members of the Executive Committee of the former Women's Organization for National (anti) Prohibition Reform will serve with her."

The National Security League raised the flag of patriotism, the Association Against the Prohibition Amendment that of temperance and law observance, the National Economy League used the mask of thrift, the American Liberty League the mask of freedom and individualism. But behind them all was the same crafty face of Wall Street, scheming to enlarge its ill-gotten gains and to protect itself from taxation (J).

WALL STREET FASCISM

The lengths to which this sinister wet Wall Street group is prepared to go came out in the hearings of the Un-American Activities Committee. General Butler's evidence was suppressed in the government report but he revealed it later and the Committee stated that it had been able to verify "all the pertinent statements" made by him (56). The plan was to organize an army of 500,000 veterans to take charge of the United States government and the leadership of this army was offered to Butler. The go-between who made the proposal was Gerald McGuire, *a bond salesman for the late Grayson M-P. Murphy. Mr. Murphy was one of the most active members of the Association Against the Prohibition Amendment. He was a broker for the House of Morgan, a director of the New York Trust, and Vice-President of the Guaranty Trust, two Morgan banks. He contributed $125,000 to organize the American Legion. Whether this was his own money or money from behind does not appear.*

McGuire had been sent abroad to study Fascist movements such as the *Croix de Feu* and his headquarters in Paris were at Morgan, Harjes Co., Paris branch of the Morgans. He suggested to General Butler that arms for the proposed army could be obtained *from the Remington Arms Co. on credit through the Du Ponts who own a controlling interest in that company.* Mr. Robert S. Clark of the American Liberty League and associated with the Morgan group, is reported also to have gone to Newtown Square, Pa., General Butler's home, with similar proposals. Butler insisted that Morgan was back of Murphy in this enterprise and made the significant reflection, *"Whatever you are fighting you will always find yourself up against the same group."*

(I may add that I happened to be talking with General Butler at Newtown Square when the telephone rang and he left the room. On returning he said "McGuire's dead." Never a more opportune death! What might this poor tool not have revealed regarding Wall St. schemes had he been brought before a Senate investigating committee!)

POLITICAL NARCOSIS

While the dominating motive of Repeal propaganda has been a tax motive there were other contributing ones. Beer is the narcotic with which it is planned to etherize radical movements. Three days before the reconvening of Congress in December 1932 a hundred newspapers over the country received and printed the advice of Mr. Walter Lippmann, "Wall St.'s most important editorial outlet," urging the immediate manufacture of beer. "Beer would be a great help in fighting off the mental depression which afflicts great multitudes and it is an unnecessary cruelty to withhold it" (57). One of the representatives of wet science at the Bingham Beer Bill Hearings, Prof. Graham Lusk of Cornell, declared that "beer makes bad food taste well. It is specially a valuable thing for the poor people . . . at this time" (58). (Beer expenditure means poor and inadequate food. The substitution of milk and good food which followed Prohibition reduced deathrate, as we have seen, among women and children.) Finally the head of the Baltimore Crusaders quoted Mr. McPurdy of the A. F. L.: "Beer would have a decidedly soothing tendency on the present-day mental attitude of the working men. . . . It would do a great deal to change their mental attitude on economic conditions" (59). That's plain enough! Trotsky turned the machine guns on the Tsar's wine cellar saying, "If men have access to liquor it will be impossible to carry through the Revolution" (Wald, "Windows on Henry St.," p. 225).

"TWO VIPERS TANGLED INTO ONE"

The reconstitution of the old liquor machine would also fortify the position of privilege. The U. S. Brewers' Ass'n, the state brewers' associations, the state and county liquor dealers' associations could, in the old days, ever be depended on to support reactionary politics. They contributed heavily to state and national campaign funds of both parties as insurance against hostile legislation and law enforcement. At the same time they were ever ready to cooperate in legislatures with the stand-pats against men with ideas and ideals (K). "There are no laboring women," wrote Mrs. Raymond Robins, the organizer of women's trades unions, "who do not know the hideousness of the political control of the liquor interests. It mattered not what bills were introduced in the state legislatures for bettering the industrial conditions of women and children, . . . the enfranchisement of women or the eight hour day, we were opposed by the liquor interests. Whether we asked to have the children of the richest land in the world taken out of mines and factories and put into the schools, whether we asked for the shorter work day or the right of women to the ballot . . . we were met by the united opposition of the liquor interests. Every worker for civic or political righteousness will bear the same testimony" (60).

WAR ON THE CHILDREN

The wet capitalists are almost as bitter against the proposed child-labor amendment as against the 18th. Captain Stayton denounces it as "infamous" (61). At the 1935 ratification hearing in Albany Mr. Guthrie, brewers' Supreme Court attorney, led the opposition. Declarations against the Amendment were filed by the wets, Elihu Root, Al Smith, N. M. Butler and H. S. Pritchett. Mrs. Cortland Nicoll, former head of the N. Y. State Committee for anti-Prohibition Reform, used the old wet phrases. "This (child-labor amendment) will send an army of snoopers to invade the home" (62). The wet Boston capitalist, Mr. Alexander Lincoln, stated before a 1930 Congressional Committee that "the same forces which were opposed to the (Volstead) enforcement act were opposed to the (child labor) amendment." Naturally! Drink drives children into the mills, where believers in cheap and unorganized labor want them. The Roman Catholic Church also backed the rich wets against the children.

THEY'VE LOST THEIR TIDE!

"This bank-note world" is every whit as obtuse as the doomed French nobility of 1789. The Republican party owed its long lease of life largely to its early moral history. It freed the slaves and saved the Union. If the Republican politicians had loyally supported and enforced Prohibition they would have had a like hold on the gratitude of the best in the nation for a generation to come. There would have been a political trade-wind blowing steadily for many years behind their sails. Enforced Prohibition would have greatly softened the contrasts between the classes and thereby have contributed to delay revolutionary movements. Personally I am glad that the great profiteers and their party have forfeited for good the backing of the substantial moral element of the country. They are now booked for the General Judgment and the drys, whom they have cheated and foiled, will sooner or later line up with the masses whom they have bled and despoiled.

Let me say that once more.

C. F. Adams, Sr., long President of the Union Pacific, commented on the narrow mentality of the big business men he encountered on Wall Street. The operations of the Du Pont-Raskob-James group against the 18th Amendment furnish a good illustration. The most precious thing in the world is the human brain and any psychiatrist could have told these financiers that the worst enemy of the brain in modern society is alcohol. Thus the renowned August Forel declared it to be "the chief producer of *Untermenschen*." But as the historian Lecky remarked "the single brain of James Watt was, and still is, the biggest wage fund that has ever arisen in the world." How many Watt-like brains will be destroyed by Repeal in days to come!

One of these Du Ponts, with incredible tactlessness, handed to each of the Nye Investigating Committee as a Christmas present a copy of "Kapoot," an account of Bolshevist social break-down in Russia. It was a Du Pont anti-Red herring (L). But, Mr. Du Pont, that will deceive no one, least of all the Christian conscience of America. This great and powerful element has no love for Moscow, or for Wilmington either. It has at last got the measure of these powder profiteers, who set nations at their ears, and whose chief title to fame is that they have destroyed one of the greatest idealisms which a people ever set its hands to realize.

POSTSCRIPT

When the first incoming tide of economic radicalism broke on Raskob-Du Pont-Sloan-Morgan property in the 1937 General Motors "sit-down strike" at Flint, Michigan, almost the first step taken by the authorities to protect this property was the *prohibition of all sale of alcoholic drink,*—beer, wine, spirits,—in state stores, beer-gardens, and private clubs, "to continue as long as the situation remains critical" and throughout the entire Genesee County. "It was feared," reported the *N. Y. Times* (Feb. 5, 1937), "that liquor-inflamed men might provoke violence under existing conditions."

This measure of defense against the liquor-inflamed, denied

to the homes of the plain people, is accorded to the investments of the rich.

REFERENCES TO CHAPTER IV NOT IN THE TEXT

1. New York Times, February 8, 1926, page 1.
2. North American Review, September-November, 1925, page 54.
3. Stewart Paton, "The Prohibiting Mind," page 72.
4. Hearings Senate Judiciary Committee, April 1932, page 12.
5. "Alcohol and Man," pages 161–162.
6. "Alcohol and Man," pages 279–80.
7. Irving Fisher, "The Noble Experiment," page 63.
8. Hearings, 72nd Congress Committee on Manufactures, January 1932, page 509.
9. Hearings, Senate Judiciary Committee, April 1926, pages 600, 604, 1189 1191, 1227 and Liberty, July 10, 1926.
10. Fabian Franklin, "What Prohibition Has Done to America," page 129 and "The ABC of Prohibition," page 55.
11. House Committee on Judiciary Hearings, February 1930, pages 176, 177.
12. House Committee on Judiciary Hearings, February 1930, page 331.
13. Lobby Investigation Report 1930, page 4225.
14. Annals of American Academy of Political and Social Sciences, September 1923, page 31.
15. "Prohibition, A National Experiment," page 177.
16. Arms Inquiry, Nye Committee, pages 1042, 1044, 1060.
17. Arms Inquiry, Nye Committee, page 2707.
18. Arms Inquiry, page 2350, and Congressional Record, pages 467–8.
19. Congressional Record, 74th Congress, pages 460–61, and Time, December 22, 1934.
20. Arms Inquiry, page 2721, Ex. 1037, page 2730.
21. Arms Inquiry, Ex. 888, p. 2327: pp. 2273 seq. and 2344 seq.: pp. 2733–35: Ex. 868, p. 2285: p. 1337: Ex. 837, p. 2255.
22. A. A. P. A. tract "Prohibition and the Deficit" and Current History, April 1928, page 21.
23. Philadelphia Public Ledger, September 6, 1933, page 26 and Scribner's, September 1930.
24. Lobby Investigation Report, 1930, page 4239.
25. New York Times, April 8, 1930.
26. Senate Report, No. 1455, page 102.
27. New York Times, June 5, 1930.
28. New York Times, May 14, 1930, page 29, and June 17, 1930, page 23.
29. Samuel Wilson, "The Scoffs of a Scofflaw."
30. Wine and Liquor Trade News, February 1934.
31. New York Times, October 14, 1930, page 3.
32. New York Times, May 16, 1930, page 16.
33. Lobby Investigation Report, 1930, page 4229.
34. Ike Hoover, "Forty-Two Years in the White House," page 247.
35. Norman Hapgood, "Professional Patriots," page 134.
36. Norman Hapgood, "Professional Patriots," page 140.
37. Harper's No. 164, "The Collapse of Organized Labor," page 167.
38. Hearings of Senate Judiciary Committee, April 1926, page 240.
39. W. Z. Foster, "Misleaders of Labor," pages 266–267.
40. New York Times, June 5, 1930.
41. New York Times, May 2, 1932.
42. Hearings Senate Judiciary Committee, April 1924, pages 5 and 20.
43. Overman Report, pages 833, 838 and 976.
44. Senate Judiciary Committee Hearings, April 1926, page 1292.
45. Malvern H. Tillitt, "The Price of Prohibition."

46. Hearings Senate Judiciary Committee, Modification of Volstead Act, Dec. 1933.
47. Overman Report, page 1306.
48. Congressional Record, January 31, 1921 (quoted in Beman "Current Problems of Taxation," page 185).
49. Hearings Modification of Volstead Act, December 1930, page 563.
50. New York Times, June 9, 1932.
51. Congressional Record, January 21, 1927, page 2089.
52. Union Signal, October 1, 1931.
53. Plain Talk, January 1932, page 29.
54. Christian Century, May 20, 1931, and New York Times, May 17, 1931, page 1.
55. Congressional Record, January 3, 1933, page 1232.
56. Investigation of Nazi and other Propaganda, 74th Congress, page 10.
57. Christian Century, 1932, page 1534.
58. Hearings Senate Committee on Manufactures, January 1932, page 158.
59. Hearings Senate Committee on Manufactures, January 1932, page 120.
60. Fred B. Smith (ed) "Law vs. Lawlessness," page 49.
61. House Hearings, Committee on Judiciary, April 1924, page 131.
62. New York Times, January 24, 1935.
63. House Hearings, Committee on Judiciary, April 1924, page 219.

NOTES TO CHAPTER IV

A.   It is not altogether easy to understand the opposition to Prohibition of some men on the A. A. P. A. Mr. Robert Treat Paine subscribed $1,000 to its funds (Lobby Investigation, p. 1075) yet he had said: "Since Lincoln signed the Proclamation of Emancipation the most beneficent event has been the decision of the American people to banish liquor" (p. 916 Hearings, April 1926). Mr. Mather of Pickands, Mather and Co. sent in a subscription of $10,000 yet his general superintendent reported to him concerning his employees: "We *know* that not as much money is spent for drink as previously. We do not have the spectacle of the mother coming to the office in tears and despair because the father has gone out on pay-day night and boozed the entire check." Mr. Maytag was the lonely representative of the A. A. P. A. in Iowa. He manufactured washing machines. The sales of these machines which, in 1919, were less than a million a year, had shot up by 1928 to six million. One would have thought that satisfactory. The secretary of the U. S. Brewers' Ass'n said of the Du Ponts that "for years they absolutely prohibited the use of intoxicants by their employees" and "now with the rush of war orders the prohibition has been clearly drawn even closer." Evidently they wanted to keep their own powder dry. But Volstead Prohibition proved even more effective than Du Pont industrial prohibition. Their percentage of employee absenteeism was in 1907 6.35; in 1924 2.96. Prof. Feldman (p. 210) pointed out that in twenty divisions of General Motors, employing 101,000 workers in twenty cities, there were but thirty employees discharged for drunkenness in Feb. 1927. This constituted only one percent of the total number discharged. What better did the fifteen directors of General Motors on the A. A. P. A. want? Haley Fiske, President of the Metropolitan Life, was member of the Moderation League. Metropolitan Life must have greatly profited by the fact that while among its general policyholders the death rate between 1911 and 1917 was 11.8 per thousand, in the Prohibition years 1921–26 inclusive it was only 8.7 per thousand (Dr. Dublin in *American Journal of Public Health*, Jan. 1928, p. 3).

The presumption is that some of these men were victims of propaganda. Others apparently calculated in cold blood that while Prohibition brought to them minor financial gains, the reinstatement of alcohol taxation would bring vastly greater ones.

B.   In an account of Prof. Pearl's alcohol super-chick discovery Samuel Hopkins Adams said of him (*Collier's*, April 7, 1923) : "He is a scientist, not a propagandist." Specialists do not agree. Dr. Fritz Lenz of the University of Munich writes, "The experiments of Pearl on hens appear to me to have no value" (*Grundriss der menschlichen Erblichheitslehre*, p. 308). And as to propaganda, when the *American Mercury* was launched in 1924 on its mission of "restoring the American saloon," Prof. Pearl was there to break a bottle over its bows. He appeared in this première with the violent wet propagandists "Jim" Reed, Darrow, and Herbert Asbury. From time to time articles by Mr. Pearl with a propaganda slant appeared in this super-wet publication. Thus he attacked temperance instruction in the public schools on the ground that it made out alcohol to be harmful. "Naturally no real evidence can be presented," he wrote. "Real evidence is the last thing desired." Professor Pearl's better-known colleagues at John Hopkins think differently. Dr. W. H. Welch described alcohol "in sufficient quantities as a poison to all living organisms," and Prof. Howard A. Kelly says that it is, "as usually used, brother to the typhoid and smallpox germs and the louse of typhus, as to all other nasty promoters of fatal disease."

C.   This capitalist concentrate was sensitive to exposure of its make-up and motive. It would pose as champion of the common people. Thus Mr. Stayton wrote that Prohibition was enacted "to exploit labor, the Rockefellers having been heavy contributors to the anti-saloon funds. This (is) enough to justify in the workers' minds all past suspicion and to breed a horde of new ones" (14). In order to appear a popular movement the A. A. P. A. claimed a large membership which it most certainly did not have,—150,000 in April 1930, although four months previously it was given as 11,000 with such specific items as North Carolina 11 members, Arkansas 3, Utah 7, North Dakota 3, New Hampshire 15, Montana 7, Kansas 13 etc. (Lobby Investiagtion Pt. 9, p. 4007). Mr. Gebhart, Sec'y of the A. A. P. A., told us that the parallel wet organization, The Women's Organization for (anti) Prohibition Reform, had in 1932 a million members (15). Believe it who can! They insisted that the plain people were backing them. The annual report to the directors of the A. A. P. A. (1931) quoted such "typical messages of good-will" as the following:

"Send one dollar. Wish I could send a million and bring back business and prosperity." " Widow's mite. God be with you." "I hope and pray that you will knock it out after all. Enclose $1 for your work" (from a clergyman).

E.   At the Republican state convention of New Jersey Morrow, in spite of a pledge to the contrary, was on hand to insist that it, too, repudiate the Republican national platform in this matter. ("The Republican party pledges itself and its nominees to the observance and vigorous enforcement of this provision of the Constitution.") This disloyalty was also treachery to President Hoover whose administration he had represented in Mexico. The resolutions committee drew up a Morrow plank, Gov. Larson clotured discussion and forced the plan through by voting the whole platform at one time. No discussion was wanted and indeed Mr. Morrow refused to discuss the question with Congressman Fort during the campaign.

F.   At the very time when Morrow stepped into the limelight (June 1930) U. S. District Judge Fake issued a temporary injunction against Federal Administrator John D. Pennington and his men from entering the Hensler Brewery in Newark. Up to April 20, 1932, this injunction had not been lifted, nearly two years afterward, contrary to usual practise. Judge Runyon of the U. S. District Court issued a similar injunction against federal officials in the case of the Rising Sun Brewery, Elizabeth, N. J., *where a federal official had been murdered.* Col. Woodcock, in testifying before a House Committee, described a near-beer brewery which ran a large pipe from its real beer tanks, underneath a street and a house, over to a garage where they had set up racking-machinery. "Is that the brewery where the judge enjoined you and the district attorney from using the evidence?" asked Senator Brookhart.

    Woodcock: "It was." (Hearings Com. on Manufactures, Jan. 1932, pp. 361, 356.)

    A federal grand jury, in a scathing presentment handed to Judge Fake, charged federal judges with obstructing enforcement, with issuing injunctions at the instigation of the liquor interests without hearing the government's side of the case, with putting men on probation who deserved sentences, with overriding the refusal of Prohibition administrators to issue brewing permits, with giving only nominal fines, with preventing prosecution by court delays (Hearings Sub-Com. Judic. April 1932, p. 88). Mr. Morrow might well have been "shocked" at such nullification on the part of the Federal Judiciary and have denounced it. Instead he denounced Prohibition which, in spite of all this double-crossing, was producing such fruits as the following:

    "The Newman Industrial Home in Jersey City, which for many years has ministered to the hungry and bedless, has closed its doors and turned its property over to the Y. M. C. A. as its peculiar *clientèle* has vanished" (Samuel Wilson, "Scofflaws").

G.   After Repeal was an accomplished fact Mrs. C. H. Sabin, leader of the rich women wets, was presented with the American Women Association's "award for eminent attainment." Miss Ida Tarbell was the appropriate chairman. A recent graph showing the close parallel between consumption of spirits and assaults of husbands on wives in Scotland during the past 35 years, might well have been hung up at this Tarbell-Sabin-Gildersleeve *fête*. These hard-hearts would no doubt jeer at Mrs. Nation's words to the bartender, after ripping up a nude painting in a Kansas joint, but *frauenhaften Frauen* feel differently: "You strip women of everything that is precious," she cried. "You strip her of husband, of sons, of home, of food, of virtue, and then you strip her of clothes and hang her naked body behind the bar, as they hung the Saviour naked on the Cross."

Mrs. Sabin's husband, Charles H. Sabin, was a director of Owens-Illinois Glass (Who's Who, 1932, p. 2007), the enormously profitable beer-bottle business of which has been re-established by Repeal. At present it also manufactures 85% of the whisky bottles of the country. Its president and vice-president are directors of National Distillers. Through its affiliate, the Owens-Illinois Can Co., it also manufactures beer cans.

The plain women of the country fear the bottle above all else. Miss Imogen Oakley has given this testimony:

"It fell to my lot to speak in college settlements to many audiences of tenement women on the duties and privileges of citizenship, and the invariable request from the women was, 'Tell us how to vote dry. We don't know much about government, or laws, but we want to be sure to vote dry because we have boys to raise and because we have been so much happier since the country went dry.'"

The largest milk-bottle manufacturer in the country, the Thatcher Manufacturing Company, was reported to have increased its output of milk bottles 35% in the first six months of Prohibition. That was really "eminent attainment" (Nat. Prohib. Hearings 1926, p. 1159).

H.   The *American Mercury* (March 1935, p. 275) says of the A. F. L.: "The majority of the leaders of this organization have long been Roman Catholics and have been the bulwark of conservatism in that ultra-conservative body." Foster speaks of Woll as representing the Catholic Church in the trade unions (p. 151, "Misleaders"). Mr. Sokolsky (*Atlantic Monthly*, Aug. 1934, p. 139) says: "The A. F. L. has never had the confidence of the highest grades of American labor. The railroad brotherhoods have kept out of it." It is, in a way, the Tammany of labor. It is said that liquor men often pay the bills of delegates from Central Labor Unions to State Federation Conventions and in some states the Liquor Dealers Protective League and the State Federation of Labor work in cooperation (Stelzle, "Why Prohibition," p. 120).

While the Wolls and Freys and Furuseths have again and again disgraced labor with their beer testimony, from other sources come other statements. Division No. 565 Brotherhood of Locomotive Engineers, in reply to a request for support to the wets, wrote: "It is somewhat of a mystery to us men engaged in the dangerous business of railroading why any wage workers would want a return to the misery of the evils of pre-

Volstead days. To say that the 18th Amendment has been a total failure, that the drink habit is as bad or worse than before, we know is simply propaganda of those interested in the return of the business that has done more to retard civilization and progress than anything in the world's history. Men in the railroad game know that we are better off morally, financially, and in every other way, by the outlawry of the booze business" (*Forum*, June 1924, p. 810).

I.   The National Association of Manufacturers and the U. S. Brewers' Ass'n are represented by their directors in the National Civic Federation. Senator Brookhart (C. R. Feb. 19, 1932, p. 3900), "There is no danger to the Prohibition cause except the insidious power of money. This power is able to control the vast majority of the public press. . . . *It puts decoy ducks even in some of the great labor organizations."*

J.   The Crusaders (the so-called Cork-screw Aiders), affiliated with the A. A. P. A., were later subsidized by the American Liberty League and affiliated with the American Legion and the Elks (who presumably represented beer and Irish Catholicism) in anti-Red drives (C. R. Jan. 14, 1935). The former anti-prohibition organization "Sentinels of the Republic," Boston (*C. S. Monitor*, Oct. 9, 1922), had similar later connections. The Black Committee showed it to be financed by the Pitcairns, wet Pittsburgh manufacturers, and by A. P. Sloan, I. Du Pont and Stotesbury. Raskob, Al Smith, Hearst and other wets back it. Its President, Mr. Alexander Lincoln, would repeal, with the 18th Amendment, the 16th, or income tax, Amendment. Also the general welfare clause of the Constitution. They oppose the Social Security Law, the Guffey Coal Act and the Income Tax Publicity measure. Two other stalking horses of this group are the Farmers' Independent Council of America and the Southern Committee for Upholding the Constitution. (See Report of the Black Committee.)

K.   Gov. Pinchot says: "For years the liquor power and the Republican party were side partners in Pennsylvania. For years the liquor power and the Democratic party were side partners in New York. . . . For years liquor has paid the bills of the dominant party in state after state throughout the nation. . . . In county after county in Pennsylvania illegal liquor still keeps the gang alive" ("Law vs. Lawlessness," p. 105).

Repeal will no doubt relieve the "sugar daddies" of Wall Street in the matter of political contributions.

L.   A letter dated August 22, 1928, from the Du Pont Co. to their Paris representative told him to go ahead with negotiations to sell powder and explosives to (Communist) Russia (*N. Y. Times*, Dec. 12, 1934, p. 18).

CHAPTER V

THE PRESS AND PROHIBITION

In the metropolitan press Wall Street has ever an agency at hand for carrying out its purposes. The method used was shown by Congressman Callaway when he asked unanimous consent for insertion in the Record of "a statement of how the newspapers of the country (were) handled by the munitions manufacturers" (1). A Wall St. group—banking, steel, ship-building, and powder interests—"got together twelve men high in the newspaper world and employed them to select the most influential newspapers in the United States, and a sufficient number of them, to control generally the policy of the daily press of the country." The purpose was to put the United States into the war in order to insure the colossal investments made in the Allied Cause.

THE SYSTEM

"These men," said Mr. Callaway, "worked out the problem by selecting 179 newspapers. (They) then began an elimination process to retain only those necessary for . . . controlling the general policy of the daily press of the country. . . . Twenty-five of the greatest newspapers (were enough).

"The twenty-five papers were agreed upon. . . . *The policy of the paper was bought and paid for by the month.*

"An editor was appointed for each paper to supervise properly information regarding the questions of preparedness, militarism, financial policy, and other things of national and international nature, considered vital to the interests of the purchasers.

"This contract is in existence at the present time (1917) and it accounts for the news columns of the daily press being filled with all sorts of preparedness arguments and misrepresentations as to the present condition of the U. S. Army and Navy, and the possibility and probability of the United States being attacked by foreign foes.

"This policy also included *the suppression of everything in*

(113)

opposition to the wishes of the interests served. The effectiveness of this scheme has been conclusively demonstrated by the character of stuff carried in the daily press throughout the country since March 1915. They have resorted to anything necessary to commercialize public sentiment and to sandbag the national Congress into making extravagant and wasteful appropriations for the Army and Navy. . . ."

Wall Street interests, which bought the press in order by war profiteering to loot the country, were without exception lined up for Repeal. It is not improbable that the press was used in some concerted way in 1926–32 also. A careful analysis of the news columns of the New York papers gives obvious indications of what Lord Bacon called "infused opinions" (A).

"FISH ARE THEY THAT LOVE THE MUD"

The wet propaganda went systematically to work to blacken its opponents. It began with the President of the United States. There were two brothers, Albert and Charles Michelson. The first devoted himself to the study of light. He was the great Michelson, the physicist who weighed Betelgeux. The other was imp of darkness. He was drawn from the staff of the tortuous *New York World* to direct a publicity bureau underwritten by Mr. Raskob. Mr. Shouse, later President of the A. A. P. A., was associated with this unique organization. From its office in the National Press Building, a few steps from the White House, it started a systematic wet campaign "to put Mr. Hoover in bad with the American people, to paint him as inept, bewildered, weak and unworthy." "We have no parallel in American history," said Congressman Tilson, "of a person being paid, set up in office and issuing such libelous misinformation about the President" (B).

A POLITICIAN BY THE GRACE OF GOD

Bishop Cannon was for years a shining mark for the press. They hated him because he could play the game and beat them in spite of every handicap. For forty years he fought the saloon and never took a cent for it. He founded the *Richmond Virginian,* a paper which for ten years led the fight in Virginia, and for its support raised $350,000, putting in himself $60,000,—all that he had. He was a business man. In earlier years he helped a church school in Virginia, selling horses, cattle, hogs, wheat, corn, timber, in the course of his management, thereby aiding numbers of poor girls to an education. One day he bought a small block of stock through Kable and Company on margin. Instantly the press of the country, which had been lying in wait for him, branded him as bucketeer and for months turned over this delicious bit in its maw. But when Bishop Cannon made the following statement concerning Mr. Hearst, and distributed tens of thousands of copies, the newspapers were silent.

MR. HEARST SETS A TRAP

"Prohibition has instituted un-American methods of spying and snooping," wrote Mr. Hearst in a manifesto, April 26, 1929. That he had little aversion to using these methods himself appears from a confidential office memorandum alleged to have been sent by him to Mr. Young of the *Los Angeles Examiner*. Follow the essential parts of this memorandum.

"In December of last year we lost a great opportunity to link Bishop Cannon conclusively with his son's affairs. Had the matter been handled properly then, it would have been of great value to us in discrediting Bishop Cannon with the general public. . . .

"Next to the World Court matter I feel that the most important duty of the Hearst papers all over the country now is the destruction of the group which Bishop Cannon represents and controls. *This can best be done by constant, though careful, assaults upon him.* In saying careful I refer to the necessity of making no errors which may have a rebound. . . . If it is possible to force other papers to lead the way in matters concerning Bishop Cannon, so much the better. The 'Old Lady at First and Broadway' (the *Los Angeles Times*) has been an admirable help to us often.

"I have come to the conclusion that it will be next to impossible to directly pin anything to Bishop Cannon. I am sincere in saying that I consider him to have the best brain in America, no one excepted. He has without exception foreseen and prepared for every attack made upon him. In the bucket shop affair there was much noise but practically no accomplishment.

"Investigations have been made of Bishop Cannon's other children and there is little hope of any news in any of them. . . . We might publish stories concerning them but the reaction of the people would be the reaction of Shuler last year,—persecution of the son of a prominent man.

"If you will carefully go over the report I sent you concerning young Cannon, you will see that there is every probability that Bishop Cannon can be successfully linked with his son's affairs by the statements of witnesses both disinterested and partial to him. . . . I am advised that young Cannon is facing bankruptcy. . . . Our play is to wait until the school is forced to the wall, then let go with all we have to connect Bishop Cannon with the organization. . . . I believe we can have the *Times* make the first plunge without difficulty, just as it did last fall. The time for the story to break should be simultaneously with the development in the new charges brought against Bishop Cannon."

Follow reports of the investigator in the course of which he mentions having entered the son's office to examine his papers. He says of this son of Bishop Cannon that he *"has excellent reputation so far as morals go and any scrape with women would have to be framed as liquor charge.* If (Cannon's son) gets (the buildings) ready for occupancy in time for school nothing can stop him. His ability as a salesman will make money for any school. . . . Believe something should be done to upset the plans unless school is to be a financial success." October 5th Mr. Cannon's office was burned, he and his wife both being in the East at the time. According to the Associated Press "the fire had every appearance of being of incendiary origin."

MUZZLING CHIEF JUSTICE TAFT

The press deliberately suppressed news favorable to Prohibition. Many glaring illustrations are at hand. On June 20, 1923, the Chief Justice of the United States put himself fairly on record as a supporter of the 18th Amendment. In this Yale Alumni luncheon speech he made a strong appeal for obedience to the law. Of this speech he wrote later to Professor Fisher: "The N. Y. World published my anti-Prohibition letters to Lincoln before the adoption of the Amendment and then nobody seemed to take the trouble to publish my speech at Yale, given after the Amendment was adopted. . . . But the result (i.e. of Prohibition) is glorious and points the only way we have to work out the problem presented."

The N. Y. *Times* gave a reasonably good summary of Mr.

Taft's speech *and put it on the tenth page.* The *Tribune* did not mention it; the *World* (June 21, 1923) garbled it shamelessly, printing its two-inch notice under the heading, "Sees Lawlessness Growing." There was no editorial mention of this mature judgment of the Chief Justice on the question which was agitating all minds. But if he had spoken *against* Prohibition!

Before a Congressional committee Mr. Horace Taft said of this speech of his brother: "I have succeeded in getting (it) into a paper through personal influence but it never goes beyond that paper. It never gets quoted. It puts him squarely where he belongs but it stops with the local paper in which I succeeded in getting it and I have brought copies here with the hope that it might put an end" to misrepresentation (2).

In other words the only way in which Mr. Justice Taft's position could be made clear for posterity was by writing it into a government document.

What a judgment on the American press!

> "FLINGING STONES AT ALL THE STEPHENS,
> STANDING FIRM WITH ALL THE EVENS,
> MAKING HELL FOR ALL THE ODDS."

Judge Britt, the chief counsel for the Prohibition Unit, declared that "it was practically impossible for Prohibition to get a fair report." Then he added: "Nothing in all American history has been so misrepresentative as the attitude of the press. With a few honorable exceptions it is impossible to obtain correct news accounts or favorable comment on anything relating to the subject" (3). An old newspaper hand, Mr. Silas Bent, confirms this: "Their (Prohibition) record (the *N. Y. Times* and *World*) is spread daily before all those who read and no one will pretend that it is creditable from the standpoint of journalistic fairness" (4). Of the *New York Times* Mr. Villard of the *Nation* wrote: "No journal has exceeded it in disseminating falsehoods, misrepresentations and half-truths . . . during the unparalleled era of wholesale lying in which the world has lived since 1913" (5).

SHIELDING THE DU PONTS

Plain Talk (April 1932, p. 13) called attention to the way the newspapers suppressed the text of the Patman Resolution "which showed conclusively how Mellon used his office as Secretary of the Treasury to aid huge private business." They have been similarly complaisant to other great capitalists. By comparing the Report of the Lobby Investigation of 1930 with the files of the *N. Y. Times* one can observe how the tender feelings of the Du Ponts were spared. The Association Against the Prohibition Amendment controlled by them was under fire. But the Du Pont and Raskob interests are dominant in General Motors and Mr. Raskob tells us that General Motors spends $15,000,000 annually in advertisements (6). It would not do to offend them, so in the *Times* for April 23rd, 25th and 26th, 1930, no mention is made of the scheme of this group to replace corporation and income taxes by a beer tax, although this was in the front of the testimony. In the May 2nd issue the whole passage relating to Irenée Du Pont's plan of tax-shifting and saving ten millions annually on one of the Du Pont plants (pp. 4165 and 4168 Lobby Report) is suppressed. No mention is made of the great political contributions, no mention of the huge expenditures in getting out the vote in Massachusetts and of course no mention of the fact that an editorial in the *N. Y. Times* was written at the request of certain prominent wets. All this front page material was thrown away and the report of the day put on the third page under the caption, "Calls Six of the Cabinet Dry Doubters." In other words a slant favorable to the wets was given to a session of the investigation which had been incomparably damaging to the wets. The report on the following day, May 3, 1930, followed the same crooked plan. It failed to report the fact that the Association vs. the Prohibition Amendment claimed to represent forty billions of capital. It made no mention of Pierre Du Pont's allusion to the *Saturday Evening Post*. Above all, again, it entirely suppressed the discussions by Senators Caraway and Robinson of the Du Pont tax-lifting scheme. All through, the central things in the evidence were suppressed and minor matters put in the foreground.

Mr. G. F. Lord, advertising agent for the Du Ponts, declares that the time when publishers were editors who endeavored to mould public opinion is past. "Nowadays the real publishers are the advertisers, since their financial support of a publication is in most cases all that keeps it alive."

"The question of properly guiding newspaper writers is, to my mind, the most serious one before the chemical industry," is a sentence which occurs in the evidence of the Munitions Hearings, Part 12: p. 2778.

WET BRAIN-STORMS

Special drives swept over the country at preconcerted times,— the killing drives, the poisoned liquor drives, drives connected with specially arranged hearings and staged debates in Congress. The Hearings of 1926 illustrated the method. Messrs. Stayton and Codman managed the Washington end, marshalling wet witnesses; the New York newspapers gave unexampled space to the extravagant propaganda there unfolded. Mr. Wm. McDonald, a lecturer in American history at Yale, says of these 1926 Hearings: "It is not recalled that metropolitan newspapers have ever before devoted solid pages, day after day for more than two weeks, to detailed reports, often verbatim, of the testimony and argument, for or against, the continuation of any national policy" (7). It must be remembered that these were not important Congressional investigations like the Pujo Money Committee or the Pecora Committee of 1933, to which persons of weight were summoned, but mere hearings at which the speakers were any who might come and often insignificant persons. It was at this time that *The Review of Reviews* felt called to caution the public against the unveracity of the metropolitan press in a quite exceptional way:

"Readers in our large cities should be warned that the metropolitan press has seriously misled the public by its method of dealing with the Prohibition question. This has been done not so much by positive errors in statement as by false emphasis and by excessive allotment of space to the wet cause, while the failure to recognize facts favorable to the laws of the country as they are today has amounted to a reckless enlargement of law violation. . . . (They are) trying to break down morale by constantly assuring the public that Prohibition is a total and hopeless failure, nullified almost everywhere and by almost everybody, and that the abandonment of the egregiously harmful system is merely a matter of that brief interval of time necessary for laws to adjust themselves" (8).

It should be noticed that unofficial votings synchronized with these wet hearings and their accompanying newspaper clamor,— the Newspaper Poll of March 21, 1926, in which 453 newspapers participated, with the April 1926 Hearings: the *Literary Digest* poll of 1930 with the wet Hearings of 1930. The sponsors of these polls knew very well that their undertakings would embarrass the government and pour oil on the flames of propaganda. Following directly on the 1926 Hearings was the Reed investigation which further increased the volume of hysterical discussion. This was undoubtedly all of a piece and purpose.

Mark Sullivan quoted the analysis of "the ablest politician in America" regarding these 1926 Hearings. He declared that for the first five years after Prohibition became constitutional there was "regard for its sanctity and deference for it," that is among the broad masses. "About the end of this period various New York newspapers turned violently wet." This observer put most of the responsibility on the New York newspapers, since besides their own direct influence they influenced minor papers throughout the country. "The activity of those opposed to Prohibition came to a head last spring in the Senate Hearings of 1926 which received lavish prominence. These hearings were printed more fully, and a greater number of newspapers printed them in full, than in the case of other hearings held by Congress in recent years. They gave the impression that Prohibition was not a settled question. They were followed by a political drive in the states" (9).

"Never have our great newspapers thrown the whole weight of their influence practically unanimously on the same side of a question before," said Congressman Fort in the House, Jan. 31, 1930. "Never have they begun to give the space, let alone the display, to any item of public controversy that they have given to Prohibition. . . . Never have they allowed themselves to show so strong a bias in the handling of news as on this subject. . . . I wonder what the great metropolitan newspapers would charge me, if I were a dealer in patent medicines, for the news-column space they now give free to the dealers in liquor" (C) (10).

THE PRESIDENT REMONSTRATES

Mr. Hoover went to New York to the dinner of the Associated Press, April 22, 1929, and reproached the newspaper men, though with utmost courtesy, for their frivolity and want of fair play. A year later, April 18, 1930, Mr. Wickersham made similar representations before the American Society of Newspaper Editors. He quoted Gustave Le Bon on "The Psychology of the Crowd." "Affirmation, pure and simple, kept free from all reasoning and all proof, is one of the surest means of making an idea enter the minds of crowds." The very quotation was an indictment of the editors to their faces. He appealed to them to use their great power on the side of law. He might have been talking to boulders on the moon.

"SCREAMING, CROAKING, BAYING, YELLING"

The "killings" drive was directed against the government enforcement agents in order to brand Prohibition as a bloody and brutal thing. The newspapers not only lent themselves to it but led it. They were largely responsible for whatever bloodshed there was. Mrs. Willebrandt testified to this: "In hundreds of cases arrested bootleggers are resisting with force officers of the law. . . . Men are arrested by state and federal officers for burglary, arson, mail-robbing, etc., for which the penalties are much more severe than those imposed for bootlegging. Yet there is no such resistance to the officers because *the men arrested know that they will get no newspaper support if they attack or kill officers of the law*" (11).

The number of deaths was infamously exaggerated. The Government year by year gave the record. Thus up to June 30, 1932, the number of officials who lost their lives in defense of law was 79; of law-breakers 173. This in a period of twelve years. Yet three years previously the *Washington Herald* declared that it had found 1360 cases, nearly seven times the official number at that time. The *Denver Post* (Dec. 5, 1929) analyzed the alleged Denver contribution to the list:

1. Norman Gould beaten to death by Rossi whom he was trying to rob. No prohibition factor.
2. Charles Ohler murdered by an unknown person. No Prohibition factor.
3. Dan Edwards shot by special officer Foster while resisting arrest. No Prohibition factor.
4. Patrolman Evans killed by Farice King. No Prohibition factor.
5. Patrolman Richie assassinated by unknown persons.
6 and 7. Patrolman Ohle and Mrs. Reese killed by Eddie Ives.
8. Junius Perkins shot by Patrolman Roy Robinson.

Prohibition had apparently nothing to do with these cases. The A. A. P. A. issued a pamphlet which listed 1360 killings and of this Mr. Curran affirmed that it had been "truthfully and carefully prepared." Atticus Webb analyzed the 114 killings attributed to Texas. In one county where there were said to have been 20 killings, not a single name of the person killed or of the killer could be given. "In all there were 31 (Texan) killings charged where they could not give the name of the one killed, and 66 killings in which they could not give the name of the one who did the killing, and 25 killings in which neither party could be given a name. Where names were given, 26 were officers killed in enforcing the law, several were counted in more than one county and several of the killings had taken place for causes with which Prohibition had nothing to do" (12).

Congressman Cooper, speaking in the House and referring to 61 Federal officers done to death by bootleggers, remarked that at no time had he heard in the House any condemnation of the criminals. But when a desperado was killed they cried "massacre." This attitude he considered largely the cause of these deaths.

"Armed to the teeth, these criminals of the liquor traffic are the most desperate and dangerous group of organized bandits in the country. A short time ago these outlaws killed a Federal officer and then poured 76 shots into the dead body of their victim" (13).

While concocting false bootlegger martyrologies the press, as Col. Callahan said, "concealed the shocking details accompanying the murder of the officers of the law in different parts of the country, which information reaches us only through special stories like the following, given out by Mrs. Willebrandt, Aug. 24, 1929." On this case Col. Callahan comments:

"The body of Richard Sandlands, Federal Prohibition agent, with neck broken, was found in Detroit River. Sandlands was guarding a motor-boat and was killed by its owner. Had the status of the victim and the boat-owner been reversed the newspaper report of the tragedy would have been a lengthy outcry against the 'murder' of a citizen by a dry officer and a demand for prompt investigation and for relief of the community from murderous officers.

"For a week the victim would have been known as a business man who owned a pleasure boat. If at the end of the week he had been revealed as a notorious bootlegger the case would have lost interest. The apparent murder of a dry officer occasions only a brief and little noticed report" (14).

But not so the deaths of criminals, and in this "the best New York journalism" was quite abreast of Hearst. The Virkula incident was played up for days upon the front page. Staff representatives and photographers were sent to International Falls, Minn., to get the story. The editors moralized and flayed the 18th Amendment as if *it* authorized murder. Then it was found that the patrolmen involved were revenue and not Prohibition officers and that Virkula, behind his little confectionery business, was a determined and practised bootlegger (15).

"Not on land or sea is a law-abiding citizen safe from the cannon and pistols, the mustard gas, the sawed-off shotguns, and the tear-bombs of dry enforcement," wrote the *Washington Herald,* April 4, 1929. "There is nothing in the history of this nation comparable with this orgy of promiscuous slaughter," said Senator Tydings. One would have thought so from the newspapers (16).

. If you read the list of law-enforcement officers killed in the course of duty you find yourself among Americans of the old stock. The bootleg dead are named with the names of Italy and Poland and Russian Jewry. Colonel Woodcock speaking in Denver made this pointed comparison: "I was recently handed a report of the Police Department of the City of New York. I opened it at the section in which is the roll of honor for distinguished service and my eye fell upon the award of a medal to an officer who was no doubt eminently deserving of it. The citation stated that the officer pursued three men attempting to escape from the holdup of a merchant at 1607 Park Avenue. The policeman shot and killed one who threatened to shoot him and arrested one of the other two bandits. I could not help but compare the fact that if this shooting had been done by a Prohibition agent it would have been the subject of wholesale newspaper condemnation and a critical investigation by this Bureau to determine whether the agent had, in fact, been within his rights" (D) (17).

THE SHOE ON THE OTHER FOOT

The press was not disturbed by the use of firearms in itself by government officials. It did not scream when Postmaster-General Hays ordered marines to shoot at sight when the mails were endangered. It did not flame out in assumed horror when he offered a reward of $1,000 to any who *killed* persons interrupting the movement of the mails. This order soon put an end to mail holdups.

Nor have the newspapers, who were so tender of the bootlegger, given publicity to the victims of an oppressive capitalism. The great steel strike of 1918 was full of harrowing episodes, constabulary attacking Slovaks leaving church, riding down pedestrians on sidewalks, and the like. In Farrell, Pa., three people were killed by these hirelings and eleven wounded, one of them being a woman shot in the back on her way to a butcher shop. Were their names in leaded type on the front page? Were they wept over on the editorial page? Did the editors denounce the coal and iron police, who were not government police at all, as they have vilified brave men on the Prohibition unit (18)?

Let me put in parallel two instances. The American newspapers tumbled over each other to show their sympathy with the bootlegging family, the De Kings of Aurora, Ill. The accidental shooting of Mrs. De King was by newspaper promotion the talk of the nation for days. But how many Americans ever heard of Mrs. C. B. Cook, of the Benton County (Iowa) W. C. T. U.?

Mrs. Cook had been active in exposing bootleggers. "She was shot dead as she sat by a window sewing, shortly after returning from a church meeting." *N. Y. Times*, Sept. 9, 1925.

Testimony of Sheriff Roy Smith after he had been threatened by Mr. De King with revolver in each hand: "I was backing out of the house with my shotgun in my hands *and with Mrs. De King waving a revolver and cursing*, when I stumbled and the gun went off. Then a minute later I was shot myself and that's all I remember." *N. Y. Times*, April 3, 1929, page 2 (19).

Newspaper pathos was, you see, reserved for alcohol shrews! How hypocritical it all was is clear from the *N. Y. Times'* treatment of the same material *after* Repeal. An Associated Press report from Pittsburgh, Aug. 24, 1934, "While attempting to prevent his young son's arrest on a liquor charge, Charles Robis, 72 years of age, was killed today by a Pennsylvania liquor law-enforcement officer" *appeared on the 34th page.* Earlier it would have floated to the front page on rivers of tears, "Father defending his only son, etc." So *N. Y. Times,* Nov. 1, 1934: "Two men, veteran smugglers, Patmo and Popez, were killed while resisting arrest on the Rio Grande." *Two inches on page 18* were deemed enough for this post-Repeal tragedy.

PRESS GANGSTERS

An endlessly repeated newspaper complaint against National Prohibition was that it was responsible for the rise of gangsterdom in Chicago and elsewhere. The truth is that the two leading wet newspapers of Chicago, Hearst's *American* and the *Chicago Tribune,* were the real initial cause of this disgraceful phenomenon. It was they who hired armed thugs to engage in their Chicago circulation wars, to intimidate newsdealers into handling their papers, and to beat up their competitors. Many who were later notorious in Chicago got their start in this way,—the Annenbergs, "Red" Connors, "Massy" Enright, Vincent Altman, "Chicago Jack" Daly, Frank McErlane, Ed Bartett, Jack Nolan. Newspaper gunmen later operated brothels and terrorized union labor. They naturally seized on bootlegging when it became clear that the Federal Government was paltering with enforcement. Dion O'Bannon, when killed in a bootleg feud in 1925, was chief circulation gangster for Hearst at $50 a week. The shooting of George Hehr, unarmed teamster, by seven *Chicago American* thugs, with similar atrocities described in Mr. Lundberg's *Imperial Hearst,* was at first unmentioned by the press; then finally attributed to union labor.

SCARE STORIES

In the Senate, Jan. 15, 1935, Senator Nye said: "We know that an American munitions company placed men in London and Paris, to send back to America scare stories about gas warfare

. . . in order to frighten the American people into an acceptance of gas warfare as a national policy."

The "killings" drive was apparently instituted to counteract the great dry victory of 1928 in the election of President Hoover. The "poisoned liquor" campaign of 1926 (Dec. 24, *seq.*) was an earlier drive of similar purpose. It gave the impression that the government was selling poisoned liquor for drinking. It was opened by Dr. Norris, the Tammany Medical Examiner of New York, in a letter to Mr. Mellon complaining of deaths from denatured industrial alcohol. Hundreds of such deaths were reported from New York and thousands throughout the country but in answer to inquiries instituted by Secretary Mellon, it was discovered that of the 337 cases of alcoholism in the New York hospitals at the time, *one only* was from denatured alcohol. Yet day after day the big three of New York journalism—*Times, World,* and *Tribune*—splashed their columns with such headlines as

Rum poisoning by government goes right on
808 rum deaths in this state so far
Nearly 500 in city

Government won't drop
Poison alcohol policy
Deaths here 400 in year

Poison liquor protest ready to rise in Senate
Death toll in U. S. grows
Edwards opens the battle against
Legalized murder, as Dry Chief
Lays issue before President.

Poison rum victims fill
Mortality lists of cities
Public outcry against deadly government denaturant in
    alcohol spreads
Reports published from 23 cities

The public outcry was newspaper outcry, pure and simple. Indeed in an editorial article in the trade paper *Chemicals,* Prof. Muehlberger, the state toxicologist of Wisconsin, spoke of the whole matter as "newspaper-made." He expressed his "amazement" at "the figures published in the daily press and the loud outcries from politicians." Census bureau figures for deaths from wood alcohol to the 100,000 in 1924 were only one tenth of one per cent. Data from one of the largest life insurance companies showed that deaths from denatured alcohol in 1926 were one third the number in 1920. This was certainly so in New York City (1929, 29 cases: 1926, 10).

The swindle was too patent and after a week the "Big Three" dropped it but it bobbed up again in the Senate in 1930, if only to illustrate how hard put the wets were for arguments against Prohibition. Senator Tydings introduced a bill to remove methyl alcohol from industrial alcohol. Now methyl alcohol had been used as denaturant since 1906. It is used in all lands, its purpose being of course not to kill but to make industrial alcohol too nauseous to drink. A skull and bones warns the illiterate. It is used because it is carried over when bootleggers attempt to re-distill industrial alcohol (the industrial alcohol, for example, which the U. S. Industrial Alcohol Co. of Baltimore, Maryland, was selling to bootleggers). The newspapers knew all this. The wet politicians knew it. Yet Senator Tydings of Maryland could bring himself to say in the Senate that "the government of the United States, driven by fanatics who have no regard for human life, advocated the death penalty for doing no greater thing than drinking a pint of liquor" and, passing to melodrama, added, "Thank God! when I sleep tonight the blood of other people will not be upon my hands" (20)!

More baying in the newspapers as of "hounds and echo in conjunction," and Prof. Harry E. Barnes characterized the drys as "sadists who demand the poisoning of liquor" (21).

COPPERHEAD FIRE IN THE REAR

What was needed above all was quiet to organize effective enforcement. To prevent this referenda were constantly put before voters and supported by the wet press. The drys naturally looked on this as tenth inning procedure, the game having already been won, and refused to participate. The consequence was an impression of rising wet opposition which of course was the purpose of the manoeuvre.

The poll of the *Literary Digest* in 1930 fitted into this program of persistent ballyhoo. In the *N. Y. Herald Tribune,* May 1, 1930, a three-column advertisement of the *Digest,* headed PRO-HIBITION in huge letters, described the poll of physicians, bankers, clergymen, lawyers, school-teachers, taken independently of the main poll. It continued: "The main poll is on. It is now at its climax. Interest throughout the nation is phenomenal. It has attracted attention in Europe. Ocean liners have wirelessed for bulletins. American newspapers and magazines have printed over 12,000 news stories and editorials." Radio broadcasts were sent out evening after evening for weeks by Lowell Thomas and Floyd Gibbons. Yet of the twenty million ballots more than three fourths were never returned (22). So little was the real interest in the thing. Names had been taken from telephone directories which contain the names of ten times as many men as women and in which urban population wholly outbalances rural. The game was from the start played with loaded dice. Mr. Orton had it "from the editor of the *Literary Digest* (Feb. 25, 1932) that from time to time attempts to stuff the ballot-box (his own words) had been observed, the evidence being in similarity of crosses marked upon a collection of ballots received at the same time" (23).

People resented this private interference in a public affair. They suspected it, coming as it did at the height of a violent propaganda attack on the Constitution. They were annoyed that such votings should be added to the numerous primary and election votings to which the public was subjected. Prof. E. A. Ross has well stated this instinctive revulsion against the *Literary Digest's* operations, a revulsion fortified by the fact that the Funk and Wagnalls Company, a firm which had established itself by selling theological reprints to Protestant ministers and which had been orginally in the forefront of the dry agitation, was now dominated by Mr. Cuddihy, a wet Catholic. Prof. Ross says:

"The taking of nation-wide polls under private auspices may be a menace to democratic government. *They are costly and can be taken only when a party with money wishes.* Their referendum is taken without safeguards. Once taken the interests which it favors will argue from it as if it were an authentic and official disclosure of voter opinion" (24) (E).

BOTTLES AND DRUNKS TO THE FORE

Press methods to discredit Prohibition were various. One was to put into even front-page prominence any discovery of stills or unpleasant statistics of intoxication. That this was a systematic and tried procedure appears from a report of the Michigan Brewery Association in the Overman Report, p. 1162. "We have been gathering from the different parts of the state reports of violation of the local option law, cases of drunkenness and things of that sort, and *every week we print up a large sheet of these reports and send out to every newspaper.*" Would the newspapers publish this unimportant stuff? A report of the Brewers' Association of the adjacent Wisconsin answers the question clearly enough: "Cultivate your home editor. . . . It will pay you good dividends. We are meeting the demands of these papers that they be given a slice of advertising. They feel better already. It is a good remedy" (Overman Report, p. 785).

The canard was their stock in trade. Mr. Broome, Superintendent of the Philadelphia public schools, read in the *Public Ledger* that a high school teacher, Dr. Maeder, charged high school students with keeping liquor in their lockers. He sent for him together with Mr. Calhoun, the principal of the school. Following is the stenographic account of the interview (abridged):

Mr. Broome. Did you state that you knew high school students to keep liquor in their lockers?

Mr. Maeder. I did not.

Mr. B. Did you ever in your experience as a teacher in the Philadelphia High School know of a single case of liquor in a student's locker?

Mr. M. No.

Mr. B. Mr. Calhoun, you were teacher in the Germantown High School for ten years. You were principal of the Roxborough High School for three years and have been principal in the Gratz High School for four years. Altogether you have been 25 years in the Philadelphia Public Schools. Have you ever known of a case of liquor in a student's locker?

Mr. C. I have not.

Mr. B.	Have you ever had reliable evidence that liquor was kept in a student locker?
Mr. C.	I have not.
Mr. B.	Do you personally and other members of your staff frequently examine the lockers?
Mr. C.	The lockers are continually supervised.
Mr. B.	Do you think it possible for the practise of keeping liquor in lockers to prevail without your discovering it?
Mr. C.	I am sure I would know of it if there were any liquor in lockers (25).

Dr. James West is executive of the National Boy Scouts. He was charged by the Associated Press with saying at the White House Conference of 1930 on Child Health: "Prohibition has not lessened drinking among young people in the United States but, if anything, the problem has been worse under Prohibition." Dr. West wrote Congressman Hudson: "I am in no way responsible for the statement made and it does not represent my personal opinion in any way, manner, shape, or form."

THE DISTILLATION OF THE LIE

A recent writer in the *Journal de Genève* has pointed out that while the lie is at all times endemic there are certain times when it breaks out in epidemic fury as, for example, in the days of the Dreyfus affair. Certainly never in American history had it been as active as in the years that led up to Repeal. It is well known that the yeast plant, of which alcohol is the excrement, dies in the 13% solution which it has itself excreted and that only by distillation can the higher percentages be obtained. The alcohol lie would be similarly fatal to itself, so self-refuting has it become, if the daily newspaper had not played for it the part of the still.

Hearst papers. Oh naturally! We were told that the nearly universal Christmas presents displayed in shops and department stores were hip flasks and cocktail shakers. "Women of all classes were pointing out that the Prohibition laws, while aimed at the drunkard, had struck down the child." They explained in one breath that the land was deluged in drink, in the next that sailors in New York were drinking *eau de quinine* strained through bread and that ether was being used for smelling parties passed from addict to addict on a handkerchief (26). To such a pass were good citizens driven by the great drought. In similar vein Senator Reed reported that men in Kansas resorted to the pumpkin gin process, packing a ripe pumpkin with sugar and sealing until a high-powered drink resulted (27). Down to a Senate Committee in Washington came Mrs. Carrol Y. Miller and testified that in her dry town in Pennsylvania the sewage system would not work because the sieves were all clogged with mash, bottle tops, and corks (28). "The half is more than the whole," says the Greek proverb and I think Senator Bingham must have listened with misgivings to his star witness, Congressman Sabath, when he testified to the horrors of Prohibition Chicago as contrasted with its idyllic pre-Prohibition conditions: "Before Prohibition Chicago was one of the most law-abiding cities in the United States. Drunkenness was hardly known. Anyone who sold to minors had his license immediately revoked. Today there are 70,000 uncontrolled 'speaks' in Chicago" (29). Of Mr. Liggett's account of Boston conditions Congressman Luce said, "The report of the Grand Jury shows that no credence should attach to his statements." He asked Congress for the publication of this Federal Jury report *"because the press of the country has spread abroad the charges that he (Liggett) made while nothing has been printed (outside New England) about the findings of the government agency in the matter"* (30).

CIVIL WAR BETWEEN THEIR STATEMENTS

Prof. Harry E. Barnes told us that "drinking had increased lamentably among virtual babes" (31) and Mrs. Robert Lovett, of Boston, before a Senate Committee insisted that "the greatest menace to our country is the drunken girl of from 14 to 18" (32). Pressed by a reporter of the *Boston Post* (March 9, 1930) for a bill of particulars "she admitted that she had no facts, had not seen any 14-year-old girls worse for liquor nor, indeed, a woman of any age in drunken condition. Had no personal knowledge of conditions under Prohibition. Members of the Women's Committee had told her this and had requested her to get it into the record." Yet this testimony was given as personal experience, a blanket charge against 14-year-old girls without a shred of evidence. Mrs. C. H. Sabin made similar allegations, charging that girls of 15 or 16 years of age were in Salvation Army rescue homes because of Prohibition, a story which, as Miss Booth said, had been "repudiated again and again, yet repeated with amazing persistency" (33). The President of the Molly Pitcher Club in Philadelphia testified regarding a detective who took 297 flasks from young people in a fraternity affair. On cross examination she acknowledged that she knew nothing of the dance, personally had not been there, was told about it by one whose name she would not divulge (34). All indeed "looked yellow to the jaundiced eye" of Molly Pitcher.

Quite in contrast to the false witness of these society women was that of Miss Jane Addams. The dance halls of Chicago before Prohibition were running ulcers. After Prohibition Miss Addams was able to report (*Survey,* Oct. 1, 1929, p. 6) that "at one of the dance halls a few months ago in one evening out of 4,500 people examined only three were found carrying flasks. Such regulation would have been impossible unless the sale of liquor had been made illegal."

Press stories of college drinking had to meet such crushing refutals as that of Prof. Clarke of the Committee of Discipline at Yale: "The change has been simply revolutionary" (35); of President Faunce of Brown, "There is less drinking among students than ever before within the memory of man" (36); and of the Phillips-Andover questionnaire sent to thirty colleges, "Drinking is steadily on the wane." When Repeal was in sight (Nov. 1932) *Brewery Industry,* a trade paper, felt it safe to tell the truth:

"Before Prohibition beer was regarded as a concomitant of a college career. (Now) not one tenth of one percent of the youth in college know what really good American beer tastes like. To them it is little more than a name. . . . The brewers should begin their publicity campaign in college newspapers as soon as it can be prepared."

"COMPELLED TO DRUDGE, THE MEANEST OF THE MEAN,
TO FURNISH FALSEHOODS FOR A MAGAZINE"

Mr. George Q. Johnson of Chicago, the man who landed Capone in Leavenworth, was quoted as saying to the Federation of Churches: "Prohibition is the cause of all crime." What he actually said was that organized crime was the biggest business in the United States, *that bootlegging was comparatively a small part of it,* that racketeering was the principal thing and gambling the next greatest source of crime (37).

Congressman Schäfer brought up in Congress (C. R. Feb. 1, 1930, p. 2979) an alleged resolution of the Charlestown, W. Va., Ministerial Association, purporting to say that "Christ belonged to a lower civilization because he used wine." This did appear in the *Charlestown Gazette* boxed. Underneath the alleged quotation were inserted the words, "Proposed for discussion by the Ministerial Association." Such a resolution had never been before the Association yet it went out over the country and was the subject of sharp debate in Congress.

The Rev. Douglas Matthews of the great Seamen's Church Institute, Coentje's Slip, New York, was asked to speak on "The Waterfront Before and After Prohibition." I read the newspaper report in my country home and remarked, "That's a black eye for Prohibition." The next time I was in New York I went to see him about this address. This was his statement: "I said that all who have to do with ships and sailors agree that there is no comparison between past and present, so great is the improvement. I also said that the Seamen's Institute turned away 90 men a day for drunkenness out of from 10,000 to 12,000 who came to the doors daily. They multiplied the 90 by 30 to get an approximation for the month and headlined the story in this fashion. Of the vast army of sober sailors they said nothing. . . . My speech was in the interest of Prohibition but their caption turned it into wet propaganda" (38).

These are samples not exceptions. Mrs. Willebrandt spoke of New York as not only the center of lawlessness but also of the dissemination of false propaganda. "There has been a vast quantity of misinformation current. Hundreds of facts are selected and circulated which bear out the impossibility of enforcement. Dozens of interviews are printed in the newspapers which reflect only wet views" (39). "No law has had as much propaganda against it," wrote Judge Kenyon of the Wickersham Commission, and by propaganda he meant crooked propaganda (40). "The metropolitan press, with rare exceptions, has written one of the most shameless chapters in the history of the Republic," was the matured judgment of Bishop W. F. Anderson (41).

Shameless is the word! The *Buffalo Times* for July 18, 1931, answered editorially an article in its columns which had described pre-Prohibition control of the press. "She seeks to strengthen her argument," said this editor, "by showing that back in the old pre-Prohibition days the liquor interests attempted to corrupt the press of the country against Prohibition. Money was paid to get wet propaganda printed in the guise of news and some editors actually sold their editorial opinion.

"There is nothing new in all this. Every industry is a vested interest to somebody and people who find their property threatened naturally put up a fight to protect their economic interests."

THE PRESSTITUTES

Little by little the venality of the public press is coming to public knowledge. The Federal Trade Commission lifted the curtain on its paid subserviency to the Power Trust; the Stock Exchange Investigation unbared bribery connected with its financial news; the 1929–30 Sub-Committee on Naval Affairs brought intimations regarding its clandestine friendships with the armament crowd: the Overman Committee of 1918 revealed it as chained to the brewery truck by brewers' subsidies; the Calder Committee exposed its cooperation with the Coal Trust to bleed the public of $600,000,000 annually in excess profits; long ago its control by the vendors of patent medicine was exposed by Samuel Hopkins Adams; and when the Tugwell Pure Food Bill of 1934 threatened fake advertising worth $345,000,000, the organized newspaper associations of America fought and defeated it.

Mr. W. H. Allen of the Municipal Research Bureau has brought to light how leading New York newspapers accept undertaxation from Tammany assessors for obvious reasons. Tweed bought up the press with "contingencies" from city money. The modern method is less obvious, a little less at least. But the most massive evidence of the crookedness of the metropolitan press has been the way it lent itself to the destruction of the 18th Amendment (F).

PAY-DAY FOR THE PRESS

The 18th Amendment cut out rich advertising for the daily press and the recovery of this source of profit must have entered into newspaper calculations. The revenue from all advertising in 1927 is said to have been $724,837,083 out of a total income of $977,648,187 (42). Mr. Scheck, appearing before the Bingham

Committee, estimated that, in 1916, $200,000,000 was spent by breweries in newspaper, outdoor and sign advertising (43). If one quarter of that was the truth it would mean a very large fraction of newspaper advertising. The present alcohol advertising of the *N. Y. Times* can not run below two millions; experts say three. This might in a pinch mean the difference between continuance and receivership to a concern whose total advertising income is put at $22,000,000. On Repeal day the press came to the cashier's grill. Just reckon what the single Repeal number of *Life* (Dec. 1933) brought to that banal and impoverished publication, those pages of expensive advertising of Martini Vermouth, Dewar's White Label, Hennessy's Cognac, of Johnny Walker, of the Continental Distilling Co., of Holloway's Dry Gin, of Moet and Chandon champagnes and of Anheuser-Busch! How quickly did Mr. T. H. Beck, President of *Collier's*, rush to the first brewers' convention after Repeal: "We are proud of the part *Collier's Weekly* bore in this long campaign," wrote that House of Morgan paper (Nov. 25, 1933, p. 58). "First and for a long time alone . . . *Collier's* presented the significant facts which led the American people to render judgment against Prohibition." And he cried to the brewers in convention: "Play up the food values, the beneficial effect (of beer) on health. The power of advertising changes customs, costumes, and habits. . . . A national campaign takes a lot of money" (44). This is the Beck of whom Bruce Barton wrote, "I am indebted to my good friend, T. H. Beck, for the title 'The Book Nobody Knows.' " Mr. Barton handles brewery advertising; in 1934 for Schlitz 296,509 lineage; for Schafer 85,694 (45). Barton describes the Lord Jesus Christ as "founder of modern business. He would be a national advertiser today." I think He would rather treat the national advertisers and their clients to an adaptation of the 23rd of Matthew:

"Woe unto you scribblers, promoters of breweries! Woe unto you brewers, disrupters of families, degraders of women, ruiners of careers, stupifiers of intelligence!"

There is little doubt that in the last analysis it was press deception that destroyed the Great Amendment. Mr. Raymond Robins was unquestionably right in saying, "Had it not been for the widespread and continuous activities of the wet newspapers of the country, the large metropolitan newspapers of the big cities . . . (Prohibition) would not have been an issue in the United

States" (46). The result was that the nation was misled completely as post-Repeal days have shown. It lost an opportunity that comes only in decades and

> "Like the base Indian threw a pearl away
> Richer than all his tribe."

The moral has been summed up for us in the words of Mr. McAdoo: "It is a tragedy that in modern civilization the agencies of misrepresentation are now so powerful and uncontrolled. Some day the means of reform must be found. Society will have to protect itself or suffer consequences greater than now appear" (47).

Finally a word about wet art.

THE NEWSPAPER CARTOONISTS AND THEIR BUTT

The English Nonconformist ministers were, in the 19th century, a chief driving force behind the whole liberal forward movement,—abolition of tests, factory reform, extension of suffrage, popular education, free trade, and all the rest. They backed Shaftesbury and Bright and Cobden and Gladstone. For some reason the novelist Dickens took a sharp dislike to them and caricatured them at every opportunity. Stiggins, the preacher-friend of Mrs. Weller, was one of his creations and little creditable to him, "a man with threadbare black clothes, a prim-faced, red-nosed man with long thin countenance," whom he represented as preaching temperance and given to rum. The British drink interest took this figure out of "Pickwick Papers" to symbolize the opposition of the Nonconformist leadership to their vile trade (G). He carries the inevitable umbrella of the Englishman and wears the tall hat of the Abe Lincoln period. The *N. Y. World* imported the exotic caricature and applied it to American drys. In the hands of the skillful draftsman, Rollin Kirby, it was more powerful than any arguments which the Swopes and Lippmanns could muster to create prejudice against the 18th Amendment. Winsor McCay used much the same figure for the Hearst papers and his adaptation of Pierre Fritel's "The Conqueror,"—1,360 corpses on either side of the lane on which advanced, instead of Alexander, Caesar, and Napoleon, tall-hatted, rifle-armed, spectacled fanatics,—was as brilliant a caricature in behalf of falsehood as ever Nast drew for honesty and good government. The

Du Pont-Harkness-James organization financed a syndicate furnishing daily newspapers with badly drawn cartoons in which this unsavory figure appeared repeatedly and listed 144 newspapers which took them in. The news-reels used the same tactics. Speakers in behalf of Prohibition were caricatured by taking their faces at an angle; by speeding up their speaking so as to make them appear laughable, while wet spokesmen were deliberate and self-contained; by picking dry leaders whose features best lent themselves to caricature. The drys were sneered at as "frumps." In the official history of the women's wet organization (Root, "Women and Repeal," p. 22) Mrs. Sabin appears with Mrs. Boole of the W. C. T. U. on the same page, by way of contrast, in a charming and youthful photograph.

AMERICA AND THE PROTESTANT MINISTRY

Froude has characterized America as "the creation of English Nonconformity" and Rhodes in his "History of the United States" says that in 1834 a third of the population of the country was of Puritan descent. It was these ministers who developed and shaped the higher education of the nation, who gave the country its peculiar idealist quality. They played their part in the Revolution,—the Mayhews and Witherspoons. They played their part in the fight against slavery,—the Parkers and Beechers. They would have lifted the burden of alcoholism from America if they had not been checkmated and cheated by Wall Street. The figure of Stiggins may pass with those who know nothing of them but with no other. After the 18th Amendment an attack was opened on them unparalleled in American history, in movie and theatre, in novel and magazine and newspaper. It was the snarl of the interests that live by poisoning mankind.

The Protestant ministers have for years been the ones to clean up after the distillers and brewers. They have helped the alcohol-sick at their own doors and in little missions. And they have been the butt of the Mencken school of slander for undertaking a rational and humane alcohol prophylactic.

THE FAMILY TEST

They say in Scotland that the real patent of nobility is birth in a manse. Much the same may be said of the United States where in the population of "Who's Who" sons of ministers far

outdistance those of all other professions.   That will balance a
good deal of what American journalists have written in denigra-
tion of the Protestant ministry.   The fathers cannot be so much
behind their own sons in character and ability.   They laugh best
who laugh last.   The *N. Y. World* is happily no more.   The Du
Ponts no doubt chuckled over the fantastic old man with the umbrella in the picture book the A. A. P. A. sent to the press.   Nine
months after Repeal found them roasting before Senator Nye's
Committee and the man who turned the spit was Stephen Raushen-
bush, son of a dry Baptist minister.

One might well compare the children of rich wets triangulat-
ing between New York, Miami, and Reno, with such ministers'
sons as President Woodrow Wilson, Chief Justice Hughes, and the
Nobel prizemen, Compton and Milliken.

THE WET OUTFIT

And what was lined up against this moral élite?   You may
little like it, dear decent wets, but it is the unquestionable truth
that everything in American life that is offensive and anti-social
and dangerous is on your side.   One has but to count them on one's
fingers,—the gamblers, the pimps, the gangsters, the brewers, the
race-track bookies, the depraved politicians, Tammany Hall and
its imitations in Boston and San Francisco, the foul United Societies of Chicago, the Jersey City Hague machine, the rotten
Republican political organization of Philadelphia, the gamblers of
Wall Street, the degenerates of Hollywood, Hearst, Vare, Roger
Sullivan, Brennan, Cermak, Curley, Hynicka, Pendergast, the underworld of lust, the upperworld of fashion, the venal newspapers,
—everything that is hateful and repulsive.   All wet!   No exceptions!   When the *N. Y. World* attempted to read the bootleggers
of New York City out of its following they would not go.   Their
vote was practically unanimous for Repeal.   That outstanding
wet, Scarface Capone, on his way to prison, insisted that conditions
for beer would be far more favorable if the 18th Amendment
should disappear.

Wet propagandists knew this well enough and to divert attention from it wove a mythical robe of righteousness for their cause.
They pictured themselves as of a piece with "that higher, holier,
earlier, purer Church."   They drank in dark "speaks" as the early
Christians lived in catacombs.   Mr. Cortland Nicoll of the

A. A. P. A. quoted Pliny's letter to Trajan (48) to find a parallel to the sufferings of the wets under dry persecution. "Christianity was a bootleg religion until the great Repealer, Constantine." Senator Edwards, who wished to make New Jersey "wet as the Atlantic," cried out: " 'No man that putteth his hand to the plow and looketh back is fit for the Kingdom of God.' Surely there can be no clearer work of God than the defense of ancient American liberty." To W. W. Montgomery of the Philadelphia A. A. P. A. the sorrows of the wets under Prohibition recalled the den of lions and Daniel (49). Others remembered the Boston Tea Party, the Stamp Act, the Alien and Sedition laws (Henry Alan Johnson) (50).

The favorite analogy, however, was that of the anti-slavery heroes, the men who withstood the Fugitive Slave law. The "Volunteer Lawyers" who proposed to defend bootleggers against the Increased Penalties Act pictured themselves as the lineal descendants of those brave men who went into the courts in behalf of hunted negroes fleeing Canada-ward. Mr. La Guardia read out the long roll of Abolitionists who would certainly have stood with him if living (51).

THE TESTIMONY OF THE ABOLITIONISTS

We of Abolitionist stock know better. The rank and file of Abolitionism was dry: so were most of its leaders. Thus Horace Greeley proposed to "cut off that liquor dog's tail *back of his ears.*" That's orthodox 18th Amendment alcoholology. In a powerful speech in Congress Gerrit Smith, whom Mr. La Guardia classified as a wet, said (July 22, 1854): "It so happened, Mr. Speaker, that my first act on this floor, after taking the oath of office, was to present a memorial praying Congress to empower the City of Washington to prohibit the sale of intoxicating drinks." Wendell Phillips lined up with "the temperance men who have funded thirty years of work in that statute" (the Massachusetts Prohibition Law) and in a speech for better enforcement said (Feb. 28, 1865): "To my mind the temperance cause is one of the weightiest, broadest, most momentous that a citizen under democratic institutions can contemplate. I contend that every man who desires the security of democratic institutions is to see to it *first of all* that every possible means be exhausted to secure, so far as human means can, a sober people." Samuel J. May on the

4th of July, 1855, spoke of the recently enacted New York State Prohibition Law in the following words:

"This is the date of a new deliverance, *a deliverance far greater than that which we have hitherto commemorated on the Fourth of July.* If the law this day inaugurated shall be maintained, perfected, and extended over our country, the anniversary of our national independence shall, in all coming time, commemorate the deliverance of the people of this state from the grasp of a mightier despot, a more deadly enemy than that our fathers of 1776 pledged their lives, their fortunes, and their sacred honor to withstand."

Of the Emancipator himself Lord Charnwood says: "His social philosophy was one that contemplated great future reforms, abolition of slavery and strict temperance policy among them." "All such questions," he is reported to have said, "must find lodgment with the most enlightened souls who stamp them with their approval. In God's own time they will be organized into law and woven into the fabric of our institutions" (52). Lincoln looked forward to *"a complete victory,"* a time "when there shall be neither a slave nor a drunkard on the earth." "How proud the title of that land which may truly claim to be the birthplace and cradle of both these revolutions" (Feb. 22, 1842).

It is Abraham Lincoln's ideal in process of realization that the corrupt metropolitan press, two generations after his death, have for the time being destroyed. Today all is still in the newspaper offices regarding this subject.

It is the stillness that follows a murder.

REFERENCES TO CHAPTER V NOT IN THE TEXT

1. Congressional Record, February 9, 1917, page 2947.
2. Hearings Prohibition Amendment, House Judiciary Committee, February 1930, page 864.
3. North American Review, September 1925, page 39.
4. Silas Bent, "Ballyhoo," page 373.
5. Villard, "Some Newspapers and Newspaper Men."
6. Pound, "They Told Barron," page 111.
7. Current History, June 1926, page 440.
8. Review of Reviews, August 1926, page 125.
9. World's Work, No. 52, page 677.
10. Congressional Record, January 31, 1930, page 2791.
11. Mrs. Willebrandt, "Inside of Prohibition," page 129.
12. Atticus Webb, "Dry America," page 116.
13. Congressional Record, January 16, 1930, page 1738.
14. Louisville Times, August 8, 1929.
16. Tydings, "Before and After Prohibition," page 104.

17. New York Tribune, May 30, 1932, page 4.
18. Adamic, "Dynamite," page 288–291.
19. New York Times, April 3, 1929, page 2.
20. Congressional Record, May 14, 1930, page 8, 918.
21. "Prohibition Against Civilization," page 35.
22. American Year Book, 1930, page 31.
23. "Prohibition Plainly Put" by Jesse Orton, page 14.
24. Quoted in R. P. Hutton, "Threshing Straw."
25. Hearings Committee on Manufactures, January 1932, page 373.
26. W. R. Hearst, "Temperance or Prohibition," XV, 24.
27. J. A. Reed, "The Rape of Temperance," page 187.
28. Hearings Prohibition Amendment, House Judiciary Committee, February 1930, page 467.
29. Hearings Committee on Manufactures, 72nd Congress, January 1932, page 236.
30. Congressional Record, February 20, 1930, page 4029.
31. "Prohibition Against Civilization," page 101.
32. Hearings House Committee on Judiciary, February 1930, page 441.
33. Hearings House Committee on Judiciary, February 1930, pages 42 and 888.
34. Hearings House Committee on Judiciary, February 1930, page 429, and Boston Post, March 9, 1930.
35. Hearings Senate Judiciary Committee, April 1926, page 1007.
36. Hearings Senate Judiciary Committee, April 1926, page 1320.
37. Hearings Committee on Manufactures, January 1932, page 552.
38. Personal Letter.
39. Willebrandt, "The Inside of Prohibition," pages 182 and 311.
40. Wickersham Report, page 136.
41. New York Times, May 4, 1932.
42. Harding, "The Degradation of Science," page 83.
43. Hearings Committee on Manufactures, January 1932, page 249.
44. American Brewer, February 1934, page 17.
45. American Brewer, January 1935.
46. Hearings, Prohibition Amendment, House Judiciary Committee, February 1930, page 841.
47. William G. McAdoo, "The Challenge," page 303.
48. North American Review, June 1929, page 641.
49. Prohibition Amendment Hearings, February 1930, House Judiciary Committee, page 302.
50. Hearings Committee on Manufactures, January 1932, page 326.
51. Congressional Record, January 21, 1930, page 2061.
52. Lord Charnwood, "Abraham Lincoln," page 75.

NOTES TO CHAPTER V

A.   The same procedure appears to have been used on other occasions. Mr. Hamill, in "The Strange Career of Mr. Hoover," says, "To put through a bill creating Hoover's appointment as food dictator and present him in a favorable light to the American public, a great campaign of Hoover propaganda was started in the twenty-five newspapers which had been selected by big banking and munition manufacturing interests to control public opinion in the United States. This was supplemented by descriptive articles in magazines of great circulation. . . ."

The campaign against the Ford Peace Ship offers at points a curious parallel to the campaign against National Prohibition. Mr. H. G. Wells calls attention (in "The Shape of Things to Come," p. 67 seq.) to the very wide response which, in Europe, met the project at the beginning. But, according to him, the press of America, and of Europe following America, was incited against it by the armament ring, fearful lest this pacifist "fanaticism" might endanger their gigantic profits. Press correspondents on the ship invented all sorts of grotesque stories on order. A ground-swell of ridicule overwhelmed the enterprise and outraged Mr. Ford felt it useless to continue.

B.   One wonders whether an article belittling Bishop Manning was not due to the fact that he was an upholder of the 18th Amendment which he characterized as "one of the greatest efforts toward moral and social betterment that has ever been made." Mr. Elmer Davis, writer of wet articles, in his "Portrait of a Cleric" (*Harper's* 153: p. 14) spoke of Dr. Manning as, among other of his alleged eccentricities, "supporting the Volstead Act as zealously as any Methodist." Was he seeking for this reason to depreciate the Episcopal bishop as Mr. Mencken the Protestant ministry?

C.   The participation of writers and scientists in the brewers' propaganda deserves a chapter by itself. Brewer Adolphus Busch once wrote confidentially, "We ought to exact a promise from every Representative and Senator whom we support, that they in turn will watch over our interests. . . . It is my aim to win the American people over to our side. This work has got to be done systematically *and the best writers of the country will have to lend their assistance. It may cost a million dollars and even more. . . . I stand ready to sacrifice my annual profits for years to come, if I can make people look upon beer in the right light*" (Overman Report, p. 1300).

(It may be said in passing that Busch himself had no exalted ideas about beer. The eminent diagnosist, Dr. Meinert of Dresden, once told me how, when he explained to Busch that beer-drinking was ruining his health, the brewer blazed out with, "I never touch beer! I drink champagne.")

Certainly those who undertake for the cause of beer cannot be surprised if they are suspected of being under retainer. Now and again these suspicions are verified. Mr. A. J. Nock expounded in the *American Magazine* in 1913 (Jan., p. 53) the Elderton-Pearson rehabilitation of alcohol and threw in, as his own contribution, his opinion "that the saloon in New York performs more social service than the churches and organized charities together." This thesis was illustrated by the following amazing sentence: "When you find bad housing, congestion, or parents of depressed morals you are apt to find it associated with good eyesight in the children. It occurred to the (Galton) Laboratory that the cause was probably the same in both cases, namely that the child spent more time out of doors. Bad living conditions tend to drive children out and *so do drunken parents*." The Overman Report (p. 110) revealed Mr. Nock as paid investigator for the brewers.

D.   Who does not remember how the Federal Prohibition agents were slammed by the press for tapping telephone wires in the course of detective work? But when Mr. Morgenthau announced that "wire tapping as a means of detecting violators of the laws against narcotics and bootlegging would be used," adding, "We do not propose to be sissies" (*N. Y. Times,* Oct. 16, 1934) not the slightest ripple of protest could be detected in the newspapers or from President Butler. It had ceased to be "dirty business."

Senator Sheppard had proposed to make the buyer as well as seller liable in the purchase of liquor. Howls from the newspaper wolves and protests that the jails would not hold the offenders! But a similar proposal before the Senate Committee on Finance, July 23, 1935, to make the buyer as well as the bootlegger of non-tax-paid liquor subject to prosecution in conspiracy, appears not to have been observed at all by the press; nor that French partial prohibition (1940) condemns the consumer as well as the seller to fine and imprisonment.

E.   The *Literary Digest* evidently chose the moment for going into action. Mr. S. E. Nicholson (*N. Y. Times,* March 28, 1930, p. 19) tells us that "the ballots were released before the Prohibition hearings in Washington were ended. Ballots should have been held until the dry hearing had been completed and the rebuttal testimony from both sides had been given." *At these hearings wet testimony was given first.*

This offensive publication interfered elsewhere. It mailed a half million double postcards to voters in California during the Sinclair governorship campaign. Mr. Sinclair recounts the various forms of trickery associated with the distribution of ballots. The estimate of electoral voting was way off but it did Mr. Sinclair "irreparable harm" nevertheless. "It encouraged our enemies, it weakened our friends and it shifted the betting odds. In short it started a chain of unfavorable events," even to changing the attitude of Roosevelt and Farley (Sinclair, "I, Candidate for Governor," p. 172–4). The ludicrous miscalculation of the Landon-Roosevelt vote for 1936 by the *Literary Digest* was followed by its demise. Drys had stopped taking it and its value as propagandist in guise of political weather-prophet was at an end.

F.   Indisputable evidence was adduced at the hearings demonstrating that in connection with pool operations *it was usual and customary* for the operator to pay newspaper writers for publicity and propaganda disguised as financial news. Senate Report No. 1455. The case of a certain publicity man named Plummer was mentioned "who expended on behalf of his pool-operating employers the sum of $286,279 for the publication of articles in the press favorable to their stocks."

So (on p. 635, Senate Com. on Naval Affairs, 1939–40), Mr. Shearer, agent of these interests, "purchased one page of the *N. Y. Commercial* for one day per week for six months to (publish) information furnished by him."

Some $40,000,000 yearly was Mr. Adams' estimate of what the newspapers received from patent medicine advertisements. When Boards of Health attempt to show what is in these medicines the newspapers refuse to print this official matter. In the newspaper contracts it is agreed that the contract lapse "if any law is enacted in your state restricting or forbidding the manufacture or sale of proprietary medicine"; also if anything appears in the newspaper detrimental to the interests of the patent medicine business. How the newspapers have been active lobbyists for patent medicine interests was illustrated in a letter sent to all the Massachusetts newspapers by the Cheney Medicine Co. of Toledo:

"Gentlemen: Should House Bills, Nos. 329, 30, 307, 742, or Senate Bill 185 become laws it will force us to discontinue advertising in your state. We respectfully refer you to the contract which we have with you."

This is but another phase of the alcohol cancer. The Warner Safe Cure is alleged to be manufactured by the New York and Kentucky Distilling Co. and Peruna is so intoxicating that its sale to Indians is forbidden by the U. S. Government (S. H. Adams, "The Great American Fraud," pp. 145–165, 21, 13 and *Collier's*, Nov. 7, 1905).

"Nothing more disgraceful can be found in recent American history," says the *Christian Century* ("Newspaper Blood Money," Feb. 6, 1935, p. 167) "than the record of newspaper publishers with regard to child labor." . . . The press "has even dared to withhold from most of the nation the fact that the President of the United States is asking that the amendment be ratified. In November the President sent out a special letter endorsing the amendment. *The Associated Press never gave it a line.*"

Mr. Brent says: "The morality of the whole press was such that it winked at the Teapot Dome deal until, two years after it was consummated, a Senate Committee exposed it." This information was in the hands of Ochs of the *N. Y. Times* and was suppressed at least for the time being ("Ballyhoo," p. 90). The *New Republic* (March 14, 1934) says, "In the last fifteen years the press made an 100% record of failure in telling the people what they most needed to know. Where was the press when Wall Street was running up stock prices to heights that had no relation to earning power? Where was the press of New York while Tammany was engaged in a riot of incompetence and corruption without parallel in all history?"

G.   Stiggins was England's most effective contribution to the wet cause in America but there were others,—as the rum fleet which lay outside New York for months, an unparalleled insult to a friendly power. Of this Mr. Borah, Chairman of the Foreign Relations Committee, said:

"When Mr. Chamberlain sent his communication to the Soviet government relating to the Zinoviev letter he said, 'You either have a government or you have not. You can either control your nationals in their effort to sow discord and violence among other people or you cannot.'

"Are we not entitled to say to the British government, 'You have a government or you have not. You can either control your nationals in their efforts to break down the policy and plant murder and misery among other people or you cannot.'

"It is quite within the power of the British government to instantly put an end to the activities of such moral pirates as would cooperate with the criminals in this country to violate law and undermine and destroy a great national policy" (Mr. Borah was referring to Sir Broderick Hartwell who had stated that he had smuggled $5,000,000 of whiskies into the United States) (*N. Y. Times,* Jan. 8, 1925, p. 30).

And there is the Right Hon. Winston Churchill. Of his anti-Prohibition utterances in the United States he says: "Every allusion was greeted with laughter and cheers." He explained to us that three-fourths of the present grave evils by which the United States is afflicted take their origin and find their explanation in Prohibition and offered to us statements such as the following:

"Anyone who has seen an American ship arrive in a free port will recall the disgusting spectacle of intoxication of both old and young American citizens, so often paraded to the contempt of foreigners" (*Collier's,* Aug. 13, 1932, p. 20 and 48).

The only precedent I can find to such impudence is the brief career of citizen Genet. How can it be accounted for?

The English economist, Sir George Paish, in a letter to Dr. W. R. Bowie of New York, remarked that "very large numbers of people in this country (England) are watching America's experiment with sympathy and hope. If it succeeds they intend to do all in their power to induce the British people to follow America's example. I am convinced that if (your) present law becomes really effective, we on this side may hope to be equally successful in persuading the British people to abandon a custom that is responsible, more than any other, for an infinite amount of mental as well as physical suffering, and for a large proportion of the poverty which now exists."

The enormously powerful drink interest of Great Britain feared the success of American Prohibition more than is commonly realized. This drink interest is one of the most powerful supports of British Toryism with which Mr. Churchill is identified. Churchill has dealt out favors to it, as for example in large tax reduction. One of his first speeches after his return from America was before the Allied Brewery Trades' Association. He boasted to these beer kegs that "he did not feel a penny the worse for his two months of Prohibition," which meant, apparently, that his alcoholic cravings, for he is no weakling in drink, were amply met with illegal liquor.

But why did not the New York newspapers give him his deserts for his unprecedented intervention in American affairs on American soil? Presumably because it fitted perfectly into their own program.

It may be added that now, after Repeal, Mr. Churchill feels called on to attack local option in America. "So long as any state is dry or even partially dry," he wrote in *Collier's* (Aug. 25, '34), "the task of cleaning up gang-ridden municipalities is made a hundred times more difficult. . . . I look with suspicion on proposals for local option." So does this champion of "democracy" denounce democratic processes.

CHAPTER VI

AN ECCLESIASTICAL INTERLUDE

On the eighth of February, 1926, Cardinal Wm. H. O'Connell sent to the press a strong anti-Prohibition statement and similar pronouncements from Cardinal Hayes of New York and Cardinal Mundelein of Chicago followed (1). As Cardinal O'Connell is ranking prelate of the Roman Catholic Church in the United States, and as his statement appeared directly on his return from Rome, it is hard to think of it as other than an expression of the official attitude of the Roman Catholic Church.

In the course of this statement the Boston Cardinal-Archbishop quoted at length from the Catholic weekly, the London *Tablet*, for Jan. 23, 1926. This was appropriate as the editor-publisher of the *Tablet* was reported at this time to be carrying on, alongside of his editorial work and under an assumed name, a flourishing liquor business (2).

ALCOHOL-CLERICALISM

The case is hardly different for European Catholicism in general. The drinkshop and the church are, in Ireland and in the countries of Catholic Europe, ever in close proximity. Real estate agents look upon this proximity as a valuable asset for the saloon-keeper. Sons of saloon-keepers form a numerous proportion of the priesthood. The saloon-keeper himself is ordinarily close behind the priest in the control, political and otherwise, of the village or town. His large subscriptions are accepted as untainted gain and the best pew in the church is at his disposal. He is the leading layman *par excellence*.

The higher walks of political life reflect the same alliance. In every Catholic land the clerical party supports the drink interest. Dr. Ignatius Seipel, the Austrian clerical leader, was its unfailing political friend. In Belgium the Rexists, a Jesuit-backed party and dripping wet, "would make Christ King" by repealing the Lex Vandervelde which prohibits the sale of spirits by the glass. In Germany the Bavarian Folk Party led by Pater Leicht and the Centrum under the lead of Mgr. Kaas, were at the forefront in the fight to keep down beer taxation (3). In the Swiss referendum of 1930 to bring the sale of spirits under monopoly control, the opposition was led by Catholic clergy. The Protestant cities put through the reform. One could write a considerable book on the breweries and distilleries operated by Catholic clergy, as for example the distilleries of the Bishop of Olmuetz, the Carmelite distillery at Ratisbon, and the great Trappist distillery at Tre Fontane close to the spot where St. Paul was martyred. Brewer Pabst of Milwaukee, writing in the *American Brewer* (Nov. 1938, p. 41), tells us that the most widely known American beers have come from the monasteries of Europe. Andech monastery draws travellers "from miles around. Here from dawn till dark monks roll beer kegs and serve foaming steins. My grandfather brought to America the, rigid adherence to a tradition of quality that he observed at Andech monastery."

Ettal cloister brewery has recently celebrated its six hundred years of beer brewing. The Moenchberg brewery, as that of Kreuzbach and Andech monasteries, is a place of pilgrimage with chapels of grace. The Benedictine nuns of Frauenswoerth Abbey make a convent liquor. Those at Schweikeberg Abbey announce that any buying ten bottles will be given two *gratis*. Even in the duodecimo Vatican City there are four bars (*Ken,* Sept. 8, 1938). The brewer is a man of spiritual eminence in Vatican eyes and I notice in the *Brewers' Journal* for Feb. 15, 1939, p. 44, that the Pope has made Mr. Guyette, President of the Harvard Brewing Co., *Knight Commander of the Holy Sepulchre.*

Cardinal O'Connell is quite right in his contention that "the immemorial beverages of the Old World" are befriended by "Catholic tradition." He must also recall that when the Eucharistic Congress was held in Dublin the hours of sale in Dublin saloons were extended into the night for the convenience of Catholic worshippers. Yet even Cardinal O'Connell, when a young curate, used to denounce the saloons as "altars of Satan."

A TRUMPET NOTE A CENTURY AGO

In 1836 the Irish Society of Boston issued an address to their countrymen. After speaking of the fact that, on coming to America, they had been admitted to all the rights and privileges of the native-born, they put the question whether they were show-ing themselves worthy of these privileges. Then, as ever, the drink question was the crux and they were urged "to take a stand calculated to prevent them from becoming a laughing-stock and by-word, a ruin to their helpless families, a reproach to their country."

That was nearly a century before Cardinal O'Connell's pro-nouncement. If only the Irish clergy had listened to the moving appeal of their laity! One thinks of such statistical material as the following: The rates of first admissions for alcoholism to the New York State hospitals for the insane were per 100,000 in 1930, —for natives 2.8, for foreign born 7.2, for Irish 22.8. Among the male patients in the Massachusetts State Hospital for the Insane in Worcester the percentage of alcoholic cases, as compared with the total number of psychoses of the same nativity, was, for the Irish 37%, the old Massachusetts stock 98%, the Jews one half of one per cent. In the Manhattan State Hospital, of 1,403 ad-missions for all types of psychoses, 29% were Irish; of the 182 cases of alcoholic psychoses 62% were of Irishmen (4).

"Whose breath blew out the light within these brains?"

"The Phelans, the Callahans, and the rest of the Irish are vanishing almost as fast as the Indians," writes Colonel Callahan, "and for that liquor is solely responsible. A few months ago I was looking over a list of the charter members of the Knights of Columbus in Louisville and it was appalling what liquor had done to us. Over twenty of the first hundred in our city have gone into drunkards' graves and, mind you, it was the very best that went that way" (5). He was writing to Kathleen Norris, the novelist, also a Roman Catholic. Mrs. Norris has given similar testimony: "In my girlhood every good mother was worrying about a drinking son. I could list for you whole families of what we used to call San Francisco's Irishtocracy, wiped out by drink." And then she adds, referring to Prohibition, "The work should have been in the hands of the Church from the beginning. For this neglect she, of all organizations, will in the end pay most bitterly."

IRELAND'S WOE

At the 19th International Congress Against Alcoholism at

Antwerp in 1928 the Rev. J. W. O'Ryan of Dublin made this statement:

"In Northern Ireland there is entire Sunday closing and a sober Sunday.   In the Free State Sunday is the most drunken day of the week.   Owing to the action of the District Justice of my county, Dublin, in extending the closing hour, I have no hesitation in stating that County Dublin on Sunday evening is the most drunken place in Europe.   With drunken motor drivers and drunken foot-passengers no one is safe.   Last year we spent for drink in the Free State £15,635,264, or £5/5 for every man, woman, and baby in arms.   There are 1,239 saloons in the country.   The worst of them is in the House of Parliament itself.   The greatest part of the revenue of the country comes from alcohol and the drink traffic has tremendous power."

The responsible lay leaders of Ireland understand this situation.   Miss Jane Addams recounts her visit to the President of Mexico and how he wished to talk only of Prohibition with her. "He thought no one thing more important than the abolition of pulque."   So of her similar conversations with members of the Irish Free State government in 1926, the year of Cardinal O'Connell's manifesto.   "They were full of plans for the improvement of Ireland, electrification of the Shannon, cooperative dairies. But every single man of the government with whom I had a chance really to converse asked me at once, sometimes wistfully, about the workings of Prohibition in America.   'How did the Irish-Americans take it? etc.'   They always closed with, 'If they could utilize the full man-power of Ireland as they hoped to utilize her full material resources all would be right' " (6).

<h2 style="text-align:center">A SAVING REMNANT</h2>

There is a minority in American Catholicism which supports the dry side.   In the Senate some years ago five of the seven Catholic Senators were for Prohibition which, as Col. Callahan says, compares well with the batting average of Methodism.   One can also quote Catholic clergy, true shepherds of souls, as the Rev. M. F. Foley of St. Paul's, Baltimore, who feels "the 18th Amendment to be what President Hoover declared it to be, a noble experiment, the most noble a great nation ever tried, to save its people from frightful evils" (7).   And there is the tender-hearted Bishop of Fall River, Dr. Cassidy, who calls "the extinction of the saloon by Prohibition, in the cities in which I move, a blessing and a benediction that no lover of truth, no lover of humanity, no lover of souls, would knowingly attempt to deny, decry, or diminish" (8).

This is in line with the utterances of Archbishop Ireland: "The Catholic Church is absolutely and irrevocably opposed to drunkenness and to drunkard making. The individual conscience has to be strengthened and supplemented by law. The claim of the saloon-keepers to freedom in their traffic is the claim to spread disease, sin, pauperism. We have seen that there is no hope of improving in any way the liquor traffic. *There is nothing now to be done (but) to wipe it out completely. We must work and bend every effort so that Catholics in political matters will always be arrayed against the liquor interest.*"

Archbishop J. J. Keane is also quoted: "I have every confidence that the arguments in favor of the Constitutional Amendment for Prohibition will receive careful consideration by the voters of the state. No other problem has wearied and tried their souls as has the liquor problem and they will be glad of an opportunity to put it out of the way definitively. Practical experience with Prohibition for even a few months has helped everyone to recognize that it is a very great blessing to be rid of the American saloon,—an infamous institution" (9).

It is with reluctance, however, that one is forced to conclude that the weight of ecclesiastical influence was thrown to Repeal. It is impossible to appraise the injuries which this has caused and will increasingly cause to their own Catholic people.

"WHY SHOULD THIS ROME, THIS ROME,
ABSOLVE THE LEFT-HAND THIEF AND DAMN THE RIGHT?"

A despatch to the *N. Y. Sun* (March 8, 1934) indicated that the Vatican at times enters American politics. "Before the election one of Mr. Roosevelt's advisers confidentially assured the Vatican that he (Roosevelt) would recognize the Holy See if he were elected. *This step is thought to have caused the Holy See to regard Mr. Roosevelt's candidacy with great interest.*" In the nature of the case the Vatican would be wary in openly condemning an amendment to the United States Constitution and the occasional mention by the press of condemnations which were coming could well have been set down to international alcohol propaganda. A boxed, front-paged despatch from Rome (Jan. 3, 1928) quoting the *Osservatore Romano,* the Vatican organ, was more significant. This affirmed that "attempts to enforce Prohibition in America have become so useless, not to say dangerous, that it would be better to abolish it" (11). "I do not think that the National Prohibition laws are any longer binding in conscience," wrote Mgr. John A. Ryan of the Catholic University, Washington, a little later. In his statement before the House Judiciary Committee in 1930 (p. 281) he practically absolved Roman Catholics from obedience to this law (12). The Catholic press with few exceptions campaigned against the 18th Amendment, the Jesuit organ *America* having distinguished itself for its acerbity.

Roman Catholic tradition, as we have seen, is indulgent to drink-selling; in Europe, at least, there are great church investments in the business; the international alcohol interests constitute a political and financial power of the first order and the Jesuit is not averse to entering into coalition with political powers. (A minor illustration of this team-work is noted in Mr. Seldes' "The Facts Are," p. 55. In 1936 prominent Catholic clergy sought to dragoon the press into opposing the Spanish Republic. "In the case of *Ken* they started a boycott *through the liquor manufacturers,* who withdrew their advertising and helped kill this publication.")

.   .   .   .

Mr. Lundberg (*American Spectator,* Jan. 1936) remarks that "the deepest secrecy shrouds the finances of the wealthy Catholic Church. . . . Its investments are held in the names of individuals and hence do not appear as Church funds on the public records." Yet *recorded* investments are enormous and extremely varied. According to the N. Y. State Banking and Insurance Department, Catholic organizations have investments in almost every firm listed in the New York Stock Exchange. In the long list reproduced by Mr. Lundberg no alcohol investments appear. Have such investments been purposely avoided? It is not certain. In a book published for private circulation, "The Occult Theocracy," page 623, one reads: "The funds of the Catholic Church (the Vatican) in the United States had been largely invested in the whisky trust by the Jew, Max Pam." Mr. Pam was a leading corporation lawyer in Chicago and, though a Jew, the founder of the School of Journalism in the Catholic Notre Dame University, Indiana (A).

It is well-known that there was a reorganization of the whisky trust in 1924, that old distilleries were bought up for a song together with trade names, proprietary rights and huge stocks of whisky in bond (F. A. C. Hearings, p. 27; Tax on Intoxicating Liquor Hearings, p. 298). There are rumors that Roman Catholic authorities were given large opportunity to invest on the ground floor in exchange for political cooperation in the Repeal movement. I can find no documentary confirmation.

When we come to the political set-up things are clearer. The nomination of Governor Smith in 1928 was the first opportunity of Catholicism to put its man into the White House. It was hoped to do this by mobilizing behind Mr. Smith the financial interests and the personal prejudices opposed to the 18th Amendment.

On January 3, 1928, the Vatican practically declared for Repeal of American Prohibition in the above quoted statement of its organ. On the 22nd of January, 1928, Mr. J. J. Raskob of the A. A. P. A. (with a fortune of $200,000,000 back of him according to "The New Dealers," p. 268) was appointed Private Chamberlain to the Pope. On March 13th Cardinal Mundelein, an opponent of Prohibition, brought to the Vatican a check of $1,500,000 to be used for the rebuilding of the Missionary College *De Propaganda Fide.* "It would have taken years to collect the huge sum . . . but American methods intervened in producing quick action" (*N. Y. Times,* March 18, III, p. 3). Of Cardinal Mundelein Mr. Brisbane wrote two years before: *"The Catholic Extension Magazine* under Cardinal Mundelein's control predicts repeal of the Volstead Act. Cardinal Mundelein is the third American prince of the R. C. Church to express open opposition to Prohibition. There is undoubtedly a well-organized Catholic movement toward modification of the Volstead law. The Catholic Church works steadily, takes its time, knows how to get results, and is never in a hurry" (13).

A month later, on the 11th of April, the Pope received Mr. Raskob of the A. A. P. A. and "imparted a special benediction upon him." On the 4th of June Mr. Raskob published a newspaper broadside against Prohibition. Then followed the nomination of Gov. Smith, Catholic layman, at the Dallas Convention, quickly followed by his unprecedented personal repudiation of his Convention's plank relating to Prohibition (B). On July 12, 1928, Mr. Raskob was chosen by the wet combination to be chairman of the National Democratic Committee. In his speech, when he took the gavel from his predecessor, he described Smith as "the Moses who might point the way out of Prohibition."

In the campaign which followed every ounce of political influence available was put forth by Roman Catholicism to elect Mr. Smith but its campaign seems to have been directed also against the 18th Amendment. "Prohibition was three times more decisive as an influence in the 1928 election than the religious issue," said Prof. W. F. Ogburn in his analysis of this campaign in the *N. Y. Times* (14). "There could be no other conclusion," wrote the Catholic dry, Mr. Callahan, "but that the hierarchy and the Catholic press were aggressively opposing the Prohibition law" (15). From Europe came in 1928 various repercussions of the American struggle. A leading moral theologian of the Roman Church, Dr. Franz Walther of Munich, issued a volume bitterly criticizing the dry movement and the heroic Father Ude of Graz, who had been insisting that alcohol was a poison, the sale of which should be suppressed by the state, was ordered to abandon his agitation throughout Austria.

THE EMPRINGHAM EPISODE

Cardinal O'Connell's pronouncement was made on the 8th of February, 1926. On the 5th of February the Church Temperance Society of the Protestant Episcopal Church came out with a statement opposing Prohibition. This was given coast-to-coast publicity in spite of the fact that the Society was wholly insignificant and not even much known in the Episcopal Church itself. Dr. James Empringham, a quondam speaker for the Anti-Saloon League, stood in the foreground of this demonstration but was really the catspaw of wet interests. The plan, devised by a well-known editor in a New York newspaper office, was to show that there were other churches besides the Roman Catholic whose official sympathies were with the wets. This would naturally heighten the force of Cardinal O'Connell's utterance that was coming three days later and to that degree strengthen the bid of Governor Smith for the Presidency. The *N. Y. Times* (Feb. 6, 1926) described this demonstration, which was really the plot of a few men, in glowing terms: "That the report of the Church

Temperance Society has given a tremendous impetus to the activities of the wet forces in and out of Congress was demonstrated today. Senator Edge said that plans were being rushed for hearings before the Senate and the A. A. P. A. announced another 'Face the Facts Conference.' Wets seized upon the Temperance Society Report as a comforting instance of their contention that public opinion was being aroused to demand change."

That this outbreak represented wet intrigue is indicated by another fact. On the second of February a meeting was held at the Church House under the shadow of Westminster Abbey to protest against the smuggling of British liquor into the United States (16). The Bishop of London presided and stated that twenty out of the twenty-four liquor ships seized in the preceding six months were British. Sir Donald McLean proposed in this meeting that a series of protests should be staged in British cities against these operations, so unfavorable to international good-will. Now as early as the 28th of January a cable from London drys had been received by the Alcohol Information Committee, New York, which ran: "Press says Episcopal Church Temperance Society preparing to make a public admission of the failures of Prohibition. Cable facts." That London wets knew what was coming was evident. The Empringham demonstration was apparently timed to take the edge off the London meeting three days before.

Disavowals came from leading drys in the Episcopal Church. Bishop Manning called on the clergy to support the law. A symposium published in the *N. Y. Times* (Feb. 6, 1926) showed five bishops favoring modification and eighteen upholding Prohibition. Yet the enormous press publicity at the disposition of the wets made of this tea-cup storm a veritable typhoon. "The Senate aroused at the news that the powerful Episcopal Church has come out for modification," and so on.

On May 25, 1927, the Church Temperance Society again broke into eruption. Among the signers was its Treasurer, Dr. W. J. Schieffelin. In the whisky trade-paper, *Mida's Criterion* (March 1935, p. 53), Mr. Hester, President of Roosevelt and Schuyler, Inc., liquor dealers, tells how just before Prohibition he bought up the cellars of Delmonico, the Ritz, the St. Regis, the Vanderbilt, and other hotels and stocked private wine-cellars for the coming years of drought. Then he went to Schieffelin and Co. and proposed that they start in with "medicinal wines and liquor." Though they were a century-old drug firm "they had no one who knew anything about this line." Hester opened a liquor department for them, coached their salesmen, and secured for them the agency of Hennessey's brandies, Moet and Chandon champagnes, the Bordeaux and Burgundy wines of Louis Lamarue, and the famous port wines of C. H. Kopke and Co. At the end of three years, in 1925, Schieffelin and Co. (Dr. Wm. Jay Schieffelin, President, Treasurer, and Director: also Vice President of the American Bible Society) had become the largest distributors of "medicinal wines and liquors" in this country.

Now "medicinal liquor" is first cousin to Plato's "medicinal lie." The eminent Lord Moynihan declares that "medical science is of one mind that alcohol is unnecessary and often harmful in the routine of disease;" Prof. Dr. Sven Ingvar of the University of Lund concurs: "The general advance of the time has simply banished alcohol from the assembly of medicines;" and Prof. Dr. Kathe, Director of State Medical Research, Breslau, says: "So far as I can see alcohol is indicated in only one kind of sickness, for delirious, sick with inflammation of the lungs, in order to ward off delirium tremens. There is no action of alcohol which strengthens health or prevents sickness."

Soon after the Church Temperance Society was formally disavowed by the responsible leaders of their church. The *Washington Times,* Oct. 18, 1928, reported the repudiation of the Society in the House of Bishops meeting at the Willard. "Bishop Freeman introduced the resolution which was greeted with cheers and the entire assembly thundered 'aye' when the question was put by Bishop Manning" (C).

(*Note on Anglican Alcohol-clericalism.* The Episcopal clergy opposed the Revolution of 1776 and for it a large contingent of them were chased out of the country. They were back in time to block the anti-slavery movement in the fifties. Since then they have been commonly the paladins of alcohol. This is an old tradition, the English Church having for centuries been largely financed by Church Ales (Coulton, Mediaeval Studies, No. 8). How clericalism, alcoholism, capitalism, war-mongering, and other evils gravitate together is illustrated by the Deed of Association of Vickers, the largest armament firm in Great Britain, which empowers it "to purchase, build, equip, improve, administer in any part of the world, works of all kind including

publications, breweries, churches, buildings, or any other works."
The churches are presumably Anglican for the Church of England
during many years invested clergy pensions funds in Vickers.

The Russian Church, in contrast to the sober Southern Slavs,
who for centuries had been under the moral tutelage of Moham-
medanism, has been characterized by age-long alcoholic degradation. Yet when Russia went dry in 1914 its higher clergy as a
body urged the Tsar to make the Prohibition permanent. How
different the common attitude of the American Episcopal clergy
toward our own National Prohibition!)

"THAT THOU MAYEST BE A HOLY PEOPLE"
Deut. 26: 19.

Then there is Israel, meant to be God's very bodyguard for
right living. In Europe the movement against alcohol owes very
much to the Jewish intelligence, to men like the late Prof. Max
Kassovitz of the University of Vienna, Dr. Roubinovitch of the
Salpetrière, Paris, Prof. Dr. Aschaffenburg of the *Akademie fuer
praktische Medizin,* Cologne, the late Prof. Dr. Henschen of the
Karolinska Institute, Stockholm, Dr. Hoppe, author of *Die Tat-
sache ueber den Alkohol,* Dr. A. Holitscher of Karlsbad, Sec'y of
the League of Abstinent Physicians, Messrs. Kohn, Davidsohn, and
others who created the movement against alcohol in German So-
cialism, the late Mrs. Eliot Yorke of the House of Rothschild, and
many more. In America one finds a few names on the right side,
Mr. Oakes of *Current History,* Dr. Emil Bogen, Mr. Justice Brandeis, Miss Lillian Wald, Prof. Taussig of Harvard and the late
Dr. Jacques Loeb of the Rockefeller Institute, but far too many on
the wrong. I asked recently at the Distillers' Institute, Washington, how largely the traffic was now in Jewish hands. "Fully fifty
per cent," was the reply. The names tell the story,—Westheimer,
Sunstein, Freiberg, Kaltenbach, Guckenheim, Rosenstiel, Fleischmann. Schenley's and National Distillers are predominatingly
Jewish (Jacobis, Levys, Weiskopfs). The office of National Distillers during Prohibition was in the Kuhn, Loeb Bldg., 52 William St. (17). Governor Lehman's firm is banker for Schenley's
(18); Mr. Albert Lasker is their advertising agent. Distillers Corporation Seagram, Ltd., is controlled by Harry, Sam, and Abe
Bronfman, ex-bootleggers (19), as Distillers' and Brewers' Corporation by Jake, Sam and Abe Ungerleider, also graduates from

bootlegging. Julius Wile's Sons are sole agents in the United States for D. O. M. Bénédictine, distilled by Catholic monks. William Goldstein is President of the Associated Wine and Liquor Dealers of America.

There are, too, those who sell alcoholized sweets to children (see *N. Y. Times*, May 22 and June 6, 1934 on liquor-candy rings) and there are whisky shavings rings that steep shavings from the insides of old whisky casks and sell the resultant concoction (20). One would not dwell on these things if there were men and women in American Jewry reacting against them, but Jewish leaders seem to count little in any *unpopular* movement.

It is said that the Rothschild fortune originated from financial operations connected with the shipment of Hessian troops to fight the American Colonists in the war of Independence (21). It would be unfair for men of our time to emphasize that fact. But it is not unfair to point out that the American people are engaged in another and equally great war of independence and that our American Jews are not helping us as they should. Thoreau has described "the demon that has acted so astonishing a part in our New England life, who first comes in the guise of friend or hired man, and at last robs and murders the whole family." The Maine Law was the symbol of our advancing deliverance from this malign spirit. Now it is broken down and in *Mida's Criterion* (22) one sees the photograph of the first legal shipment of liquor into that state for eighty-five years,—four cases of Seagram's (Jewish) whisky.

When Rabbi Wise tells us that "the only hope of the world is that Israel and Christendom stand together" we ask, "Why then did you not stand with us? Why did you not rise up and rebuke those who were destroying the 18th Amendment,—the Cellers, the Sabaths, the Siroviches, and Dicksteins; the Ochses and Lippmanns and Swopes?"

The big-wigs of Schenley's and National Distillers are but sellers of potato schnaps in the villages of Eastern Europe, immigrated to America and here established. *Coelium non animum mutant.* Our Jewish leaders should disassociate themselves and their community from them, for they are still Eastern European, with little understanding for American ideals of law and decency and freedom.

REFERENCES TO CHAPTER VI NOT IN THE TEXT

1. New York Times, February 9, 1926, page 9.
2. Alliance News, June 1924, page 92.
3. John Bond, "St. Alcohol," *passim.*
4. "Alcohol and Man," pages 296, 297, 364.
5. The Callahan Correspondence.
6. The Survey, October 1, 1929, page 54.
7. Hearings, House Judiciary Committee, February 1930, page 627.
8. Hearings, House Judiciary Committee, February 1930, page 1006.
9. Ramsdall, "Catholics and Prohibition."
10. International Pamphlets, Stevens' "The Church and the Worker," page 32.
11. New York Tribune, January 3, 1928.
12. "Questions of the Day," page 36, and Prohibition Amendment Hearings, January 1930, pages 269–281.
13. New York American, February 11, 1926.
14 New York Times, January 19, 1930, page 22.
15. Callahan Correspondence.
16. Christian Science Monitor, February 3, 1926, page 1.
17 N. Y. Times, February 2, 1934, page 1.
18. Plain Talk, March 1935, page 29.
19. N. Y. Times, December 12, 1934, page 14.
20. N. Y. Times, June 5, 1930, page 12, and December 10, 1933, Sec. IX, page 1.
21 Conti, Rise of House of Rothschild, pages 5, 8, 11, 12, 21.
22. Mida's Criterion, January 1933.

NOTES TO CHAPTER VI

A.   *The Brewery Age,* Oct. 1935, page 55, publishes a picture of two monks from an Oregon Benedictine Abbey who raise hops. They had come to the Cincinnati Brewers' Convention in search of customers. *Mida's Criterion,* Oct. 1936, page 14, mentions the Sacred Heart Novitiate of the Jesuits at Los Gatos, California, which operated all through Prohibition in sacramental wines "and so was able to offer aged wines to the public when Repeal came." The monastery of the Christian Brothers, Napa, California, advertises "a great American brandy of old world quality, blended with unhurried skill" (*N. Y. Times,* Oct. 15, 1941). It is also reported that the San Miguel brewery of Manila is partly owned by the Rev. Michael O'Doherty, Archbishop of Manila.

B.   It is a mistake to think that in the Democratic Convention in Madison Square Garden in 1924 Mr. Smith was opposed primarily because of his Catholicism. The wets back of him, Hague, Brennan, Olvaney and the rest, were indeed Catholics but the objection to them was a moral one based on the type of politics which they represented. Most Americans do not care to see a man in the White House with the backing of the underworld of drink and public knavery. That such was Smith's case is obvious from the names of subscribers to his governorship campaign of 1926,— Ehret and Ruppert each $2,000, Doelger $1,000, Mara, race-track gambler $1,000, Tex Rickard, gambler, $5,000, Cavanaugh, king of book-makers, $1,000, and so on.

The *New York World* declared McAdoo a Kluxer. He was not. He was a dry and for that reason alone this super-wet organ opposed him. When the break came on the 102nd ballot McAdoo sought to throw his voting strength to Senator Walsh of Montana, a Catholic and a dry: the Smith votes went to Senator Underwood, not a Catholic but the spokesman of the whisky interests in the U. S. Senate. The Catholic delegates from Massachusetts, New York, and New Jersey declined to vote for their fellow-churchman, Senator Walsh of Montana, one of the most attractive figures in American life, just as at Baltimore they had refused to vote for the dry Catholic, Gov. Burke of North Dakota, and supported Marshall, Presbyterian and plaything of Indiana brewerdom. It may be added in this connection as an indication of how largely what is supposed to be anti-clericalism is anti-alcoholism, that when some years ago Senator Walsh of Montana was opposed for re-election by a dry Methodist Republican, Dr. Clarence Wilson of the Methodist Board of Temperance made a special trip to Montana in order to support Mr. Walsh politically as against his fellow-Methodist. Dr. Wilson also tried in every way to secure a cabinet appointment for the dry Catholic, Col. Callahan of Louisville, from Mr. Hoover (Callahan Correspondence).

C.   Dr. Empringham earlier met the arguments of his wet fellow-churchmen:

"We are not concerned with what men eat or drink but with what people sell. You can drink sewage, carbolic acid, whisky, or any other poison and we will not seek to restrain you by force. But if you attempt to sell any commodity injurious to the health of the community, no matter whether it be infected milk, diseased meat, or dangerous drugs, your act ceases to be an individual matter and becomes a social problem" (Cong. Record, Feb. 22, 1926, p. 4357).

CHAPTER VII

PRESIDENT HOOVER AND ENFORCEMENT

Mr. Hoover's antecedents were dry. His Quaker mother evangelized the Iowa frontier in the early days and fought the saloon. The election of 1928 gave him a mandate of unprecedented weight. His oath of office, taken on a Bible open at Proverbs 28: 18, "Where there is no vision the people perish; but he that keepeth the law, happy is he," significantly reinforced the pledge of his inaugural address: "I have been selected by you to execute and enforce the laws of the country. I propose to do so to the extent of my own abilities."

His first move went to the center of things. In his speech at the Associated Press dinner, New York, shortly after his inauguration, he asked the Press in so many words for fair play for Prohibition. On June 6th he sought from Congress the reorganization and concentration of Federal bureaus connected with Prohibition enforcement. In his message of Dec. 3, 1929, he appealed for further legislation,—a joint committee of Congress to collaborate with executive agencies in preparation of enforcement legislation, provision for relief of congestion in Federal courts by simplification of procedure in dealing with petty cases, corrective legislation for the District of Columbia which, as he said in this message, "should be the model of city law enforcement." Of certain conditions in the national capital he added, "It is urgent that this be remedied."

Evidently Mr. Hoover wanted immediate action but the first step made for delay. The Wickersham Commission was rather a study of the history of the previous eight years of Prohibition than a help to the making of history. The transferring of enforcement to the Judiciary, theoretically right, led to reorganizational delays so that it was not until towards the end of the term that Attorney-General Mitchell had his forces in first-class order. Nevertheless enforcement continually improved in many directions and was moving, at the end of Mr. Hoover's administration, to a far

(161)

higher level. His major appointments, Col. Woodcock and Attorney-General Mitchell, could hardly have been bettered. It is not improbable that another four years of Hoover administration would have vindicated the policy and satisfied the nation of its utility and practicability.

THIS LAW AND OTHER LAWS

The story told by Col. Woodcock to the Committee on Manufactures (Jan. 1932, p. 343) is sufficient answer to those who think that Prohibition cannot be enforced as well as other laws. With one exception more convictions were registered in National Prohibition cases than in any other coming before the Federal courts in 1931. The percentage was, in *National Prohibition cases, 85.9%*.

White slave cases	71.6%
Peonage	50%
Customs	82.1%
Internal Revenue	64.6%
Postal	80.2%
Regulations of Commerce	83.6%
Banking and Finance	68.7%
Liability and Insurance	66.2%
Public Lands	77.4%
Foreign Relations	96.3%
Not specifically classified	73.7%
Other liquor cases	84.3%

In 1932 the number of convictions reached the still better percentage of 89% (1).

"Of course the number of Prohibition cases is large but one Federal judge, Judge Letts, told me that (they) cause him no concern . . . and I believe that is generally true, because we try to make these cases so good that the defendant generally pleads guilty. I do not think, therefore, that Prohibition cases actually absorb the trial time of Federal courts and it is an interesting fact . . . that from 1900 to 1920 the percentage of Federal crimes in Federal courts increased more rapidly than the percentage of increase due to Volstead cases. . . . I think we can be very much more effective against the commerce in liquor than we are today and, as you know, the bureau is operating with only one half the increase that the Wickersham Commission recommended" (A).

Asked whether the bureau had any way of dealing with large scale operators Mr. Woodcock replied: "Our special agents' group is set up for that purpose and I think you will find in every community that . . . the violators are eventually caught, whether they be big or small" (2).

THE COST OF PROHIBITION

"We are just getting to the point of efficient administration," continued Col. Woodcock. How efficient it was can be gauged by its cost. The appropriations were in 1931 $9,623,390. "We collected in fines and penalties a total of $3,447,558; in taxes, $586,149; and from the sale of seized property $104,592; making the money returned $4,138,211. Then in the (federal) cases prosecuted in state courts there were fines imposed of $1,091,996. With those deductions the net cost of the Bureau of Prohibition was $4,234,282. But the appraised value of the property seized was $21,484,730 together with automobiles valued at $3,218,323. This is the value of the sugar, alcohol, copper, electric motors, machinery, etc., turned over to the War, Post Office, and other departments through coordination in kind. Our statistical department estimates that the Bureau of Prohibition actually costs the Federal Government nothing to operate" (3).

IMPROVEMENT OF PERSONNEL

There had been in later years a great improvement in the personnel of the Prohibition Bureau. Asked by Senator Norris as to this Mr. Wickersham said: "I think the service has been greatly improved, first by the continuous process of sifting out, second by giving employees better status under the Civil Service and then by giving them better compensation." After referring to these "straightforward, honorable, upright, vigorous, fine officials," he continued, "I have wondered how you can get such men for the salary. Even the best salaries are not large." Then he described the social ostracism to which they were subjected because of their work (4).

These men were almost all veterans of the World War. Their ostracism was unquestionably due to newspaper abuse which pictured them as Apaches, cut-throats, and sneaks.

After declaring Prohibition enforcement "one of the most

difficult problems in organization ever put up to any country,"
Mr. Wickersham further declared that "the whole tendency is
toward a very improved enforcement . . . even in the course of
the ten months that we have been looking at the subject. . . ."
Government training schools and correspondence courses in criminal investigation and law enforcement had greatly developed the
effectiveness, intelligence, and *esprit de corps* of this arm of the
Federal service. The finger-print and criminal record of every
person convicted of a felony under the National Prohibition Act
gave a closer check on the habitual bootlegger.

The Coast Guard had pretty well cleaned up importation by
sea. A few more first class destroyers at its disposal, the addition
of several hundred men, the equipment of patrol boats with silenc-
ing devices, etc., and this phase of enforcement would have been
beyond questioning (5). After Jan. 1, 1926, the Bureau of Prohibition limited the production of industrial alcohol during the year
to 12% less than during the fiscal year ending June 30, 1927.
Each industrial alcohol plant was allotted its share. In this way
the amount manufactured might well have been kept down to
legal needs. The distilling business had been concentrated in 49
plants owned by less than 21 companies, in order to facilitate
control.

THE RAILWAYS COOPERATE

There had been, in the first period, some violation of the
prohibition of transportation. The government retorted by libeling cars which, by delaying railway equipment, caused friction.
It therefore undertook negotiations with leading trunk-line officials in various cities of the country. These proved singularly
successful. "Friendly interchange of views across the conference
table brought immediate results. The carriers in practically all
cases pledged their active support and this has been honestly fulfilled." Yardmasters, railroad police, and special agents were ordered to cooperate. Shipping clerks assisted Federal officers in
their investigations. Constant access to railroad yards, day and
night, was given to Federal agents. Employees, who in previous
years had helped bootleggers, were in some cases discharged. The
government began to receive tips from the railroads themselves regarding illicit operations. The Pullmans stopped drinking on
trains. "Often it has happened that the connecting link in per-

fecting a case against liquor conspirators has been supplied by a faithful railroad worker in railroad transfer yards where carloads of liquor may have been camouflaged as merchandise." The express companies, too, cooperated. Their employees in all parts of the country were under orders to give Federal enforcement officers every assistance possible in tracing violators. Their books were open to Federal officials. This information helped to locate rings of smugglers. As a consequence of all this, liquor-smugglers found it extremely difficult to obtain railroad equipment for unlawful purposes and even express shipments by trunks became negligible. Smuggling in railway cars coming from Canada ceased. "The shipment of liquor by rail," says this government document we are summarising, "is no longer a serious problem for enforcement authorities in large sections of the United States."

Bootleggers were banished from the highways through the revocation by traffic officials of their permits to drive. Such outlaws found it next to impossible to recover a license. Earlier they had driven cars of the finest type, bought on installments, but later they were black-listed as dangerous risks by practically every auto-financing agency in the United States. Accident insurance companies also refused policies to any known to be engaged in rum-running.

The U. S. Shipping Board cooperated to prevent American vessels being transferred to foreign registry for liquor smuggling. Foreign registry by many vessels was cancelled. The illegal use of radio by smugglers was stopped by successful negotiations with foreign governments. Cooperation with Cuba and Mexico rendered smuggling from those lands insignificant.

PADLOCK INJUNCTIONS AND REALTY MEN

The use of padlock injunction led to widespread eviction of "speaks" by real estate boards; this through a provision incorporated in leases forbidding the use of property by such violators. Federal Prohibition administrators negotiated these agreements with representative real estate boards in many places and the practise became general. Rental losses in Philadelphia, for example, became so heavy because of padlock proceedings that the members of the Philadelphia Real Estate Board joined eagerly in a conference called by the Prohibition Administrator to discuss the question of realty cooperation. In Chicago the Real Estate Board stood for the fullest possible cooperation with the Federal government by removing tenants and by handing on information to the Government (6).

Distilleries on farms were closed by injunction as well as those in city buildings. For the successful operation of a still in a city a warehouse or store is needed, preferably in the heart of the city. Padlock proceedings forced the criminal into the city's outer area where he worked at disadvantage. The placard, "Closed for One Year" had a restraining effect on wide circles of the lawless. It made the public at large realize that the law was being upheld. At one time 18 out of 20 night clubs in New York City were closed by injunction for a year and the other two went out of business. A hotel in Albany opposite the railroad station was an object-lesson to tens of thousands of travellers during its sabbatical year (7).

SUSPENDED SENTENCES

Suspended sentences proved in Massachusetts an effective way of cooking small fry. In most cases the violator was ready to plead guilty wthout trial on condition of escaping prison sentence. After a session with the probation officer he was put by the judge on probation for from one to five years. Commonly a fine was paid, also, for seasoning. The probationer had to report once a month and if arrested a second time the prison sentence went into effect. This course was so effective that nine out of ten never got back to the Boston courts. It closed criminal careers of this type, kept men out of overcrowded prisons and helped to clear court dockets (8).

The needed machinery for enforcement was gradually provided,—civil service rating, training schools for agents, the Increased Penalties Act, the right to stop cars without search warrants (Carroll v. U. S.), treaties extending the right of search at sea to 12 miles, taxation of bootlegger-income which put extensive evidence into government hands, right of agents to seize account books for evidence (confirmed by Supreme Court, Marron v. U. S.), a treaty with Canada.

FURTHER POSSIBLE HELPS

What was done with ever increasing success did not exhaust the means and methods of enforcement. Col. Woodcock (strongly seconded by Mr. McAdoo in the *Review of Reviews,* March 1928) proposed a subsidy to states, conditioned on their bringing their law enforcement agencies to a certain standard (B)—this by analogy to the method by which the Federal government finally brought order and system into the various state militias. He also advised the formation of a special staff in each district to make investigations and to lay the evidence without expense before the local prosecuting agencies. A decision of the Supreme Court, Nov. 24, 1930, according to which "petty offenses might be proceeded against summarily before a magistrate sitting without a jury" opened the way for simplification of legal process in petty cases. As Senator Capper had said "the promise in the Constitution of the right to 'a speedy and public trial' will be more nearly carried out if the (Wickersham) Commission recommendations are adopted (trial before a Commissioner with right of jury trial reserved to defendant) than under our present system which encourages delays (and) congested dockets" (9).

Other simple improvements which, without material expense, would have tightened up enforcement were:

Coordination of evidence-gathering agencies,—six in the Treasury, one in the Department of Justice, one in the Immigration Service, and one in the Post Office. (This has since been effected for liquor revenue tax collection. See Treasury Release Aug. 14, 1935.)

A unified border control of the Customs, Immigration, and Prohibition Enforcement services into a body like the Canadian Mounted Police.

Search and seizure laws modified to enable Federal officials to enter houses where distilling was going on.

Deportation of aliens convicted of bootlegging.

Provision making it a felony to forge permits or to use, or possess, such permits willingly.

Legislation empowering supervisors to inspect the records and processes of customers of permittees manufacturing products from specially denatured alcohol.

The institution and maintenance of a definite program of educational publicity conducted directly by the Bureau of Prohibition with a view to informing the public of the actual facts relating to enforcement.

Improvement of juries with dismissal of old alcoholics from

service; also improvement of the quality of U. S. Commissioners.

Enlistment of the Dept. of Agriculture with its authority over counterfeit labels and adulterated products.

Enactment of ouster laws for the removal of incompetent and negligent officials as in some states.

Elimination of independent denaturing plants.

Change in equity proceedings to make substituted service in padlock cases also liable.

Refusal on the part of the Federal government to issue industrial alcohol permits in states without enforcement codes. This would have soon brought great industrial states that were nullifying the law, as Maryland and New York, to terms.

THE NATION'S CAPITAL

But while enforcement improved it is hard to understand why at certain points it was not better. The capital city of the nation was the touch-stone for Mr. Hoover's enforcement. Any laxity there would encourage the lawless everywhere to believe that the Federal government was insincere. Wets made maps indicating vast underground operation. Mr. Woodcock surveyed the city carefully and found some 181 places, mostly negro homes (*Current History*, March 31, p. 8) where drink could be obtained through a taxi driver (10). "I have heard much, since I have been in the Senate, about the debauchery and corruption and crime in the city of Washington," said Senator Wheeler (Jan. 24, '31). "I must confess I have never seen it. I am honestly of the opinion that Washington is one of the cleanest cities in the United States today."

Nevertheless there were conditions of which the Chief Executive ought certainly to have been cognizant. On the 21st of February, 1923, Secretary Mellon declined to make public figures regarding importation of liquor into the United States by foreign diplomats. Nine years later Senator Howell could say: "I found that persons of diplomatic status were securing the unlawful delivery in Washington of hundreds of thousands of quarts of liquor annually by virtue of permits and protection afforded by the executive branch of the government. . . . I found that one foreign distillery delivered in Washington, by virtue of executive permits, 13,000 quarts of diplomatic whisky" (11). During all these years the lawless traffic had gone on unhindered of Mellon.

What Governor Pinchot said of President Coolidge was applicable to Mr. Hoover: "The free and unlimited importation of liquors by diplomatic representatives is a chief cause of the wetness of Washington. If the President, following the far stronger precedent set by the British government years ago in the matter of slaves, should suggest to all foreign governments that he would regard it as a friendly act if they would instruct their representatives to import no more alcoholic liquors but conform instead to the law of the country to which they were accredited, the atmosphere and attitude of official Washington respecting the 18th Amendment would change over-night" (12).

Senator Howell charged that the Board of Commissioners, the legal administrators of the District, had no legal concern respecting the enforcement of Prohibition nor were anxious for any. "I found that 97% of Washington's police had no duties whatever in connection with liquor violation except the apprehension of intoxicated motorists and pedestrians. *Four police with one old auto* were detailed to stop bootleg liquor filtering into Washington by 24 highways. Of the hundreds of Federal agents of the Prohibition Unit not more than three or four were actually on duty in the national capital. . . ." (13) One wonders at the degree of success which enforcement attained and it was no slight degree. One wonders more when one reads what went on at an earlier date. In the 1924 (March) Hearings on Firearms and Intoxicants, page 51, a police official, Mr. Simonton, was asked by Congressman Blanton:

> "Do you know that the officers here have testified that a man is arrested and he frequently puts up collateral from $10 to $25 or even $100 and never goes to court and he is permitted to forfeit his collateral and then to go and open up his place again?"

Simonton. "That is right."

Blanton. "Is that the law or just a custom that has grown up?"

Simonton. "It is more a custom than a law. This forfeiture of collateral goes to the police fund for disabled policemen and the maintenance of those injured in the service."

The Sheppard Act, it was claimed, had been repealed by implication on the passage of the Volstead Act, and no police regulations for the city of Washington had been passed to take its place. This very adequate and powerful act contained in its 23rd section the provision "that if for any reason any section . . . or part of this act shall be held unconstitutional . . . that shall not destroy any other section . . . not in and of itself invalid." Yet the Corporation Counsel for the District, finding that the Supreme Court had invalidated one provision of a similar law in another jurisdiction, proceeded to invalidate the entire law of the District by his own unauthorized fiat. This in spite of the Willis-Campbell Act, Nov. 23, 1921, which provided that "all laws in regard to the manufacture and taxation of the traffic in intoxicating liquors and all penalties for violations of such laws that were in force when the National Prohibition Act was enacted, shall be continued in force as to both beverage and non-beverage liquor" (14).

Police neutral, enforcement legislation treated as repealed, courts giving inconsiderable fines and rarely prison sentences, search for stills and stored liquor allowed only on evidence of sale, rare use of injunction against liquor nuisances, and this in the capital city! Senator Howell laid the responsibility at the door of the White House. "The President of the United States is all-powerful in the city of Washington. He appoints officials of the city and under the law can remove those officials when he sees fit, no matter if they are confirmed by the Senate. . . . In my opinion if the President called the Commissioners of the District of Columbia before him and said, 'Gentlemen, I have secret official service at my command. If they discover anything in Washington in connection with the violation of the Prohibition law . . . you are out,' there is no question what the result would be" (15).

CORN SUGAR

Again during the Prohibition era there was a steady and large increase in the consumption of corn sugar. Wets attributed this to the increase in home-distilling. But there were few establishments in the United States which manufactured corn sugar and their output could easily have been controlled by a handful of Federal agents. Mr. Denny speaks of the "near omniscience of the Hoover Intelligence Service (Dep't of Commerce) in economic warfare" as far surpassing the Intelligence Service of the nations during the war, and illustrated it with an incident from the Japanese earthquake of 1923. A relief conference was immediately held in Washington and the question of the rice market came up. Mr. Hoover took out of his pocket a single sheet of paper on which were typed the statistics regarding the precise position of the rice trade Saturday at noon, the very moment of the earthquake. Why was Iowa corn sugar not under as close supervision as Far Eastern rice? Did the President's Argus eyes lose their keenness when he passed from his Secretaryship to the Presidency (16)?

The present administration is doing what its predecessors failed to do. Mr. Mellot of the Internal Revenue service writes:

"The Treasury is taking other means of combatting the bootlegger which we believe will go a long way toward eliminating him. Liquor is made from a certain limited number of commodities such as sugars, syrups, molasses, corn meal, cider, and oak chips. We are now checking on the producers of these commodities and on the sales which may be suspected of going into illegal liquor. Still seizures during recent weeks have decreased in the same proportions as the sales of these commodities have decreased. . . . Most of the manufacturers of these commodities have co-operated splendidly. *Having checked the daily records of the concerns handling such commodities and having noted and investigated suspicious sales we have in many instances made seizure of the very first lot of alcohol produced. This is a most effective weapon. The purchase of commodities which might go into illegal liquor has been cut down tremendously*" (17). In June 1936 Deputy Commissioner Berkshire declared the leak now "negligible."

This was done under legislation passed June 18, 1934 "to protect the revenue by requiring information concerning the disposition of substances used in the manufacture of distilled spirits." Why was this simple and practical device for cutting out illegal distilling by the roots not urged upon Congress by Mr. Hoover?

Similar methods might have been used against illicit brewing. A Detroit brewing expert is quoted in the Cong. Record Dec. 20, 1932, p. 803, "There are but 15 or 16 maltsters in the United States and perhaps not more than a dozen dealers in rice and corn products used in the manufacture of malt products. It is easy to see how little work would be necessary to discover the amount of material shipped to manufacturers. This would enable the government to get a complete check-up at very nominal expense. This method would at once eliminate the wort manufacturer, alley-brewer and home brewer" (abridged).

To prevent the diversion and sale of denatured alcohol the Treasury Department which under Secretary Mellon had failed to muzzle these abuses, under Mr. Morgenthau "asked for legislation authorizing the Commissioner of Internal Revenue to require manufacturers and users of denatured alcohol and products manufactured from denatured alcohol *to report their sales, shipments and consignments of such alcohol or manufactured products under the system that is applied to materials like molasses, sugar and yeast.*" This legislation was enacted by Congress in August 1935. Another effectual weapon which should have been given to National Prohibition!

OTHER ENFORCEMENT IMPROVEMENTS AFTER PROHIBITION

In order to *protect revenue* the administration following Mr. Hoover's secured legislation which could have been provided for Prohibition defence. A Treasury release for Aug. 14, 1935, states that "through diplomatic channels action was taken to close to smugglers' activities the nearby foreign ports which were being used as bases of supply. As a result of those efforts most of the foreign ports in the Western Hemisphere, notably those of Cuba, Newfoundland, the French port of St. Pierre, Puertos Varrios in Guatemala, and Belize in British Honduras, were effectively closed to smugglers' operations." Further the Anti-Smuggling Act of 1935 empowered the President to establish customs enforcement areas not more than *fifty nautical miles outward from the outer limits of customs waters.* Penalties for smuggling were increased and the laws respecting the boarding and searching of suspected vessels strengthened. "Highly effective" air guard has been developed which during the year to June 1936 located and destroyed 402 illicit stills. The growth of this branch is indicated.

	1934	1935	1936
Miles cruised	219,572	527,755	837,696
Hours in air	2,752	5,709	8,958

Experiments are even being made to detect yeast cells in the air in order to locate moonshine plants. The old denaturating formulas of the Treasury nullificationists have been replaced by three new formulas (July 1, 1936) which are believed to be impregnable.

Federal protection has also been secured for present-day revenue officers which was denied brave Prohibition enforcement officers. Legislation became effective May 18, 1934, providing punishment for killing or assaulting Federal officers. Section 2 reads:

"Whoever shall forcibly resist, oppose, impede, intimidate, or interfere with any person designated in section 1 hereof (U. S. marshals, coast-guards, officers of custom or internal revenue) while engaged in the performance of his official duties or shall assault him . . . shall be fined not more than $5,000 or imprisoned not more than three years or both, and whoever in the commission of any of the acts described in this section shall use a deadly or dangerous weapon shall be fined not more than $10,000 or imprisoned not more than ten years or both."

A later Bill, HR 9185 Sec. 2b (Collection of Revenue from Intoxicating Liquors) provided for penalty of *20 years imprisonment* for those who, while violating the laws in respect of intoxicating liquors, *have in their possession* machine guns or sawed off rifles or shotguns (18).

The June 26, 1936, bill also contained a clause which if enforced in Prohibition days would quickly have ended brewery nullification. "For flagrant and willful removal of taxable malt liquors for consumption or sale without payment of tax thereon, all the right, title, and interest of each person, who has knowingly suffered or permitted such removal, or has connived at the same, in the lands and buildings constituting the brewery premises and bottling house, shall be forfeited by a proceeding *in rem* in the district court of the United States having jurisdiction thereof" (Cong. Record, May 19, 1936, pp. 7660 and 7667). The report of the Attorney-General for 1938 (p. 93) mentions the usefulness of this post-Repeal method. "The forfeiture of real estate used for the operation of illicit stills has been continued. In one case in the northern district of Illinois the forfeiture of a farm comprising 151 acres was secured."

Mr. Robert Barry was Vice-President of the A. A. P. A. in charge of its public relations. He is now Director of Public Relations of National Distillers. In *Mida's Criterion* (June '37,

p. 37) he writes: "Given a nod from the White House under Mr. Coolidge or President Hoover, and a commission to clean up bootlegging such as he received from Mr. Roosevelt to clean up kidnapping,—J. Edgar Hoover and his government men could have done the job."

POLITICAL HESITANCY

Senator Borah declared President Hoover to be "all right on the 18th Amendment. I have had many talks with him and I have never reached any other conclusion after leaving him." Then he illustrates how Mr. Hoover "let I dare not wait upon I would." He wrote the President:

"I believe the people would overwhelmingly support you in an *announced* policy that you would feel free to select men purely upon their fitness and regardless of Organization or Senatorial recommendation (i.e. to U. S. District Attorneyships, the key enforcement positions). I feel furthermore that if such a policy were announced a good majority of the Senate would support the practise. . . . Everybody must realize that such a course has become absolutely indispensable to clean and efficient and able public service. In my opinion it would make a change, the benefits of which cannot be overestimated. . . . All this vicious practise of Organization and Senators impressing their views on the appointments is outside the Constitution, beyond the law, and in my judgment too often results in crowding the public service with a vast number of political accidents, political incompetents, not to say corrupt officials" (19).

But the President after consultation with various Senators declined to move. He feared "the young revolution" in the Senate which he was told it would precipitate.

"AND WHISPERING I WILL NE'ER CONSENT, CONSENTED"

Was Congressman Patman right when he said: "The President is a victim of the reactionary leaders of the party to which he belongs. Mr. Mellon is running the country as far as the administration in power is concerned"? (20) Who knows? Mr. Beck with his relationship to the Vare political interests, Mr. Walter Brown, politician of Ohio who had helped Mr. Hoover in the 1928 campaign and was made Postmaster-General in return, Mr. Ogden Mills in the Treasury with the influence which his money carried in pivotal New York state, were all bitter wets whose influence in the 1932 campaign was to be foreseen. The terrific wet propaganda which followed Mr. Hoover's election could hardly have been without influence on Mr. Hoover's mind. One cannot but feel that there was a certain loneliness in his position. The press were as hyenas. He all along felt that he had little effective backing from the official drys. As the administration advanced it became obvious that new and enormously powerful groups had taken position against the 18th Amendment. One who was seeking Republican renomination would hardly care to offend Wall Street. If Mr. Hoover had but thrown himself on the immense dry constituency which had put him into office; if he had stated his determination to nail the flag to the mast; if he had made it clear that the charges of trimming thrown at him were without justification, how different things might have been. But men on the march cannot rally about a sphinx.

Mr. Hoover's advisers and political intimates made drys wonder about Mr. Hoover. Why had he selected for his cabinet men like Mr. Lamont, a member of the Ass'n vs. the Prohibition Amendment, and Messrs. C. F. Adams and Walter Brown, both wets. Why his political intimacy with Col. W. J. Donovan of the N. Y. 69th, who appeared later as marshal of the Walker Beer Parade? When Donovan dug out a war-time letter of Mr. Hoover's in which he disapproved the ban on beer "because it takes a lot of beer to make a man drunk" drys were disturbed. When his secretaries, Newton and Hyde, ostentatiously asked the Census Bureau and the Treasury what effect legalized beer would have on unemployment and revenue, they naturally concluded that the President was considering modification (21). He has been charged with directly taking the edge off a dry statement by secretarial interpretation in the rare instances that he made dry statements (22). "He used words about Prohibition," said the *Christian Century*, "which sounded as if he were dry but which skirted the issue so cleverly as to commit him to nothing but law-enforcement to which his oath bound him" (23). His managers and spokesmen are said to have given assurances to both sides. Col. Woodcock tells me that he never met President Hoover but twice during his term of service. That was not the attitude of one really interested. Whatever the reason he seemed to vacillate, to have receded from the uncompromising position which he took at the start.

It was a tragic *dénouement*. If he had but led the American people into the final solution of the alcohol question as Abraham Lincoln did into the settlement of the slavery question, his renown would have been little less than Lincoln's.

THE LOST LEADER

The crisis came and he wilted. A National Group of Subscribers to Former Republican Campaign Funds had been organized early in 1932, pledging its members not to contribute unless the Republican Convention took formal stand for Repeal (24). "Pennsylvania as well as Wall Street refuses to give to the Hoover campaign without Repeal," said Mr. Hoover's most intimate political manager to an acquaintance of the writer, *"and you know which end of Pennsylvania I mean"* (presumably Mellon's). If Mr. Hoover had but explained this to the nation and rallied the conscience of the nation against its money-bags! Senator Borah went to the President and asked for a statement regarding his position. The reply was, "See Mills and Brown." "Then I'm through," said Mr. Borah and the President had lost his greatest campaigner.

According to Borah's speech somewhat later in the Senate it was Brown and pre-eminently Mills who shaped the plank in the Republican platform. "It was written in this vague contradictory way . . . because they were seeking to please two classes of voters. . . . Just as soon as the campaign is over the reasons for placing that plank in the platform will have disappeared and the party, in my judgment, will stand unmistakably for the repeal of the 18th Amendment" (25).

But Mr. Hoover did not wait for the close of the campaign to throw over the Amendment. His convention plank was discarded for straight-out repeal in his acceptance speech. In that speech he used the strongest words that ever crossed his lips regarding the great evil which the 18th Amendment was designed to end. He spoke of "the saloon system with its corruption, its moral and social abuse which debauched the home, its deliberate interference with those states endeavoring to find an honest solution, its permeation of political parties, and its perversion of legislatures which even touched at the capital of the nation." He

C.   Mr. Ogden Mills had been charged by both Maurice Campbell and Major C. F. Mills, Prohibition Administrators in Southern New York, with having systematically interfered to break down Prohibition enforcement. Had Mr. Hoover never read of this in the nation's press? Corrupt agents were reinstated in office through Mills' influence. Special emissaries sent from Washington betrayed the secrets of the Prohibition Administrator's office in New York. "I told all the facts to Ogden Mills, I told them to General Andrews, and heard them told to Col. W. J. Donovan, the confidential campaign manager of Herbert Hoover. It would surprise me to know that Mr. Hoover was not made aware of them at that time." *New York World,* September 11 and 8, 1930.

CHAPTER VIII

THE TRIUMPH OF GAMBRINUS

I. THE BEER CONGRESS

The brewer was the essential cause of the Eighteenth Amendment. It was he who owned the saloons, corrupted politics, defied decency. His product constituted in volume 90% of the liquor sold. When he was outlawed the limit of alcohol toxicity was set at one half of one percent. It was placed that low in order to safeguard the public. Justice Brandeis defended this arbitrary standard in the case of Ruppert v. Caffey. The brewer had shown himself defiant of law. No chances were to be taken with him.

When he sought to get back by legislative enactment he plead for but a slight increase of alcoholic content, a harmless modification. In the early days of state and national Prohibition, when brewery iniquity was fresh in men's minds, these efforts were thwarted in the referenda. Beer bills were defeated in Oregon in 1916 by 54,636 majority, in Washington the same year by 145,556 majority, in Colorado by 65,792. In Michigan in 1919 the anti-beer majority was 202,520, in Ohio 29,781 (in 1922, 189,-520) and in California 65,062 (1). During 1924 sixty bills were introduced into Congress which sought to legalize 2.75% beer by volume. In 1926 the increasing propaganda encouraged the brewers to ask for higher percentages, namely 2.75 by weight which is 3.45 by volume. Federal laws use volume not weight as the standard of measurement in statistical tables, etc. To measure alcohol strength by weight and not by volume was to establish a new precedent. But in this way the brewers were able to disguise the extent of the advance asked for. Near-beer became nearer-beer *pari passu* with the propaganda. A. A. Busch wrote to a Committee of Congress that 2.75% weight beer would be rejected by the masses, that is by the brewers (2). When the politicians in Congress thought by the universal hubbub that the people were ripe for it they took the last step and legalized 3.2% (weight) beer which was 4% by volume.

They insisted that it came within the Constitutional requirement regarding intoxication. Yet it was practically the draught beer of pre-Prohibition saloons and drunkenness. The dam was now sawed open and the other intoxicants soon followed through the breach.

BIEROLOGISCHE WISSENSCHAFT

They brought their scientists to Congress to prove the non-intoxicity of beer. Dr. H. A. Hare, Professor in Materia Medica, displayed the evidence which he had offered years before in the defeated Feigenspan and Ruppert cases, before the Supreme Court. (3) Professor Yandell Henderson, physiologist of Yale, was introduced as "an expert on poisons." He told the Congressmen that beer will extinguish a fire, in contrast to 50% spirits, a rather rough test for present-day laboratories (4). His testimony was a string of *ipse dixits,*—that beer of about 4% is not appreciably more intoxicating than an equal volume of coffee . . . that no beverage which in common usage implies the absorption of 80 cu. cm. of absolute alcohol into the blood in an hour can properly be denominated as intoxicating (A). . . . that good wine running from 8 to 20% cannot be defined as intoxicating (5). These paradoxes made the steins rattle as the fist struck the table but fist-play does not make things so.

He explained how he became a recognized authority on this subject. He had been asked by a colleague to give a definition of "intoxicating." "As I happened to have a morning when I was not very busy I wrote the statement and gave it for publication in the college paper, in the innocence of my soul. To my surprise it was republished in nearly every paper in the country, including the Congressional Record. I believe that it is partly upon that impartial scientific statement that the bill before your committee is based" (6) (abridged).

The press is indeed on the watch for pro-alcohol science. Any wild untruth will find nation-wide response.

"INNOCENCE" ABROAD

"I have seen hundreds of people in Munich beer-gardens drinking beer and none have come out drunk," continued Prof.

Henderson.   Does he think that in these days of travel others have not seen the blank and idiotic beer faces in the Kindlkeller and Hofbraukeller?   The great psychiatrist Kraepelin was in charge of an institute for psychiatrical research in Munich for many years.   He is a responsible scientist who has dealt with Munich alcoholism in all its phases.   This is his testimony.   "In the production of alcoholism in Germany beer undoubtedly plays the chief rôle.   It must be conceded that beer is capable of producing typical delirium tremens" (7).

But Prof. Henderson is not alone unfamiliar with the European authorities.   He seems to know as little of American ones. At the Congressional Hearing he was asked by Senator Hatfield regarding certain classical experimentation on alcohol's minimal action.

	"Doctor, are you familiar with Dr. Walter R. Miles' experiments in the Nutrition Laboratory of the Carnegie Institute?
Prof. Henderson.	In a general way, yes. . . . I could not give you any particular details of them offhand.
Hatfield.	I take it that you do not agree with his conclusions.
Henderson.	I do not remember in detail what his conclusions were.
Hatfield.	You cannot tell the Committee briefly what these experiments were?
Henderson.	No" (8).

PROFESSOR MUENCHENHAUSEN

Travel pictures made safer testimony.   Henderson harked back to Munich.   He thought that few cared "to distend their stomachs quickly with more than a pint (of beer). . . . I should think that the average rate of ingestion in Munich was a quart in not less than an hour."

Hatfield.	"What quantity of 4% beer must be consumed in your judgment to reach a state of intoxication as you define it?
Henderson.	I should say, eight to ten quarts. (Laughter.) These people in Munich were never drunk."

"WHY STREWEST THOU SUGAR ON THAT BOTTLED SPIDER?"

Others talked in the same vein, physiologist Lusk of Cornell, for example. "There is no drunkenness in France except that of visiting Americans. I have myself consumed three quarts of beer in an evening in Munich without feeling any effects from it." Dr. Martin Dewey, President of the American Dental Association, declared that "one of the most important factors to good teeth is the proper dentition of the mother in pregnancy. . . . The importance of beer as an article of diet in pregnant mothers cannot be overestimated." One rubs one's eyes in amazement. Have these Americans never heard of von Bunge's discoveries concerning the effect of parental alcoholism on the capacity to nurse in daughters, with their sidelights on caries of the teeth? They constitute a very cornerstone of the European study of alcoholism. Dewey actually compared the teeth of Europe to our disadvantage. Has he never been in English cities? Dr. Charles Norris, Chief Medical Examiner of New York, told the Committee that alcohol is converted into energy. He would have a hard time to prove it (cf. Chauveau's experiments and the recent and absolutely decisive ones of Le Breton and Schaeffer at Strassburg). He declared beer to have certain valuable extractives, lupulin among them. But lupulin makes contribution to the stupefying effect of beer (B). Dr. W. G. Morgan, ex-President of the American Medical Association, affirmed in the face of all the exact and convincing experimentation on the subject that four glasses of 4% beer wouldn't in any way impair the equilibrium of one writing on a typewriter and would have no effect whatever on a person operating an automobile or in charge of dangerous machinery. This was too much for common sense (9). Senator Brookhart broke out with:

"After training 26,000 riflemen under my own personal direction for the championship of the world I found that one could not do his best if he used any percentage of beer, wine, or other intoxicant. I absolutely prohibited its use and after a little the men themselves were so thoroughly convinced that I had no trouble at all in enforcing the prohibition" (10).

EXPERT COUNTER-TESTIMONY

Near-beer is not habit-forming, hence its slight commercial value. The brewers during Prohibition advertised this non-in-

toxicating beer as "even better than the old. It is brewed by masters. It has the same age, the same flavor, same quality and
purity. . . . *Alcohol was always a small factor in beer"* (adv. in
Chicago Tribune, Oct. 5, 1930). The President of the U. S.
Brewers' Association in similar vein described his near-beer as
"brewed and aged in the famous way to give all the old-time
tang, snap, and incomparable flavor" (11). All in vain. Near-
beer is fly-paper without the tangle-foot.

The only way to get large and permanent sale was to induce
habit and this could be done only with actual intoxicants. But
then there was the Constitution and back of the Constitution
honest, experimental science.

Hollingworth, for example, whose intelligence tests, motor
control of speech tests, memory tests, were all made with 2.75%
beer: "The laboratory measurements identified effects from very
small doses, effects of a kind to interfere with industrial efficiency
or to prove a menace to person and property. To limit the term
intoxication to instances where the casual observer can easily see
that something is wrong is to invite distresses under the name of
harmless effects" ("Alcohol and Man," p. 262). Dr. Miles went
to Washington on invitation of the House Committee and at his
own charges. . . . He gave to Congress what is probably as near
absolute truth on the subject as can be obtained. The chairman of
the committee said to him afterward, "I know nothing of these
things. I am a dry but I am obliged to bow to the party decision."

What did Prof. Miles tell the Congressmen, who for party
reasons were about to nullify the Constitution? He told them
that there was a marked influence of a 2.75% solution on pulse
rate, averaging over 8% in the two hours after drinking. This
meant so much additional burden on the heart. In an hour and
five minutes after taking a pint and three-fourths of 2.75% solution unsteadiness in standing increased 20%.

He told them that alcohol had a marked affinity for the
nervous system. "Inject a solution of alcohol with a dye that will
stain and you find that the nervous system is chiefly stained."

He told them that alcohol does not wait to pass through the
stomach into the small intestine, as food does, but goes right
through the wall of the stomach and appears in the blood un-
changed.

He told them that this 2.75% solution put the seven medical

students serving as subjects of experiment out of commission. "I would not have dared to let them drive an ambulance. I would not have dared to let them administer an anesthetic or attend to any of their hospital duties."

He told them that an increased accident proneness of only one-tenth of one per cent would wipe out the whole gain they were looking for from taxation (12).

Similar testimony came from others. The summary by Prof. Reid Hunt of Harvard of the Dodge-Benedict experimentation dealt with the alcoholic equivalent of one to one and a half liters of beer of somewhat less than 2.75% by weight of alcohol. The protecting lid reflex of the eye was delayed by 7% and extent diminished by 19%. Patellar reflexes, which give the best indication of the condition of the nervous system, were delayed 10% and extent (determined by muscle-thickening) 46% (13).

Dr. Joy Elmer Morgan of the National Educational Association enforced these conclusions: "It is a question of a split-second whether when a child runs in front of an automobile the man can stop in four-fifths of a second or three-fourths. . . . More children of elementary school age are killed today by automobile accident than by all other causes combined" (14).

The 18th Amendment was put into the Constitution to protect society from this dangerous poison. It had the very best theoretical justification. The Johns Hopkins psychiatrist, Prof. Adolf Meyer, affirms that "even with the low alcohol fermented drinks it is difficult to specify any form of production and any product that could not become socially disturbing or actually intoxicating" (15), and the medical director of the New York Life Insurance Co., Dr. Oscar H. Rogers, with his immense practical experience declares that "there appears to be no limit within which alcohol may be entirely harmless. It is as if there were a direct relation between the amount of alcohol used and the amount of damage done to the body" (16).

"WHY PUT A MUZZLE ON A TOOTHLESS DOG?"

Court decisions in the Georgia Court of Appeals (O'Connell v. State) and the Wisconsin Supreme Court (Briffit v. State) had held ordinary beer to be intoxicating. Senator Borah called attention to the fact that when the demand was made for higher per cent beer the explanation the brewers' attorney gave was that only therewith could they compete the bootleggers out of business. "How could you compete against intoxicating beer except with intoxicating beer?" asked the Senator (March 16, 1933) (17). That the politicians knew very well that 3.2% beer was intoxicating and its relegalization un-Constitutional appears from restrictions they offered upon its sale. Senator Bingham for example: "No draught beer was to be sold; all beer was to be bottled in pint bottles and packed in cases. No beer was to be removed from original packages or cases except in public hotels and restaurants" (18). One would have thought they were dealing with dynamite. Wet La Guardia was asked in a Congressional Hearing, "Suppose they permitted this beer to be sold as soft drinks without a license?" "I can't imagine that. It would be a very unsafe thing to do. . . . I firmly believe that all alcohol-containing beverages ought to be under regulations" (19). As soon as it was put on sale wet Ickes, Secretary of the Interior, refused to allow its sale on Indian Reservations and even the Tammany Fire Commissioner of New York barred it from the buildings of the fire department of that city (20).

In the debate on the beer bill, Dec. 20, 1932, Mr. Sanders of Texas asked a series of pertinent questions: "Why should Congress protect the dry states from importation of 3.2% if the beverage is not intoxicating? Why prosecute all seizures and forfeitures under the Volstead Act's harsh provision (i.e. in a dry state)? Why oblige brewers to pay a license of $1,000 for making a harmless, non-intoxicating beverage?" (21)

"Strange," said Congressman Stalker, "that after six Congresses have convened and adjourned, it is just now discovered that 4% beer (in volume) is not intoxicating" (C) (22). And then he pointed out that the real purpose of the bill was to make the Volstead Act unenforceable as the prologue to repeal of the 18th Amendment. The brewers would, of course, never have stopped at "modification," as any subsequent Congress might have easily restored the one half per cent standard of intoxicity. The bill had been reported to the Ways and Means Committee as a tax measure. This was a subterfuge. It had been previously demonstrated that a favorable report could not be obtained from the Judiciary Committee which had jurisdiction over Prohibition legislation. As it was, the chairman and five other members of the Ways and Means Committee refused to have any part in this action. They quoted the Constitution and their oath at length. "I do not believe that the government should obtain revenues through the violation of the Constitution," said Chairman Hawley. "My feeling, after listening to many discussions and the recent hearings, is that the liquor interests are planning by this measure to secure again the existence of 90% by volume of the liquor traffic, the repeal of the 18th Amendment, and the return again of the sale of all intoxicating liquors with attendant and acknowledged evils. . . ." (23)

"IT IS THE FUNCTION OF GOVERNMENT TO PUT RINGS
IN THE NOSES OF HOGS"

Jefferson.

"Behind (this bill) is the whole weight of the inter-allied, world-wide liquor interests," said Mr. Finley of Kentucky (24). "I hold in my hands a letter from Anheuser-Busch outlining the legislation which Congress should adopt," said Mr. Tarver of Georgia. "Levi Cooke, attorney for the Brewers' Association, participated in the formulation of this measure in collaboration with the Legislative Counsel of the House. . . . They are coming to Congress and in effect saying, 'We are violating the law; you haven't stopped us and you can't stop us. Therefore, pass a law which makes our racket legal' " (25).

Even wets expressed disgust at their insolence. Mr. La Guardia got up in the Ways and Means Committee, where the brewers were mobilized, and broke out with, "The quicker the brewers and distillers get out of Washington the better it will be for the American people. No brewer and no distiller should be consulted or have a word to say in the writing of legislation pertaining to the distribution of liquor. . . . It was the control of legislatures and, in the old days, of Congress, the activities of the lobbies of the liquor interests which brought about Prohibition. . . . We see the old activities coming back" (26).

So we do, Mr. La Guardia. And you were one of those who gave "the long call" which brought these *porci tedeschi,* as your co-nationals call them, trotting back.

"TRUST NOT THOSE CUNNING WATERS OF HIS EYES"

"During the Hearings," said Chairman Hawley, "the brewing interests stated that they had no desire for the return of the saloon.

But a motion to prevent this by refusing to permit beer to be sold in such places was voted down in committee" (27). The wet bloc in Congress had agreed upon a tax of $7.50 per bbl., the brewers finding this satisfactory. This was now scaled down first to $6 and then to $5, in spite of the fact that the bill was framed to raise money by taxation (D). No one not a licensed brewer was to be allowed to brew for home use. "A complete monopoly, second only to that of oil for its effectiveness and power to levy on consumption," was turned over to the brewers "for a paltry license fee" (28).

Article Five of the Constitution provides that "the Congress, whenever two thirds of both Houses shall deem it necessary, shall propose amendments to this Constitution." Congress only four months previously had passed on this question and by a vote in the House of almost 3 to 1 had declared that they did not deem it necessary to submit an amendment for repeal of the 18th Amendment. "After having failed to pass a resolution submitting the 18th Amendment to the states for its repeal, as the first act of this last session of the 72nd Congress, the wet forces of this House now propose to nullify the Constitution by act of Congress" (Congressman Guyer) (29). The revelations of the Overman Committee had shown the brewers to be crooked to the marrow. Their lawlessness continued under Prohibition and found its legislative sanction in the law of March 21, 1933, by which a wet Congress and a wet President thumbed their noses at the Constitution. As soon as this law went into effect consignments of beer and pretzels came to President Roosevelt from St. Louis and Milwaukee brewers. The truck that brought the first barrels to the White House, *and significantly to the National Press Club,* bore the words: "President Roosevelt, the first real beer is yours." Real beer meant intoxicating beer and therefore un-Constitutional beer. (In a letter to Congressman S. B. Hill regarding certain other legislation Mr. Roosevelt said later: "I hope your committee will not permit doubt as to constitutionality, however reasonable, to block legislation.")

Nevertheless the essential matter is not the intoxicity of a glass of beer over which wet physiologists were so ready to quibble before Congress. It is a question of the domination of the nation by an unutterably corrupt and extremely powerful group. Before Prohibition they contributed to the campaign funds of both parties

for special favor and protection. After Prohibition in certain
areas and for a time they appeared to have secured themselves in
much the same way. As the Wickersham Report said of pre-
Prohibition conditions: "The corruption of the police by the liquor
interests was widespread. When proceedings were taken to forfeit
saloon licenses, because of violation of the law, it was a common
practise for the brewers to procure surety bonds and provide counsel to resist forfeiture. *The liquor vote was the largest unified
deliverable vote."* The Report also mentioned the hang-over of
brewery politics in the Prohibition period. "When conspiracies
are discovered from time to time they disclose combinations of
illicit distributors, illicit producers, corrupt police, local politicians,
—making lavish payments for protection. . . . *These things have
been particularly evident in the distribution of beer"* (30).

Repeal was a capitulation to the knaves who sell alcohol and
the dupes who buy it. It is going to make law-enforcement as
against the brewers tenfold as difficult as it was before the 18th
Amendment. They may well say, "If we with our Wall Street
allies can pry Prohibition out of the American Constitution we
can break down any form of restriction or control in state or
city with impunity."

Unless we retrace our steps we are in for trouble with these
lords of the underworld (E).

II. THEIR "MOST POWERFUL RECRUIT"

"With all your main and all your might
You back what is against what's right."

In the weeks preceding the 1932 national convention of the
two major parties the nation was treated by the wets to an unparalleled display of fireworks. It began with a rocket which General
Pershing sent up from Paris, declaring his disapproval of Prohibition (31) (F). This was followed by another from Mr. Chrysler.
Then came the glare of the Rockefeller Roman candle, a pin-wheel
from Dr. John R. Mott, two more rockets from Mr. Sloan of
General Motors and Mr. Firestone. The newspapers were primed
to give this demonstration the widest possible publicity and the
coming conventions were, in so many words, asked to believe that
the bottom had fallen out of the dry cause. The letter of Mr.
Rockefeller was especially important to the wets, not because of

its contents—these were but newspaper patter,—but because there was a general idea that he was the financial support of the dry side. The newspapers in order to heighten this opinion talked of the fifteen to thirty millions which he had given it, so that Mr. Rockefeller himself had to explain that his total gifts, together with those of his father, had in *twenty years* been inside of $350,-000 (32). His letter was hailed with transports of joy from social registerite down to underworldling. Mrs. Sabin, wife as we have seen of a director of the whisky bottle manufacturing concern, Owens-Illinois Glass, wrote, "We are all more than delighted. He is our most powerful recruit so far" (33)(G). Similar commendation came from Mr. Hearst, the yellow journalist:

"It will do more than any document which has appeared to bring the nation to conviction of the ineffectiveness of Prohibition." When Repeal was an accomplished fact Mr. Shouse said, "It was the Rockefeller letter that settled the matter."

The letter was addressed to Dr. N. M. Butler as if in reference to the latter's letter in the morning of the same day outlining a wet plank for the Republican platform. But the fact that it was coming was known in the newspaper offices weeks before. The *N. Y. Times* on the following day explained its purpose. In big headlines it said: "Leaders of 2,500,000 wets unite to fight for Repeal spurred by Rockefeller. Plan political pressure. Great mass-meeting will be held in Chicago on eve of the Republican convention. What appeared to be the most powerful drive against Prohibition developed yesterday with the publication of the letter of John D. Rockefeller, Jr., to Dr. N. M. Butler." It was indeed the overture to the Repeal symphony of the Republican Convention. The usual publicity of Ivy Lee was supplemented in this case by nation-wide talkie publicity. Mr. Rockefeller, certainly for the first and only time in his life, was to be seen on thousands of screens, turning over sheets of paper, as he read his pronouncement.

A CRUSHING ANSWER

Col. Woodcock answered Mr. Rockefeller for the Government and his reply was annihilating. Mr. Rockefeller had stated that the amount of consumption had increased under Prohibition. Woodcock showed that in 1929–30 it could not possibly have been more than one third of the 1914 consumption, if that.

Again, Mr. Rockefeller affirmed that the speak-easies had replaced the saloons probably twofold, if not threefold, a shamelessly reckless assertion. Woodcock came back with careful surveys in New York and Detroit which proved how relatively few the speaks really were (H). He had spoken of a great army of lawbreakers financed on a colossal scale by the illegal sale of liquor. Mr. Woodcock quoted the Attorney-General of the United States:

"The assertion has been made that the principal source of gang-power is the profit derived from illegal liquor traffic and that the elimination of this source of revenue would put an end to racketeering. In the recent income tax prosecutions against a number of the organized gangsters it was developed that on an average not over 20% of their revenue came from liquor traffic and this has been diminishing" (35).

Never did man bear false witness more inexcusably than Mr. Rockefeller that June afternoon when he read his Repeal letter to the millions in the darkened movie theatres throughout the United States.

Why did he do it?

It was suggested that "to Mr. Raymond B. Fosdick belongs the honor of having brought Mr. Rockefeller over to the wet side." Certainly Mr. Fosdick is a wet of the wets. In the early days of National Prohibition this agent of Mr. Rockefeller publicly protested against arrest of bootleggers by New York police: "It is peculiarly unfortunate that Gov. Miller should hold the Police Commissioners responsible for Prohibition enforcement" (*N. Y. Times* Jan. 25, 1921, p. 2). More official, perhaps, is the story in *Life* (April 27, 1942) of how Mr. Nelson Rockefeller "helped abolish Prohibition. At dinner one evening Mr. John D. Rockefeller affirmed that the speakeasy problem had been exaggerated by the press. Nelson took the other side of the argument and won it by escorting his father on a tour of 25 blind tigers on the very site of the proposed (Rockefeller) Center. As a result John D. Rockefeller made his memorable and influential statement in favor of repeal."

"The very site of the proposed Center" was owned by Nicholas Murray Butler's university!

A report current at the time, that the Rockefeller letter represented a Wall Street deal, is declared by Mr. Rockefeller's attorney to be "insulting and libelous." We must conclude, then, that the impulse to publish came from Mr. Rockefeller alone; that his statistics were not handed to him but were of his own discovery, or of investigators chartered by him (if indeed he had any investigations made. I get no reply from him, or his attorney, on this point); that the date of publication, so obviously timed for the forthcoming Republican convention, was chosen by himself; and that his descent from Olympus to the film studio and the innumerable little movie houses, was not imposed upon him by any agreement.

His little homily on bootlegging was addressed to that champion of "the Higher Lawlessness," Dr. N. M. Butler, brother-in-law of three large-scale bootleggers who had pined in stripes for two years each, in a New Jersey jail. There is piquancy, also, in the fact, a fact of which Mr. Rockefeller declares himself unaware, that at the very time of his abjuration of National Prohibition as the parent of bootlegging, his own major company, the Standard Oil of New Jersey, was entering into negotiations with National Distillers for the formation of the Standard Alcohol Company, for the manufacture of alcohol from petroleum waste. These negotiations were consummated on a 65–35% basis. The Standard Alcohol Co. has for some years had its offices at 26 Broadway. (See Moody's Manual of Investments, 1935, p. 1371 and Poor's Industrial Investments, 1937, p. 640.) Among its directors are Mr. Bedford, head of the Standard Oil, and Mr. Seton Porter, king-pin of the whisky trust.

And who were National Distillers, Standard Oil partners? Congressman J. J. O'Connor, long adept in the study of whisky operations, charges them with having been, during Prohibition, large scale whisky jobbers for bootleggers (Cong. Record, Jan. 4, 1934, p. 97).

"YOUR DAGGERS
HACKED ONE ANOTHER IN THE SIDES OF CAESAR"

The propaganda tactic was to start the bellwethers, well knowing that the follow-tails would rush after. Black ram Pershing and the Golden Fleece led off. Then followed Mott and Sloan and the rest above-mentioned. Dr. Mott, who has relations to Mr. Rockefeller, advocated a referendum on the ground that the young people had had no opportunity to express their opinion on Prohibition. (Nor had they, for that matter, on slavery or the Bill of Rights) (37). Mr. Sloan is a director of Du Pont de Nemours Co. and of General Motors. The tire man Firestone also had automobile contacts. From this it can be seen how limited the great demonstration really was. But the enormous publicity at the disposal of enormous wealth gave to the uncritical the desired impression of a great uprising. On July 27 appeared throughout the land in the leading newspapers a full page advertisement from the humor paper *Life,* blackguarding the 18th Amendment and calling for an avalanche of telegrams to let the (Republican) Convention know that "an aroused and irate *majority* demands out-and-out repeal" (38). At this time *Life* was being recommended to Mr. Raskob to help finance its wet propaganda (39).

III.   THE BEER PARADE

These occurrences of the early summer of 1932 illustrate again the solidarity between Tammany and Wall Street. While the kings of finance were libeling the 18th Amendment in their way, the sidewalks of New York were echoing with the shufflings of the Beer Parade (May 14). East Side and West Side, "the squalid sides filled with immigrants who had not the courage or ability or sense to make for the virgin lands and become self-respecting farmers," mobilized their sordid following under the marshalship of Col. Wm. J. Donovan of the Irish 69th Regiment (I). The Tammany Society was, of course, out in full strength with everything alien that could be mustered,—Polish Falcons, United Hungarian Societies, County Tipperary men, Celtic Circle folk, Lithuanian-Americans, Ukrainian Veterans, Portuguese-American clubs, Russian-American clubs, Swiss Vereine, United Bavarian Societies, Sachsenvereine, Landwehrvereine, Platt-Deutscher Volkfest Vereine, Unaffiliated German-Americans, ready, at drop of hat, "to speak German at the ballot-box" (that is vote for beer) as they had been admonished by their leaders. Then there were Tchekoslovak Societies, the Order of the Sons of Italy, Jewish War Veterans, all the unassimilated population of Europe, so unconscious of American ideals, fermenting on the East Side. And there were Elks Club bands and the Knights of the Sacrament Band to provide martial beer music: and the contingent from the Fulton Fish Market proud with the memories of their former member, Gov. Smith. There was a large body of Knights of Columbus and numerous posts of the American Legion. There were New York political grafters fresh from the grillings which Judge Seabury had given them, with Walker at their head. The League of Locality Mayors turned out in a body with beer-mugs in their hands and posed for the photographer. The parade was called "The Beer for Taxation Parade." The sheep huddled confidingly around the multimills of the A. A. P. A., waiting to be sheared with a beer tax. Millions of out-of-works were calling for bread. The slums cried for beer and taxes. They "walked with Walker" for beer and only stopped long enough to stand one minute, bare-headed, in honor of—the Lindbergh baby! It was a grotesque, yet forbidding, spectacle, an illustration of the burden of political immaturity which Europe has loaded on our shoulders (40) (J).

IV.   THE BEER CONVENTION

It has been said that President F. D. Roosevelt's "one rebel yell" was when, as member of the New York Senate from Dutchess County, he protested the candidacy of Boss Sheehan of Buffalo for the U. S. Senate. Apart from this he has ever been the indulgent friend of Tammany. He vetoed the state legislature bill for its investigation. "Never once during all the months in which disclosure has been piled on disclosure of the unspeakable corruption of government in New York, have you voluntarily denounced those Tammany leaders who hold power in your party and office in this community," was the judgment of two of New York's best citizens, Drs. Wise and Holmes, on Roosevelt and the Seabury revelations. Roosevelt's answer was a crudely phrased insult. But when Olvaney resigned, taking with him a fortune from public life, Mr. Roosevelt went out of his way to make eulogy of him. He refused to remove McQuade or recommend the investigation of Theofel, and his wife was one of a committee asking the unspeakable Walker to run for mayoralty re-election in 1929 (41).

CHICAGO SEWER RATS

One who could be so indifferent to the shame of Tammany would not be likely to protest much against the Sullivan Democracy of Chicago. Roger Sullivan had organized the gamblers, brothel-keepers, pre-Prohibition saloon-keepers, and criminals into a political machine for mutual protection from the law. His right hand was J. F. O'Malley, dive-keeper and murderer. His immediate successor was Brennan, a scoundrel of the corrupt wet type, who died in 1928. Cermak, Brennan's understudy, who had behind him the Catholic Poles and Bohemians as Brennan and Sullivan the Catholic Irish, was perhaps the vilest figure in the whole group. He was leader and patron of the United Societies which the brewers financed for political ends. The horrible brewers' dance halls of Chicago, which promoted drunkenness and seduction among Chicago's young people, were carried on under their auspices. The Juvenile Protective Association estimated that 1,200 girls were betrayed every night in these halls. The *Chicago Tribune* put the number much higher (K). In 1931 Cermak was chosen mayor of Chicago. It was the throning of indecency and corruption. His property was at one time valued at seven million dollars although he had never other large source of income than city office.

The forty-four members of the Illinois Legislature from Chicago were absolutely controlled by Cermak. He also controlled the third largest delegation to the Democratic National Convention of 1932. He forced his party in Illinois to adopt a resolution for unconditional Repeal. Then he went to New York and conferred with Curry, the Tammany Hall leader, and with Hague, the head of the corrupt Jersey City machine. After these interviews he announced, "Governor Roosevelt is wet enough for me."

The Convention reflected this triple alliance of corrupt machines and political black-legs. The underworld of the cities was stretching its hands towards national power. "A great drive is being made," wrote Mr. McAdoo ("The Challenge," p. 29) "by an alliance of all the political machines in the section of the country where they are strongest, to gain control of the Federal Government. This drive is being made under the guise of an attack upon the 18th Amendment and the Prohibition laws. That this issue should have been chosen by the machine politicians for their purposes is not unnatural. The connection between machine politics and the criminal liquor traffic has always been particularly close. . . . It is asserted, and perhaps with truth, that many machine politicians in our great centers of population maintain speak-easies in order to retain their connection with this class of supporters and to form the indispensable basis for their political operation. Of course politicians of this stamp are opposed to Prohibition. They are fighting for their lives. Not only would Prohibition, if properly enforced, break up their centers of power but, as the population becomes more sober, more thrifty, and reaches a higher plane of comfort through the abolition of the liquor traffic, it would be much less susceptible to machine deception."

THE KING-MAKER

In the Democratic Convention of 1932 Cermak played the leading *rôle*. It was conducted on the approved beer-garden models of the Tammanyized cities. Drys who attempted to speak were howled down. Senator Walsh of Montana, Convention chairman, appealed to Cermak to intervene when this treatment was being applied to Mr. McAdoo. Senator Cordell Hull was unable to continue and sat down. He explained the Convention later as "the culmination of four years of use of the Democratic Organization by affiliated organizations, equipped with vast moneys, to quietly hand-pick many delegations and pack the National Convention with reference to the anti-Prohibition movement."

Governor Roosevelt in Albany sent his approval of the Repeal plank. When the break came and his nomination was announced he took airplane to his disreputable Convention. Cermak made for the airport, ushered him into the Stadium, and heard him declare, "From this hour the 18th Amendment is doomed" (42).

It was the supreme triumph of brewery and underworld.

When the Illinois jackpot Legislature of 1909 voted for Lorimer, Cermak was one of his electors. Lorimer "made" the Senate but Theodore Roosevelt refused to attend a public banquet until the invitation sent to Senator Lorimer was withdrawn (43). The last time the infamous Cermak appeared in public was when he and F. D. Roosevelt, hobnobbing together in Miami after the election, were both shot at by an underworldling.

And that's the difference between the Roosevelts!

REFERENCES TO CHAPTER VIII NOT IN THE TEXT

1. Annals of the American Academy of Political and Social Sciences, September 1923, page 97.

2. Modification of Volstead Act Hearings, December 7, 1932, page 604.
3. Hearings Committee on Manufacturers, January 1932, page 280.
4. Hearings, Modification of Volstead Act, December 1932, page 98.
5. Yale Alumni Weekly, October 14, 1930; Manufactures Hearings, page 34.
6. Hearings, Committee on Manufactures, January 1932, page 26.
7. Hearings, Committee on Manufactures, January 1932, page 335.
8. Hearings, Committee on Manufactures, January 1932, page 35.
9. Hearings, Committee on Manufactures, January 1932, pages 146, 148, 252, 254, 43, 44, 83.
10. Hearings, Committee on Manufactures, January 1932, page 86.
11. Samuel Wilson, "Beer,—Is it Intoxicating?"
12. Hearings, Modification of Volstead Act, Ways and Means Committee, page 502 seq.
13. Modification of Volstead Act Hearings, Ways and Means Committee, December 1932, page 616.
14. Hearings, Senate Committee on Manufactures, January 1932, page 369.
15. "Alcohol and Man," page 275.
16. Annals of American Academy for Political and Social Sciences, September 1923, page 7.
17. Congressional Record, March 16, 1933.
18. Hearings, Senate Committee on Manufactures, January 1932, page 3.
19. Modification of Volstead Act, Ways and Means Committee, December 20, 1932, page 230.
20. New York Times, April 4, 1933.
21. Congressional Record, December 20, 1932, page 756.
22. Congressional Record, December 20, 1932, page 767.
23. Congressional Record, December 20, 1932, page 775.
24. Congressional Record, December 20, 1932, page 773.
25. Congressional Record, December 20, 1932, pages 763 and 764.
26. Hearings Modification of Volstead Act, Ways and Means Committee, December 5, 1932, page 229.
27. Congressional Record, December 20, 1932, page 775.
28. Congressional Record, December 20, 1932, page 811.
29. Congressional Record, December 20, 1932, page 787.
30. Wickersham Report, pages 6 and 37.
31. New York Times, May 27, 1932, page 1.
32. New York Times, June 8, 1932.
33. New York Times, June 8, 1932.
34. "Upton Sinclair Presents William Fox," page 149.
35. Letter to Senator Sheppard, New York Times, June 29, 1932, page 11.
36. William H. Allen, "Rockefeller, etc.," pages 278–286.
37. New York Times, June 9, 1932.
38. New York Times, June 27, 1932, page 9.
39. Lobby Investigation Report, page 4002.
40. New York Times, April 18, 1932 and April 19, 1932, page 8.
41. N. M. Thomas and Paul Blanshard, "What's the Matter with New York?" pages 184, 295, 178, 179.
42. Fletcher Dobyns, "The Underworld of American Politics," pages 42, 44, 186, viii, 114, 133, 135, 136, 128, 137.
43. Fletcher Dobyns, "The Underworld of American Politics," pages 140, 141.

NOTES TO CHAPTER VIII

A. This is, Professor Henderson explains, about one third of an ordinary small tumbler of 100% alcohol (*Yale Alumni Weekly*). In the traveling anti-alcohol exhibitions of Germany one often sees a bottle with heating apparatus below and glass tube in the stopper. After two minutes the alcohol in ordinary brown beer passes through the stopper and burns for a considerable time.

Dr. Arthur D. Bevan testified before the Bingham Beer Bill Hearings (p. 388): "You can produce complete anaesthetic effect with beer so that a man is dead drunk in the same sense that he sleeps as he would under ether. Alcohol belongs to the same group as ether, chloroform and verinol."

Prof. Henderson is a specialist on noxious gases in mines and tunnels. The danger from beer in such places was made clear April 28, 1942 when the Hudson River tube train crashed and burned 75 feet underground, killing five passengers and injuring 217 others,—the worst wreck in this company's 35 year history. The motorman had at meal-time drunk five glasses of beer (one for each passenger subsequently killed)! Chief Walsh told the court that after the crash *"the man fell asleep and was very comfortable."* *Boston Herald,* April 29, '42.

B.   Sir Wm. Osler in an address at the Workingman's College, London, 1906: "Whether or not the yellow resinous narcotic powder found in the blossoms of hops is responsible, it seems to be a fact recognized by the most careful students that alcohol with a lupulin content is a peculiarly vicious member of the notoriously vicious alcohol family."

C.   Mr. Rainey, floor-leader: "In Sweden they have been able to study the liquor problem more thoroughly than in any other nation. In Sweden 3.2% beer by weight is not considered in any degree intoxicating" (C. R. Dec. 1932, p. 748). On the contrary the experimentation of the Swedish physicians Dr. Liljestrand and Dr. Hammerstén, has proved the intoxicating character of this percentage and Swedish government documents which I have translated elsewhere ("The Dry Fight in Europe," p. 224), exhibit the general disaster which it brings.

Senator Bailey called attention to the fact that statutes passed by Congress for forty years had without exception declared beer of a content of 3.2% to be intoxicating. Thus Act of August 8, 1890, "that all *fermented,* distilled, or other intoxicating liquors transported into any state . . ."

Act of March 1, 1913: "The shipment or transportation in any manner or by any means whatsoever of any spirituous, vinous, *malted, fermented,* or other intoxicating liquor."

Act of March 3, 1917: "No letter, postal card, circular, newspaper containing any advertisement of spirituous, vinous, *malted, fermented,* or other intoxicating liquors."

Act of March 4, 1909: "Any officer, agent, or employee of any railroad, express company, or other common carrier, who shall knowingly deliver any spirituous, vinous, malted, *fermented,* or other intoxicating liquor" (Cong. Record, March 16, 1933, p. 496).

D.   The Hull-O'Connor Beer Bill provided for a tax of $10 per bbl. Representative Rich: "You have heard time after time on the floor of the House that you would tax beer $12 or $18 per bbl." (Modification Hearings, Ways and Means, Dec. 1932, p. 644).

E.   Mr. Robert A. Woods described how futile efforts at control were

in the decade before Prohibition: "For four years I worked with others with final success to secure legislation to eliminate saloon practices leading to intoxication. During this whole period the entire power of the Massachusetts liquor trade, in all its branches and with all its methods, *strongly reinforced from outside the state,* was brought to bear to thwart an effort to cleanse the saloon and reduce in some degree its responsibility for the huge burden of drunkenness and related forms of law-breaking. A little later I was appointed one of the three members of the Licensing Board of the City of Boston. My object was to reduce the total of drunkenness and to drive a wedge between the liquor business and prostitution. In both directions practical measures were devised which demonstrated that good results could be increasingly secured. But the Board met the unyielding opposition of the liquor trade at every point and the two members (of the Board) actively interested in this policy were finally displaced through the power of certain great brewery interests" (Annals of the Am. Acad. of Polit. and Soc. Sciences, Sept. 1923).

It was a capital mistake after the adoption of the 18th Amendment to allow the brewers to brew anything. The demand for near-beer was insignificant. It but masked law-breaking. The breweries should have been dismantled and torn down and the making of near-beer allowed only in homes. When the brewers were caught with strong beer they explained that it had not yet been de-alcoholized. When they were conforming to law they sold the excess alcohol to bootleggers. At the approach of agents they would switch off the strong beer and disclose only near beer. Within half an hour of the successful raid the brewing of strong beer would be proceeding again.

They operated under false names and labels. Carloads of beer would be apprehended but because of false names in the railroad records it was impossible to trace the source. Truck drivers, apparently under instruction, would, when caught, not know whence they came or whither they were going. They corrupted the police. They maintained a detective system by which Federal officers were under observation. They would subsidize a whole neighborhood so that it would be almost impossible for a government agent to get within a few blocks of a brewery without his presence being known. When the police were in league with them, as in New York, they would inquire of a loitering stranger, suspected of being a government agent, as to his business in the neighborhood, and if unsatisfactory answers were given, they would oblige him to reveal his identity at the nearest station.

They patrolled their premises for a radius of ten miles with motorcycles. They protected them with high board fences and wire entanglements. They employed professional gunmen as guards and to act as outposts and escorts to fleets of beer trucks. They threatened government agents with death. At times, as in one New Jersey case, they actually beat up Federal agents and took a truck from them. In some places they worked with gangsters who went to jail for them, as in case of the Sieben Brewery, Chicago.

All this and more, and they did it because, as Anheuser-Busch wrote to the President of the United States, *"they operated in the security of a special dispensation from Washington"* (*Ladies' Home Journal,* May 1924, House Hearings 1924, p. 320 seq. Wayne Wheeler, Campbell in *N. Y. World* Sept. 9, 1930, Haynes, "Prohibition Inside Out," Gunman Hearings 1925, p. 25, "Prohibition, a National Experiment").

F.   General Pershing might have told the nation what National Prohibition had done for the army. In the period 1907–16 the hospital admissions for acute and chronic alcoholism were 16.1 per thousand. In 1920–29 it was 7.84, a clean drop of one half ("Alcohol and Man," p. 416).

G.   Mr. Fosdick is friend and supporter of wet Gov. Smith. As Chairman of Training Camp Activities of the War and Navy Departments, he opposed features of the Army Bill for the protection of the troops at home and in France from the drinkshops.

Mr. Rockefeller wrote of his mother and grandmother, "They were among the dauntless women of the day who . . . were found with women of like mind praying on their knees in the saloons in their ardent desire to save men from the evil that so commonly sprang from these sources of iniquity." For such women Mrs. Sabin would have little sympathy. Mr. Rockefeller, when serving on the Grand Jury investigating the white slave traffic, said: "As foreman I discovered that the sale and use of alcohol beverages had a very vital and intimate relation to the white slave traffic. I doubt if it would have flourished without drink."

Four doors south of Mr. Rockefeller's Broadway office was, about the time of his jury service, a Mr. Adolph Keitel, maltster, who sent out a circular letter describing certain activities of the brewers: "I can cite instances where representatives of breweries, or managers of their branches, were not only abetting, but actually operated themselves, houses of prostitution and were engaged in the white slave traffic" (Modification of Volstead Act Hearings, Dec. 7, 1932, Ways and Means, p. 624).

The brewers, as Mrs. Sabin, were "delighted" with Mr. Rockefeller's letter.

H.   In March 1931 the Detroit Police Department made a survey of the number and location of the premises suspected of illegal sale of liquor. In April, 1931 they reported 1,561. They took immediate steps to have them vacated by the owners under threat of temporary injunction. A recheck in August, 1931 showed that 777 had been voluntarily closed, leaving 884 still under suspicion. It had been stated by the newspapers previous to this survey, that there were 28,000 open saloons in Detroit.

On April 11th, 1932, *two months before the Rockefeller letter, the* Prohibition administrator of New York made a survey of the borough of Manhattan for the purpose of locating all premises suspected of selling liquor. The result showed that there were 3,494 places where liquor *might* be sold. Of these 2,182 were speaks, 927 restaurants, 286 cordial

stein a second time in crescendo. "I object," said Mr. Dickstein a third time (4). The Lower East Side had it.

"In pushing through today under suspension of rules, with only twenty minutes of debate on each side, you are not only breaking the precedents of 150 years but you are not showing proper respect to the office of the President of the United States," said Mr. Snell, the opposition leader. "To guard against the saloon and for the protection of dry states I believe, if the Democratic majority would give us an opportunity to present such an amendment, there are votes enough to adopt it. But the Speaker has flatly denied us that right and openly said, 'Take it or leave it'" (5) (abridged).

Yet these stipulations, too, were in the party platforms of 1932. "The Speaker is primarily responsible for this precipitate action," added Mr. Moore of Ohio. "If you will search the history of this country you will not find any legislative action so ruthless as that which we are about to take,—a thing like this where we have had no debate, where this resolution was not even numbered until we came this morning, where not one fourth of the membership of the House has ever read it, where we can make no amendments, where we have not had any hearings, where a new method of submitting it to conventions is set" (6) (abridged).

Gag rule in the House; muzzle in Committee. The Judiciary Committee, elected by the House and vested by its ruling with jurisdiction over legislation of this type, asked permission to work out and submit a plan with least disturbance to the national welfare. The request was denied (7).

THE STARTER

The Democratic leader in the House stood on the floor of the House, stop-watch in hand, during those fateful forty minutes, announcing, "I leave one quarter of a minute to the gentleman from Michigan," "I yield one half minute to the gentleman from New York," "I yield one half minute to the gentleman from Texas." So was the 21st Amendment, the wet amendment, to be crowded through (8).

Mr. Thatcher of Kentucky, after noting that members had had no opportunity to see the printed resolution until after the House convened and then just when the motion for suspension of rules was made, also declared the thing without parallel in Amer-

ican history. "Even in the adoption of by-laws for a private corporation some advance notice is required and full opportunity is
given for discussion and amendment. Yet it is now and here
proposed, under these unexampled conditions of gag rule and
haste, to submit a proposal for the naked and unconditional repeal
of an Amendment to the Federal Constitution which was ratified
by 46 of the states" (9).

There are those who can quote Scripture even for such a
situation. Mr. Beck, abandoning Shakespeare and Sophocles as
without requisite unction, broke out with, "Now is the accepted
time and this is the day of salvation" (10). "Today we are
making history," he said later. Yes, and what kind of history!
A member of the Judiciary Committee was more appropriate in
his quotation. He repeated the admonition to Judas Iscariot,
"What thou doest, do quickly" (11).

ANOTHER TURN OF THE SCREW

The assault of Dec. 5, 1932 failed. The wets lacked 14 votes
of a two thirds majority. When the Repeal Resolution was
brought up again, Feb. 20, 1933, Speaker Garner took no chance
but put the Democratic party under binding caucus control. Again
both parties repudiated their party platforms. "Never in the
political history of the United States was there such a betrayal,"
said Representative Guyer. The Republican platform pledged
"to safeguard our citizens everywhere from the return of the
saloon." The Democratic platform gave similar assurances.
"The Speaker, having failed the first hour of this session to jam
a naked Repeal resolution through the House, has now resorted to
the secret caucus (that last relic of parliamentary slavery) to force
his party in the House to repudiate the platform upon which he
was elected" (12).

This time the wets won,—289 to 121 with 16 not voting.

They said they were but carrying out the mandate of the
people. But the election of 1932 was not fought on wet-dry
lines. There was no possible opportunity for an expression of
opinion because both parties had declared for the same thing.
The election actually threw out many of the worst wets in Congress,—Blaine, Bingham, LaGuardia, Hull, Schafer, and Clancy.
The issue was primarily economic. The huge majority for change
was the agonized cry of a people struggling with bitterest need.

"The strategy of the wets," said Mr. Garber, "is to politicalize the depression in order to repeal the Amendment. In the very midst of this cataclysm of economic conditions without precedent, the demands of the brewing and liquor interests (are) given the right of way, when workers are in need of every penny to buy milk and food for their children" (13). Mr. Summers of Washington put the dot over this i. "You talk of revenue. I know and you know that this is not the sound, unselfish judgment of the American people but the hue and cry of paid propagandists. This is the culmination of a deep-laid plot of heartless millionaires to shift the tax burden from their pockets to the cravings of the helpless" (14).

GNAWING FILES

In the Prohibition decade wet lawyers brought forward every objection legal subtlety could concoct to undo the constitutionality of the 18th Amendment. Mr. Eliot Tuckerman argued it unconstitutional because it was resolved in Congress by two thirds of a quorum instead of two thirds of the whole body,—an argument which would have dragged down with it other preceding constitutional amendments (15). It was attacked as violating inalienable rights; also as denying a republican form of government to the two states, Rhode Island and Connecticut, which refused to ratify (Mr. Henry Alan Johnson) (16). Yet the Amendment, by smashing brewery-saloon government, tended more than anything in recent times, to assure a republican government to the states. In a more ingenious mood Mr. Johnson sought to draw a distinction between an amendment to the Constitution and a statute which is passed after the manner of making a constitutional amendment (17). He insisted that the 18th Amendment was a law which went astray and found itself in the Constitution when it should simply have passed Congress and received the President's signature.

Mr. Meyer of Chicago contended that the states, or 45 states, could not take from the 46th state by their collective action any right that was reserved in the Constitution of that state (18). Mr. Hardgrove held that the 18th Amendment, though prohibiting manufacture and sale by individuals, could not prohibit manufacture and dispensation by the state itself. This on the ground that, unless expressly stated, a statute does not bind a sovereign.

A bill in the N. Y. Legislature which provided for the sale of liquor by a state commission on the ground that the state could do what an individual could not do, found support from Mr. Coudert of the Voluntary Committee of Lawyers, Inc. (19). The seven year time-limit attached to the 18th Amendment by the wets in the hope of extinguishing it, was now pointed to as an undue restriction on the right of the ratifying agency to deliberate calmly and with sufficient time.

But the hopes of the wets finally centered on the argument of Mr. Bacon (approved by the Voluntary Committee of Lawyers) which, on Dec. 16, 1930, was upheld by Judge William Clark of the Federal Court of New Jersey. This held that the 18th Amendment was void because it had been ratified by state legislatures instead of by state conventions, an objection which, if valid, would hold against other preceding amendments to the Federal Constitution. In vain. All these refinements of legal dialectic were relentlessly thrown aside, one after another, by the Supreme Court (20).

WET INNOVATORS

But these wet "strict constructionists" were well prepared to play patron to novelties and to show themselves the loosest of constructionists when it suited their ends. They were first to attach a time-limit for ratification to an amendment to the Constitution. They first undertook the repeal of an amendment in the nation's fundamental law. They first substituted ratification of an amendment by conventions, which were indeed but plebiscites in the guise of conventions, rather than, as heretofore, by legislatures. Now everyone of these three radical innovations was prompted by the exigencies in which the alcohol capital found itself.

It was the same group that had sought in vain to find a flaw in the 18th Amendment,—the Voluntary Committee of Lawyers headed by J. H. Choate,—and which had earlier offered to give legal defense to bootleggers caught by the Increased Penalties Act, for which they might indeed have been subject to government prosecution as accessories (21). The plan of ratification by conventions was drafted by them before the 72nd Congress passed the Repeal resolution and indeed before there seemed any likelihood of its doing so (22). Mr. Dowling describes their action as a striking illustration of how legislative development of the law may be advanced by private organizations. They were on the ground with legislative drafts and the legislatures in practically all the states followed their guidance. The plan favored was election of delegates at large. This took place in 22 states, and in others in combination with local representation. It was sheer innovation. Although half of the state constitutions contain specifications regarding constitutional conventions, not one provides for a convention of delegates at large solely (23). The usual procedure is that of the state conventions of 1787 which ratified the Federal Constitution, namely to select delegates in the number and manner of the lower houses of legislatures (24).

MOBILIZING THE ALIEN VOTE

Senator Hastings of Delaware, who was on the Resolutions Committee of the Republican National Convention of 1932, describes a conversation with two residents of Delaware (presumably Du Ponts) who had " done more to steer the country to the point of having anything written in the platform with respect to the 18th Amendment than any other men that I know" (25). They were advocating ratification by conventions. "What they propose and what they hope to carry through is that the populace of the cities, most of whom are wet, shall be arrayed against those in the country, most of whom are dry; and in order that they may get a majority of the wets on one side they propose that the subject shall be submitted in that form." Senator Bingham was perfectly frank about this. "It has been brought to my attention," he said, "that in many states the members of the legislature are elected year after year and hold a kind of hereditary seat in the legislature, due to their ability; that most of them have a record of having voted dry always; that it would be extremely difficult for them to change their votes, even to meet changed public opinion" (26).

It was this serious substantial American leadership which was to be swamped by the alien votes of the cities. And the election of delegates at large was to be part of the machinery. It should be noted that the Senate voted for ratification by state conventions contrary to the advice of the lawyers of its Judiciary Committee (27).

There were practical reasons against this innovation. Senator Norris protested against "putting upon tax-payers millions of dollars of expense to carry out this simple mandate" in a time of hunger and bankruptcy (27). But the Repealers, who affected such indignation at modest enforcement expenditures, could not wait. So New York had to pay out $805,689 for this extra election and other states accordingly, a total of not less than ten millions.

More serious were the constitutional objections to this method as parodied in practice. The essence of a convention is deliberation. The 1787 conventions debated the question before them on occasion for six weeks and the shortest debate was a full three days. There was not, and there could not be, any deliberation in the 1933 conventions. The delegates were, to all intents and purposes, pledged. Mr. Noel Dowling wrote in the *American Bar Association Journal* (29) that there was "a common purpose to make the popular vote as nearly binding as possible. In nearly all states candidates were nominated without party or political designation and on the basis of 'for' or 'against' ratification. Most of the states required the candidates to file a written acceptance of the nomination 'for' or 'against' as the case might be. Several required written pledges of the candidate, others an oath, and Arizona prescribed a criminal penalty for violation of the instructed vote."

Now the Constitution makes no allowance for amendment by popular vote. It will not do to say, as Mr. Dowling suggests, that the required deliberation took place in Congress. That was just what did not occur there in the forty minutes allowed. Mr. Rainey, in moving suspension of rules and introduction of the Repeal Amendment actually said: "A Member of this House is not voting wet or dry when he votes to submit this amendment. He is simply conceding to the States the right of petition" (30). Not only, then, did Congress not deliberate on the essential issue. It did not even vote on it according to this floor leader.

In the case of Hawke v. Smith, the Supreme Court ruled that an amendment to the Federal Constitution cannot be ratified by a referendum. "The framers of the Constitution might have adopted a different method. Ratification might have been left to a vote of the people or to some authority of government other than that selected. The language of the article is plain and admits of no doubt in its interpretation. It is not the function of the courts or legislative bodies, national or state, to alter the method which the Constitution has fixed."

Deliberation and discussion were needed above all things. The country had for years been subjected to a propaganda unexampled for its ruthlessness and deceit. It controlled the press. Newspaper, radio, and movie were closed to the dry side except when the dry side could be held up to ridicule. All defense of the 18th Amendment was to be choked off in these fake conventions, and Repeal ratification rushed through by what were practically unconstitutional referenda.

"THAT DISHONEST VICTORY
AT CHAERONEA . . . FATAL TO LIBERTY."

In the elections for the conventions every imaginable lever was moved. Repeal was pictured as the necessary cure for the agonizing depression. We had been told by Mr. H. H. Curran, President of the A. A. P. A., that with the disappearance of Prohibition "the Federal income tax of everybody who pays, down to the smallest and up to the biggest amounts, would disappear overnight" (31). Postmaster-General Farley capped this promise with a threat. "Unless the 18th Amendment is repealed every income taxpayer in the country will have to contribute six to ten dollars out of every $100 earned" (32). A survey by Bradstreet of the business leaders of the country alleged that two thirds of them believed recovery would be hastened by Repeal (33). Men of position insisted that the moral results would parallel the financial. Thus President Hopkins of Dartmouth felt that Repeal was "fundamentally vital to the welfare of the country. . . . My concern and deep solicitude are for the welfare of the oncoming generations" (34) (B). The faces of alleged "dry Sauls who had become wet Pauls" (the phrase was Congressman Beck's) (35) appeared on the front pages of the public prints. Everything possible was done to give the impression that the 18th Amendment was doomed. Skillful political manoeuvring had been at work repealing state enforcement codes, one by one, until fifteen states were without this defense, among them dry states such as North Dakota, Colorado, Oregon, and Washington. Beer had been made widely legal where it hitherto had been illegal because of the 3.2% legislation of Congress. From all sides came disquieting news. Gov. Rolph proposed to release a thousand more bootleggers from

California jails (36). The Attorney-General slashed the personnel of the Prohibition Bureau by one half, dismissing 1,300 agents (37). The Administration, through the Bureau of the Budget, cut enforcement appropriations from $12,440,000 to $5,860,000 in anticipation of Repeal. To heighten further this sense of foregone conclusion, a Federal Alcohol Control Administration was established on Nov. 22, 1933, by the National Industrial Recovery Act (June 16, 1933), when the votings were actually going on.

All this naturally created an ever denser atmosphere of fatalism and discouragement. The newspapers redoubled their clatter. The nation, as Professor Farnam put it, was racing down a road into a swamp because a sign-post had been turned by some one. That "some one" was the metropolitan press.

BRIBING AND WHIPLASHING THE STATES

The order of state votings was clearly arranged so that wet states should come first as far as possible. Early wet victories would thus increase the defeatist sentiment. Repeal was to be carried in "one whirlwind chaos of inane hurrahs." In the depth of the depression only the liquor interest and its ally in high finance could provide money for a suitable campaign. The nation was bribed in the National Recovery Act, for by Sec. 217 important taxes were to be removed providing Repeal became an accomplished fact (38). Thus the 5% tax on all stock dividends was to cease; also the one tenth of one per cent upon each gallon of gasoline sold, and the 5% tax on corporation profits in excess of the 12½% tax provided by the revenue laws of the United States (C). This actually brought a remission of $227,000,000 of taxation in the following year (39). One can easily see how the prospect of this recoupment would invite subscription to Repeal campaign funds.

And this was not the only way the dice were loaded. Governors and representatives of states are reported to have been told in so many words by the Roosevelt administration that their states need not look for Federal favors and appropriations unless they ratified the Repeal Amendment. Newspaper men in Washington affirmed that the Governor of Kentucky, seeking Federal relief appropriations, got the run-around until he promised to make Kentucky vote for Repeal. The Governor of Colorado had a similar experience, as he stated to Mr. McBride. South Dakota asked for Federal relief for its hungry. They were told that if they legalized beer they would be able to feed their poor with the revenue therefrom. The Repeal election in Idaho was not desired by the people of the state and was brought about largely by pressure from Washington. "Both in Montana and Idaho members of the Methodist Conference rose and stated that the dividend checks received from the Montana Power Co. and the Idaho Power Co. on July first were 5% less than usual, the amount lacking having been deducted as a Federal tax at the source. The statement accompanying the dividend said that this tax would be removed whenever the Federal budget was balanced *or the 18th Amendment repealed*" (40).

PRESIDENTIAL INTERVENTION

"The President in effect made the scuttling of Prohibition a rider on his measure for economic recovery." Postmaster-General Farley was sent from state to state as the President's personal representative to urge the states to repeal. Southern dry Democrats were told that it was a matter of party loyalty to fulfill this platform pledge; that it would be a personal disappointment to Mr. Roosevelt if they balked. Never before, as Senator Morrison of North Carolina said, had a party sought to coerce sovereign states in the matter of amending the Federal Constitution, and this with the assistance of the chief executive of the nation.

And what was going on in high places was paralleled by doings in low places. Thus the wets had a sixteen to one victory in Memphis, for it was important that Tennessee should vote wet in order to influence the Kentucky election following. In one Memphis ward 660 votes were cast for Repeal against three opposing, a ward in which only 153 votes had been cast in the preceding hotly contested gubernatorial election. Mr. R. E. Johnson, an engineer in Memphis, says of this electoral steal that put Tennessee in the wet column:

"Shelby County, which is for practical purposes the City of Memphis, is credited with giving Repeal candidates a majority of 30,515 votes. . . . I want to say that it is my sincere opinion that not more than 18,000 people went to the polls in Shelby County and that a large portion of them were not entitled to vote. . . . Names were copied on the poll sheets from the registration books and the personal appearance of the voter was not obtained."

The polls in Eastern Tennessee closing at 4 P. M. reported heavy dry majorities. Thereupon "the election thieves in Memphis, where the polls close at 7 P. M., got busy and wrote the results."

That indirect Federal bribery was at work appears from a despatch of the Universal Service from Knoxville, July 21, 1933 headed:

"Two Counties Getting Largess (i.e. Federal appropriations) Bolt Repeal." "Of the four East Tennessee counties in the Cove Creek Dam area expected to benefit from the 35 million dollar government expenditure, only Clairborne and Union gave majority for Repeal. Anderson and Campbell gave big dry majorities."

"Offence's gilded hand" was obviously at work in the corrupt currents of the New York election as so often in the past. The Act providing for the Convention election stipulated that the Bi-partisan Board of Elections should supersede the Board of Supervisors. This change was objectionable in that the election inspectors were not two wets and two drys but two Republicans and two Democrats. In the cities this would generally mean four wet inspectors and no dry ones. The figures from the election gave grounds for suspicion,—367,782 blank ballots cast and 482,338 declared void (41). In New Jersey crooked politicians fixed it so that wet candidates had no county opponents whatever in eleven counties. As two days only were left for a check-up there was no chance for protest (42).

Repeal swept the country. The conventions assembled, voted and went home.

President Butler of Columbia, who had shown such solicitude for the Constitution in the Prohibition years, who indeed, "on a dull dark day in March 1920," when Root and the brewers were seeking to overthrow the 18th Amendment in the courtroom of the Supreme Court, had vowed to defend the Constitution from this very Amendment, was elected as delegate to the New York Convention. But he now had so little concern for constitutional usage that he did not even attend the convention's sessions but sailed for Europe, sending later from Paris a cablegram in which he "welcomed the end of Prohibition as the beginning of true temperance" (43). The Utah Convention, the 36th ratifying, showed a similar disregard for the dignity of the Constitution. A Salt Lake City newspaper man read to the convention a forged telegram to the effect that Maine delegates were planning to put the clock ahead, in order to beat Utah in the race for the honor of dealing the death-blow to Prohibition. To forestall this supposed action, the Utah Convention suppressed the speeches and discussions which were planned for the evening session and ordered immediate voting. "In this way," said the forger gleefully to his colleagues in the North American Newspaper Alliance, *"The Salt Lake City Telegram* got the story for its last editions, and the Eastern states got their liquor four hours earlier than they had expected" (44) (D).

It was indeed an appropriate closing of the campaign to lie the 18th Amendment out of the Constitution.

REFERENCES TO CHAPTER IX NOT IN THE TEXT

1. Personal letter.
2. Congressional Record, December 5, 1932, page 9.
3. New York Times, January 30, 1934 and Hearings on H. R. 10933, March 18, 1936, page 27.
4. Congressional Record, December 5, 1932, page 7.
5. Congressional Record, December 5, 1932, page 8.
6. Congressional Record, December 5, 1932, page 9.
7. Congressional Record, December 5, 1932, page 35.
8. Congressional Record, December 5, 1932, page 11.
9. Congressional Record, December 5, 1932, page 19.
10. Congressional Record, December 5, 1932, page 9.
11. Congressional Record, December 5, 1932, page 20.
12. Congressional Record, February 20, 1933, page 4512.
13. Congressional Record, February 20, 1933, page 4519.
14. Congressional Record, February 20, 1933, page 4511.
15. Joseph P. Pollard, "The Road to Repeal."
16. The Century Magazine, April 1928, page 643.
17. Hearings Prohibition Amendment, House Judiciary Committee, February 1930, page 394.
18. Hearings Prohibition Amendment, House Judiciary Committee, February 1930, page 341.
19. Hearings Prohibition Amendment, House Judiciary Committee, February 1930, page 1175.
20. Eliot Tuckerman, "A Fight for the Federal Constitution," pp. 6, 28.
21. House Judiciary Hearings, February 1930, page 1176.
22. Literary Digest, November 25, 1933, page 8.
23. American Bar Association Journal, July 1933.
24. Elliott's Debates on the Federal Constitution.
25. Congressional Record, February 15, 1933, page 4167.
26. Congressional Record, February 15, 1933, page 4166.
27. Canon William S. Chase's Brief, page 40.
28. Congressional Record, February 15, 1933, page 4161.
29. New York Times, January 21, 1933.
30. Congressional Record, February 20, 1933, page 4508.
31. Lobby Investigation Report, page 3998.
32. New York Times, May 25, 1933, page 2.
33. New York Times, November 9, 1931.
34. Congressional Record, April 15, 1932, page 8277.
35. Congressional Record, February 23, 1932, page 4547.

36. Hearings Modification of Volstead Act, Ways and Means Committee, 1932, page 409.
37. New York Times, June 28, 1933, page 17.
38. Document 76, 73rd Congress.
39. Tax on Intoxicating Liquor Hearings, December 1933, page 301.
40. Pacific Christian Advocate, September 14, 1933.
41. Canon William S. Chase's Brief, October 1933.
42. New York Times, May 6, 1933, page 18.
43. New York Times, June 28, 1933, page 1.
44. Editor and Publisher, December 9, 1933, page 12.

NOTES TO CHAPTER IX

A.   Mr. Celler was brought up in a whisky atmosphere. He describes his father (Hearings on H. R. 12005, April 8, 1936, p. 27) as a maker of "bad whisky . . . sold as the very cheapest."

The underworld was watching its Congress. They sent bullying letters to those who opposed them. Mr. Clarke of New York read into the Record threatening letters sent him for voting against the Garner gag resolution: "Traitor! Should be hung!" He received great numbers of them. "Some of our papers are doing a bad job in inciting their readers," was his comment. Mr. Blanton also read a sample: "We are sending you an ultimatum. Vote right or we are going to bump you off" (Cong. Record, Dec. 20, 1932, p. 805).

B.   The strictest safeguards were promised for future sale. Mr. Julian Codman, an active wet, proposed the following for the state of Massachusetts: "All intoxicating liquor to be sold by a state corporation composed of men of the highest character and with no other business. No profits, no advertisements. Taxation according to the intoxicity of the liquor. Distilled liquors to be sold in strictly limited quantities and only for delivery at the house of the purchaser whose name with hour of sale should be registered. No public drinking. Local option. Part of the profits to be used for temperance instruction" (Feb. 3, 1932, p. 3304, Cong. Record).

C.   This was made the basis of solicitation of campaign funds. Thus an official of the A. A. P. A. wrote Sept. 12, 1933: "Dear Sir: We hereby request your company to make an appropriation of $250 in the interest of your stockholders, to be used in bringing about the Repeal of the 18th Amendment." After stating that remission of taxes was contingent on Repeal, he adds: "Heads of corporations feel justified in appropriating a reasonable sum to bring about a situation which will save a considerable sum to stockholders."

D.   Yet Governor Dern of Utah had testified: "Prohibition has been beneficial. Conditions in mining camps are greatly improved. The shiftless class is to a large extent disappearing." Mr. M. H. Welling, Secretary of State for Utah, had declared Prohibition "an amazing improvement, infinitely better than the old conditions," and the Hon. J. W. Cherry, Chief Justice of the Supreme Court of Utah, "It is the best method of dealing with the intoxicating liquor problem we have found."

CHAPTER X

ROOSEVELT AND REPEAL
(A STUDY IN BROKEN PLEDGES)

"All that I have done . . . to prepare this country morally . . . for whatever contingencies may be in store, I submit to the judgment of my countrymen" (F. D. Roosevelt's Acceptance Speech, July 19, 1940).

When the distillers' program of Repeal was fairly realized they acclaimed the leader of Repeal. On his following birthday a great IN GRATITUDE broadside in the *New York Times,* with his portrait, announced a complimentary dinner given by the National Organization of the Wine and Liquor Industry (1). ("In the hope for *the continued* success of his constructive labors in the interest of our industry, the following organizations join in wishing our honored President many happy returns of his birthday.") On the first anniversary of Repeal Schenley's Distillers' Corporation also displayed a picture of the new Emancipator who had struck the shackles from four million beer kegs. "Due to your dauntless leadership a great American industry was born a year ago today" (2). Mrs. Roosevelt stood shoulder to shoulder with her husband. She went to Kansas and said in public address: "The average girl of today faces the problem of learning *very young* how much she can drink of such things as whisky and gin and sticking to the proper quantity" (3). Yet of Mrs. Roosevelt's own youth a writer in Harpers (Jan. 1940, p. 131) writes: "As an orphaned young girl she carried a load of shame on her slender shoulders for her two attractive uncles were such inveterate drinkers that her grandmother could not entertain guests."

As competent politician Mr. Roosevelt winced at this publicity and ordered it stopped (4).

The cabinet followed their chief's lead. Tugwell wrote (5) that the New Deal stood for a more abundant life, specifying "wine, women, and song." This in practice has meant beer and prostitution. With two millions from P. W. A. funds and an additional $520,000 for operation, Secretary Ickes developed a rum distilling monopoly on the Virgin Islands, having a potential output of four million gallons. The Secretary of Agriculture sponsored an experiment station in Florida for the distillation of brandies from orange and grape-fruit culls (6). Annual expense to the nation,—$150,000. Postmaster-General Farley is son of the saloon who naturally thinks Repeal "a major accomplishment of the Democratic Party" (A).

The Secretary of the Navy, with the President's approval, reestablished the sale of intoxicating liquors in officers' quarters, clubs, and messes at naval stations and of beer in men's canteens. The War Department is now permitted to open beer canteens on military reservations (7).

Never has the country seen such a let-down. When the President released the green light not only brewer, distiller, and saloon-keeper came racing down the street but track gamblers, bookies, and the loose generally. It opened what Mr. J. Edgar Hoover has called "the most terrible three-year period of criminal history in the life of America" (address at International Association of Chiefs of Police, Kansas City).

"THIS IS OUR STORY"

In the general rum-rush the Roosevelt family was well to the fore. Even before Repeal was an accomplished fact, ex-bootlegger Ungerleider had organized Distillers' and Brewers' Corporation (capital $7,500,000) with Mr. Dall, President Roosevelt's son-in-law, on the Board of Directors (8). Other tie-ups of the Roosevelts with the alcohol interests were exhibited by the *Saturday Evening Post* of July 2, 1938. Shortly after F. D. Roosevelt entered the White House, the fire insurance policy of National Distillers, one of the largest fire insurance policies in the world, some $75,000,000, was taken away from W. T. Shackelford of Baltimore and turned over to the President's son, James Roosevelt. In addition to this he was presented with the lion's share of the business of insuring liquor imports. This made him the biggest insurance man in America. It was perhaps meant to insure distillers against other things besides fire—against high taxation, possibly against a government monopoly.

Mr. Roosevelt's political intimate, Mr. Joseph P. Kennedy, son of an East Boston liquor-dealer, went with James Roosevelt to London. Contact was made with British Distillers, Ltd.

"Jimmy was regarded as something like an American Prince of Wales. He helped Kennedy to reach the two great positions which he now holds, that of Ambassador to London and that of premier Scotch whisky saleman in America." His appointment as Roosevelt's personal envoy to the Pope's coronation followed later.

"Kennedy was enabled to get a flying start in the whisky business with the aid of two enormous permits for the importation of Scotch whisky *before Repeal. These were brought in under medicinal permits granted in Washington.* When America officially turned wet, Kennedy was on the market with one huge shipment of Haig and Haig 'medicine,' and another huge shipment of John Dewar 'medicine'!"

After this one could expect anything of the Roosevelt family and when James Roosevelt, because of his moving picture relationships, felt it necessary to withdraw from this profitable whisky insurance business, his mother, Mrs. F. D. Roosevelt, was on hand to take charge of the directorship her son had resigned (*N. Y. Times* Dec. 15, 1938). About the same time son Elliot, radio magnate in Texas, telegraphed to Congress to kill the Johnson bill which would end liquor advertisement on the air (9). It may be added for completeness that Mr. W. Forbes Morgan, whom the distillers hired to head their Spirits Institute at an annual salary of $50,000, was not only nephew of J. Pierpont Morgan, but uncle by marriage to Mrs. F. D. Roosevelt.

"CALL THE JOCKY, CALL THE PANDER
BID THEM COME AND TAKE THEIR FILL."

That girls are "learning very young to drink" and thereby to make their little contributions to the Kennedy-Roosevelt incomes appears from the March 1937 Report of the Juvenile Protective Association of Chicago:

"Since January 1934 when the sale of liquor in taverns was licensed, we have been increasingly conscious of the menace of the taverns." (Chicago has now 9,012 retail liquor outlets with but 6,377 police to watch them!) "They have not only the evils of the old saloon but a host of new evils as well. To sell their liquor and attract patrons the tavern-keepers need girls, the younger the better. They are usually employed on a commission basis, drinking with patrons and inducing them to spend freely. One out of every twelve taverns has 'girl hostesses' " (the brewers' shocking degradation of two lovely words).

"These 'hostesses' soon lose any respect they may have had for men and 'play' every man for all the money he has. As long as they look attractive, which isn't for long, unless they are caught as victims of alcohol, narcotics, or venereal disease, which is often, they get along. Patrons are protected from observation by 'Venetian blinds' supplied without cost by brewers in return for purchase of their brand of beer. Young people frequent tavern back-rooms and engage in drinking, petting, and immoral dancing. It is no infrequent occurrence to see young girls as well as boys carried from these places too intoxicated to walk."

Mr. Walter Cromwell reported in March 1939 for the same Juvenile Protective Association on "the unceasing flow of complaints from parents, welfare-workers, parent teacher organizations, civic and business groups, church groups, and individuals,—complaints of indecent entertainment, of distribution of indecent literature, of fathers spending their earnings for liquor and gambling, of mothers keeping rendezvous with taverns while children suffer, of grave venereal threat to public health in tavern prostitution." So Dr. Parran (*Shadow on the Land,* p. 216) writes of "the growing (syphilitic) menace of roadside taverns and night clubs." (At the present time there are 21,600 groping and stumbling blind in the United States who owe their affliction to prenatal syphilis. "Cost and Loss from Syphilitic Blindness" in Reprint No. 110 from Venereal Disease Information.)

Mr. C. R. Cooper's "Designs in Scarlet" is written on the basis of Department of Justice material. He tells us that "cities, towns, and countryside are full of pitiless leeches who are fattening on the helplessness of our children. . . . Many keepers of hot spots seem to have assumed that all laws pertaining to morality, decency, and protection of minors were repealed with the death of the Prohibition Amendment. . . . There are more percentage girls and female hangers-on in one of the Eastern cities than in all the Atlantic Coast cities during the speak-easy period. A new low in the degrading of Repeal is a combination of bar and brothel in which girls act as bartenders, leaving the work when possible to engage in prostitution" (pp. 13, 98, 132).

The brewers could stop these revolting things by refusing

to sell their products to law-violating taverns. They never will. President Roosevelt could easily end them by making brewers take out federal permits revocable if beer were sold to dives, night-clubs, or brothels. He never will.

"We have a rendezvous with debt," says ex-President Hoover referring to his successor's rake's progress through our national solvency. But the rendezvous with drink is going to prove even more serious. What a contrast does Mr. Roosevelt offer to the statesman-president of Mexico. Mr. Cardenas is fighting not only clericalism, to which Mr. Roosevelt is so complaisant, but drink, gambling, and vice. He is working on a plan of progressive pro-hibition and, on the last Anti-Alcohol Day, shut up 1,600 bars. He has the measure of the alcoholic royalists.

" 'TIS NOT THE MANY OATHS THAT MAKE THE TRUTH
BUT THE PLAIN SINGLE VOW THAT IS VOWED TRUE"

THE ROOSEVELTIAN PROGRAM, NO. I

In his proclamation announcing the adoption of the 21st Amendment (Dec. 5, 1933) Mr. Roosevelt specified various items of policy which were to characterize the era of Repeal. Let us examine them one by one:

The first read: *"I call specific attention to the authority given by the 21st Amendment to the government to prohibit trans-portation or importation of intoxicating liquor into any state in violation of the laws of such state."*

Five days after his inauguration, Mr. Roosevelt had Congress convened in special session in order to re-legalize beer. But two and a half years passed and no word came from him, no step was taken towards the passage of an act to enforce this clause of the new amendment. When the Federal Alcohol Administration Bill was before Congress, July 23, 1935, Mr. Tarver of Georgia re-marked: "I have read this bill very carefully and find no pro-vision in it intended to carry into effect that of the 21st Amend-ment which prohibits the importation of liquor into dry states. The amendment (I offer) is in the exact language of the 21st Amendment (with penalties). I know of no reason why we should not vote to incorporate such a provision into the statute for the enforcement of that Amendment" (10). Yet,—the Tarver amendment was rejected 69 to 33.   One of the aims of the bill was stated to be enforcement of the 21st Amendment!

In the following month (Aug. 30, 1935) the special $1,000 excise tax, first imposed by the Revenue Act of 1918 upon persons manufacturing or selling liquor in dry states or localities, *was repealed* and another thoroughfare thereby opened for illegal sale. Not until June 20, 1936 *when the Presidential election was pending,* was "an act to enforce the 21st Amendment" quietly slipped into the Federal statute books, and signed by the President while the National Democratic Convention was in session in Philadelphia. *There was no debate on it in Congress.* The *N. Y. Times* referred to it *in three lines on page 30 of its June 21st issue.* The press is determined that we shall forget the whole subject (B). The politicians, too, evidently felt it best to let sleeping dogs lie. In this way they were able to say that they had fulfilled the promise in the Roosevelt party platform of 1932. *One clause of the law repealed the Reed "bone-dry" amendment which forbade personal importation into dry states.* The new law is wholly inadequate and in 1938 attempts made by the Lee amendment to make it effective failed (C).   All of which recalls President Lincoln's words of Oct. 11, 1858, in the Douglas debate, "If you withhold that necessary legislation for the support of the Constitution . . . do you not commit perjury?"

LOADING THE DICE

Mr. Roosevelt presumably aimed to delay the passage of this legislation until state prohibition also should everywhere be broken down.   The Federal Government set the pace by repealing statutes which protected American citizens and the nation's wards in Alaska, Hawaii, Porto Rico, the Canal Zone, and elsewhere.   In his testimony at the Tax on Intoxicating Liquor Hearings, Mr. Choate proposed, *and Mr. Roosevelt, it is said, was behind him* (*N. Y. Tribune,* Dec. 17, 1933, p. 5) that the United States government should collect the whole gallonage tax and distribute some of it to the states, adding "I would certainly say that these payments ought to be limited to those wet states from which the tax income arises."   Mr. Lowry (p. 54) "assumed" that this would be "an incentive to repeal their dry laws in order to get that revenue."   As this income, starting at 20%, might after the analogy of the estate tax rise to 80% of the internal revenue from drink the bribe, together with local license taxes, might well be decisive. Nor would it end there. At the same hearings Mr. Toll of the American Legislators Association urged that while one half of the gallonage tax should go to the Federal Government and one half to the states, *the state should give half of its share to the cities and towns that voted wet* (11).

Chicken feed for wet counties: nothing for dry ones. Chicken feed for wet towns: nothing for dry ones, in spite of the fact that they, too, are heavily burdened by the asylums, relief, prison, and other expense resulting from the drink traffic. An ideal method, certainly, to put a crimp in local option as well as in state prohibition.

The liquor men began working to wear down the people's patience in the few remaining dry areas. California voted all power of control and prohibition to the state, effectually estopping attempts at local option. In North Carolina, in spite of its magnificent dry vote in 1933, the legislature enacted in 1935 (at 3 A. M. without prior notice to dry members) a liquor-control law which allowed 17 counties to vote on the establishment of county package sale, thereby voting themselves out of the existing state prohibition system (12). A correspondent of the *Brewery Age* (April 1935, p. 22) wrote of this (desiring to be) Prohibition state: "I crossed North Carolina where beer if more than 3.2% was illegal. I'll venture the statement that every brewer in America, who could, by hook, crook, or secret rebate, get a distribution in North Carolina, was openly violating the law there. The brand I saw most carried the name of an individual who stands high, very high, on the National Code Authority. The second most popular brand came out of our national capital. I am told the same condition exists in Georgia. Our only excuse is 'everybody is doing it.'" As ever the beer way to change a law is to nullify it. Repeal legislation then follows. It's the method of Sir J. Bernard who, in 1784, in view of the approaching election, moved the repeal of the oath against bribery on the ground that it was merely an occasion for general perjury. Five percent beer is now legal in North Carolina. The law has been ham-strung.

In Alabama repeal was defeated by a good majority. The legislature then legalized liquor by local option in twenty-five counties, as in North Carolina. In Georgia and Arkansas the same procedure was used. In Tennessee the Crump machine forced repeal through the legislature by one vote over Governor Cooper's veto. In Illinois they are seeking to admit beer into 715 dry districts.

The *Brewers' Journal* (March 1935, p. 25) is perfectly frank about it. "We take the position that the brewers from New York to California or Minnesota or any other part of the country, however distant from Alabama (till recently a dry state), have an interest in the laws of that state as they relate to the manufacture and sale of beer and *this industry should not rest until every state in the union legalizes beer.*" They first opened breweries in old Prohibition states as at Minot, N. D., to make "non-intoxicating beer"; then attacked the law. The *Brewers' Journal* (Sept. 1935, p. 192) announced: "There are about 5,500 retail establishments in Kansas for the sale of beer that *have been licensed by the Federal Government*" (that is, by the Roosevelt administration). In 1937 these were legalized by the legislature on the ground that 3.2% beer is not intoxicating, the trick used for breaking down National Prohibition by the Roosevelt administration. Yet Kansas in 1934 had reaffirmed constitutional prohibition by 89,000 majority. So by devious political methods was the legalization of illegality secured.

These brewers recall the Greek admiral, Dicaerchus, who was wont to set up altars to lawlessness wherever he landed.

"SPREADING RUIN AND SCATTERING BAN
SPLASHING AND PADDLING WITH HOOFS
LIKE A GOAT"

THE ROOSEVELTIAN PROGRAM, NO. II

Mr. Roosevelt's second request reads: "*I ask the whole-hearted cooperation of all our citizens to the end that this return of individual freedom shall not be accompanied by the repugnant conditions that obtained prior to the adoption of the 18th Amendment.*"

Nevertheless the stomachs even of unwrung wets turn at the consequences of "the return of individual freedom." Mr. Clarence Darrow, erstwhile wet propagandist, wrote: "I cannot recall a situation that so tended to *invite* consumption of liquor. It seems as if I had never seen such display. There is nowhere any effort to place restrictions on sale. I do not believe legislation should *encourage* the consumption of alcohol. This is being done to an alarming extent" (13).

The country is deluged. In California a mere $10 license permits the sale of beer and wine to a consumer in amounts up to a barrel of 52 gallons of wine at a single sale. Barrel-houses have consequently sprung up all over the state (14). "Millions of jugs are in daily use, women ordering for the home. Cars drive up and put their filled jug in the rumble-seat" (15). Long distance beer trucks cross and re-cross the country as those sixteen with huge trailers, running from a Pueblo (Col.) brewery to points between Dallas, Texas, and South Dakota. The drivers are expert salesmen, paid $7 a day. The *Brewers' Journal* notes the advertising value of these trucks, their constant suggestion to eye and mind in their passing (16). The brewers have indeed discovered that they can transport beer in tank trucks from Canada to Florida with a variation of but 2% in temperature, enabling them to bottle and sell two thousand miles from the brewery (17). None are safe from the beer nuisance. Steam launches deliver beer to Alaska and the Eskimos are petitioning the Territorial Board of Liquor Control again to make it a crime to give Eskimos drink (18). They are after the Indian trade. The *Cong. Record Index*, p. 13, 1934, mentions Senate Bill 2892, "to allow the use of 'medicinal liquor' to Indians;" also after minors of the C. C. C. camps where 3.2% beer is allowed sale by the government on the ground that it is not intoxicating (19). The late Mr. Brisbane of the Hearst press even urged free beer at these camps at government expense (20). According to the Juvenile Protective Association of Chicago (1936, p. 10) parents are having to prosecute proprietors of school-supply and lunch rooms for selling liquor to their children, "a violation which in some cases has had most tragic results." Liquor men, indeed, "have no more mercy than milk in a male tiger." Mr. Sturges of their Distillers' Institute said to the T. N. E. Committee of Congress (Hearings Part 6, 2660), "I have complaints coming to me *all the time* of children's cocktail parties in hotels and taverns." Alcohol kindergartens!

Mr. Roosevelt is interested in the conservation of forests, top soil, waterpower. In his message of April 27, 1937, he said, "The greatest single resource of this country is its youth." Yet not once has he lifted finger to protect youth from the great danger of alcoholism. I judge the reason for this neglect can be found in his words regarding wild life conservation: "Into this we can enter heart and soul *because there is no political partisanship in an activity whose object is to preserve the life of our great out-of-doors.*"

No political dangers in protecting birds: in protecting boys and girls, very grave ones!

I would commend to Mr. Roosevelt the words of the eminent Swedish economist, Prof. G. Cassel, *when speaking for National Prohibition:* "The best political economy for Sweden is to fill the land with bright, active, healthy young people."

On the 28th of December, 1934, Mr. Choate announced a hearing on *tequila,* an alcoholic drink made from agave cactus. "It is believed that there is a substantial demand for tequila and similar distilled beverages among the Mexican population of the United States." He wished "to ascertain the extent of the demand" (12). Brewers have even gone so far as to introduce into the House of Representatives a bill to legalize curb-selling of beer to motorists on the streets of the nation's capital (*N. Y. Times,* July 25, 1939, p. 12).

MAKING BEER SLUTS OF AMERICAN WOMEN

Minors, Indians, and *women!* "To reach the women," writes *Brewery Age,* "we scheduled the advertising for the same days as the chain food ads which run usually on Thursday and Friday afternoon." On p. 20 they write that "nursing mothers constitute a large market" and describe the transformation of an abstaining woman into a lover of beer. "Every year millions of American mothers nurse babies. Imagine what an insurance policy on the continuance of the brewing industry the brewers could write if they could design advertisements to capture a considerable part of this market. It would be pretty difficult to dislodge an industry that had sold itself to American mothers" (22). They would be wet voters in local option contests.

So they set up The Modern Science Institute in Toledo (23) to dispense Gambrinized science and secured Miss Jean Stewart, trained in Boston University, and "one of the most accomplished newspaper women in the country," to get "the feminine slant" for the brewers (24).

The effrontery of the liquor men scared even Mr. Choate.

When Park and Tilford, distillers, published their "Open Letter to the Women of America" in the *N. Y. Tribune,* he called their attention to the Capper Bill forbidding alcohol advertisements (25). "The advocates of this bill urge it on the ground that advertising is increasing drinking among women. . . . You have only to continue for a short time the publication of such matter (to) build up an opposition to your business against which the friends of freedom and moderation will be helpless." A despairing article in *Harper's Magazine* pictures the effects of Repeal in women's faces already. It speaks of "ladies who become embarrassingly loose and even sluttish" under the influence of drink.

"One thing is certain—there is not a child who can bear the thought of his mother being even the most infinitismal shade altered by drink, *and that is what happens to the vast majority of women if they drink at all"* (26).

This was in 1936. Walter Davenport describes these ladies at a later stage, in 1939. The lascivious had become maniac. An attendant hired by a "souse-trap" (sanitarium for drinkers) to strait-jacket women in delirium tremens said to him: "Look at my nose. See that arm? Them's teeth marks. I been kicked in the stomach so often with number five triple A's that I gotta wear a special belt. When a lady gets the horrors she could lick a circus gorilla." "He showed me a ragged scar on his scalp. 'No more D. T. dames for me!' " (*Collier's,* Sept. 30, 1939) (D).

The effects of Repeal are indeed, as Dr. John Haynes Holmes says, working themselves out "like maggots in rotten meat."

CONGRESS TOUCHES BOTTOM

The low level to which Repeal has brought us is reflected in Congressional discussion. The whisky trust is tied up with the glass bottle manufacture. The representatives from Arkansas and Missouri (barrel-stave states) seek by legislation to secure a part of the container trade for the barrel men in spite of the fact that this would mean facilitating illegal sale. Containers are now the center of interest and not protection from the terrible protoplasmic poison.

"The minute you give them the right to peddle liquor out of a barrel," said Mr. Massingale in the House, July 23, 1935 (27) "you have a hog-wallow in every alley, in every little town in the country, and you will have around such a place every cheap gambler and bootlegger in the community," and Mr. Robertson "When we write into this bill permission for any little fly-by-night hotel or club to sell, by retail, liquors from barrels, we are writing a barroom bill." He can "sell indefinitely out of that barrel by drawing out a part of it and bringing more and refilling" (28).

Day after day the cooperage and bottle representatives in Congress wrangled over this bone. The 74th Congress was a worthy successor of the 73rd (Repeal) Congress.

The scourge of the French countryside is the *bouilleur de cru* —the home-distiller. The Roosevelt-Choate alcohol administration has paved the way for this personage in the United States. From a Treasury release, May 28, 1934, one learns that "farmers who possess home-made natural wine not exceeding 14% alcoholic content, produced from salvaged grapes of their crop last season, will be permitted to pay the internal revenue tax of ten cents per gallon on such wine and dispose of it through legal channels or . . . may qualify as wine-makers." Now mark the difference. Dr. Alexis Carrel, asked by the French government to suggest a program of national regeneration, gave as the first item, "The suppression of the liquor traffic as in Scandinavia," referring presumably to the prohibition of home distilling (*N. Y. Tribune,* Dec. 15, 1939). Since then the French government has taken this prohibitory step (*N. Y. Tribune,* Aug. 7, 1940).

THE ROOSEVELTIAN PROGRAM, NO. III

President Roosevelt's third request ran: *"I ask especially that no state shall by law or otherwise authorize the return of the saloon either in its old form or in some modern guise."*

In pre-Prohibition days it was the fashion in certain circles to speak with respect of the saloon. "It fulfilled an important social function." Dean F. G. Peabody of the Harvard Divinity School felt that "substitutes" should be provided for it before we could proceed to its destruction. (So gentle Mr. Gandhi. "I would die before I would kill (plague-carrying) rats. *We should by strict observance no less than by sanitation* prevent rats from breeding.") In an article in the *Survey* by the Rev. F. C. Laubach it was said of "the Church" that it had much to learn from this useful social institution. "Three fourths of the saloon's patronage are impelled thither by one of the finest cravings of the soul" (29).

When, however, the 172,000 drinkshops of the nation shut down not the slightest social disturbance was observable. Mr. Robert A. Woods, the Nestor of social workers, described how the home automatically replaced the saloon. "As soon as men got the alcohol out of their systems they began to rediscover themselves as domestic beings. The profoundly moralizing result was so wide-spread as to show its effects on the whole character of tenement neighborhoods" (30).

"NEVER AGAIN"

Now the curious thing is that after the saloon disappeared none could characterize it too harshly. Everyone protested with vehemence that it should never, never, come back. Governor Smith, saloon politician and Tammany sachem, described it as "despised of right by the American people" (31), and in his speech of acceptance affirmed, "I will never approve any law which, directly or indirectly, permits the return of the saloon." The fiercest wets in Congress pledged the nation on this point. Senator Copeland, speaking before the Tammany Society, insisted that "under no circumstances must the baneful evils of the corner saloon come back to haunt us." Senator Edge was certain that "legal saloons will never return. Public opinion would not permit it" (32). Senator Tydings was ready "to fight against its return with every bit of energy at my command" (33). Mr. Anderson of the Wickersham Commission declared the saloon "as completely a thing of the past as human slavery" (34). Congressman Oliver of New York proposed that "hereafter no saloon shall be maintained anywhere in the United States under the penalty of two years in jail," and if there was a wetter wet in or out of Congress than Mr. Oliver, it would be hard to lay hand on him (35).

In his debate with Senator Borah, President Butler declared that after Repeal, if it came, he would ask the state of New York ("and thousands and thousands would do the same") for "the absolute prohibition of the saloon" (36). Mr. Rockefeller had said the same: "The saloon must never return."

"HE KEPT US OUT OF THE SALOON"

As for Mr. Roosevelt, his words were: "There must be some definite assurance that by no possibility, or at any time, or in any place, the old saloon can come back" (*N. Y. World*, Sept. 8,

1930). This he reaffirmed in his Seagirt acceptance speech of Aug. 28, 1932. But our thirty-second President is kin to the French politicians of whom Henri Rochefort said: "Before elections they swing the sword of Brutus. In the Chamber they use it as a paperknife." Honest Senator Glass offered to the Senate an amendment prohibiting the drinking of liquor where sold, in order, as he said, to forestall "the return of the vile institution" (38). It was not understood why Democratic senators voted against this amendment until word came that President-elect Roosevelt had let it be known that he "supported Mr. Garner's unwavering demand that submission should not be complicated by emasculating amendments." (Yet he had written to Senator Wagner, *before his election*, advocating a constitutional amendment prohibiting the saloon. Lindley's "F. D. Roosevelt," p. 275.) When the time came he sat down and signed the Act for the District which provided for the licensing of 1,800 drinking-places, one to every 300 persons in the nation's capital (39).

THE PRESIDENT INTERVENES

President Taft once described the "infesting beer-shops" of his day as follows:

"The temptation to the lazy, *prompted by distillers and brewers lending credit,* forces upon the community saloons everywhere, because even in a hole in a wall a considerable daily income can be earned. The political machine of liquor-dealers wields, through the ubiquitous saloons, a vicious influence over voters" (*Ladies' Home Journal,* May 1919). Recently the Senate Committee for the District and the Commissioners of the District, attempted in some degree to check this evil of credit sales. Wet Senator Tydings spoke of "all sorts of disreputable concerns in the beer-selling business. . . . *(It) ought to be put on a cash basis* so that it may be controlled to a greater extent than is possible under *the extended credit system.* . . . Breweries have set men up in the business and *completely financed them* . . . until in their desire to have more and more outlets for the sale of beer they have pulled down the standards of every man in the beer business" (Cong. Record 1939, pp. 9355 and 9351).

Congress passed this modest measure of control. *Mr. Roosevelt vetoed it.* As far as I have observed this is the only time he has condescended to deal with legislation on this subject.

It is as when a demented man opens every water faucet in the house and resists all attempts to turn them off.

And the faucets of the nation as well as of its capital city have been tampered with. In 1938, on the very eve of Washington's birthday, House bill 8115 was slipped through the House. The report of the Senate Committee favoring it contained a letter from the Post Office Department (Hearings March 5, 1938, p. 2) to the chairman of the Committee, with these significant words, *"It has been ascertained from the Bureau of the Budget that this report is in accord with the program of the President."* This bill, if passed by the Senate, would have made every one of the 44,877 post offices of the nation an agency for the sale of liquor, by the mailing of half-pint samples. No limit was set to number sent, to frequency of mailings to same address, to age of those receiving, to number of fictitious addresses. Every home in the land was to be opened to half-pint pocket flasks of gin, rum, whisky, and wine.

WET INVISIBLE GOVERNMENT

THE ROOSEVELTIAN PROGRAM, NO. IV

"The policy of the government will be to see that the social and political evils that have existed in the pre-Prohibition era shall not be revived nor permitted again to exist," continued Mr. Roosevelt. *"Failure to do this honestly and courageously will be a living reproach to us all."*

The political evils of the pre-Prohibition era came from the political activities of the liquor men, now lined up behind you, Mr. Roosevelt. Mayor Kelly of Tammanyised Chicago may well have expressed their grateful sentiments when he said, "I'm for a third term for Roosevelt and a fourth and a fifth" (E). Their power before Prohibition interpenetrated our whole political life. "Regulated, unregulated, or absolutely prohibited, the liquor traffic is," insisted Mr. McAdoo ("The Challenge," p. 3), "the very heart and center of the spider's web of corruption, dishonesty, and dereliction of public duties, which has for so long undermined the effectiveness of popular institutions throughout a large part of the nation." "There was a time," said Mr. Borah, "when it was literally true that a man aspiring to public office, if it were no higher than that of member of the school board, had to go and bow to the saloon in order that he might realize his aspiration for the place" (40). After National Prohibition had largely broken brewer hegemony, Mr. Bryan, who certainly knew what was in the background of politics, said: "I have been in politics for about forty years and it is a great relief to have something else beside the liquor question to talk about when one goes to a convention. For years it was true in all parties,—the first thing to find out was whether the liquor men were in control. If they were you couldn't do anything except protect the saloon" (41). An illustration of electoral fear of these "liquor men," even during Prohibition, came from President Coolidge. In a message to Congress he had written,—"The American people very wisely outlawed the liquor traffic" but a telegram from the White House directly cancelled this sentence after it had been actually set up in many newspapers (42).

This sinister power is even stronger today than in the old days. Formerly the German brewer took the lead: now the Jewish whisky-truster runs neck to neck with him. National Distillers, the backbone of the whisky trust, is tied in by interlocking directorates, complementary stock interests, etc., with Adams Express, American Medicinal Spirits, U. S. Industrial Alcohol, Owens-Illinois Glass, Fleischmann Yeast, Canada Dry Corporation, and the enormous manufacturing and distributing concern, Standard Brands of the J. P. Morgan Co. (43) (F). National Distillers and allies are reported to be pressing the Federal Alcohol Commission to refuse permits to independent distillers (G). According to Mr. Landes, attorney for the New York wholesalers, "They have tried to usurp the wholesale liquor dealers' business by selling direct to the retail liquor dealers. They have even tried to cripple the business of the retailer by selling whisky to the consumers and, last but not least, are starting to invade the importing business. They sell retail to hotels, clubs, and restaurants" (44). Their ideal is a totalitarian business. This trust with its powerful interlockings promises to make anything like regulation or control wholly illusory.

"TRYING TO WIPE CLEAN THE NOSE OF THE LIQUOR INTEREST"
Congressman Dingell

The wets acknowledge it. Congressman J. J. O'Connor of New York said in the House, July 1935, "Some of us here who fought for the Repeal of the 18th Amendment would not raise one finger again to do the same, because the whisky trust has control of the whole situation" (45). Senator Lewis of Illinois warned these "masters of the whisky trust" lest they be wiped out again. Repeal did not license them "to continue the immorality, the vulgarity and the corruption they are initiating in the great cities" (46). The brewers' increasing power has gone to their heads also. They again flout laws. Anheuser-Busch was indicted Dec. 18, 1934, just a year after Repeal, for furnishing equipment to a chain store of 17 bars selling their beer exclusively (47). Yet in 1932, the year before Repeal, Mr. Busch promised the Ways and Means Committee, if allowed to brew beer again, "to do all possible to promote the cause of temperance by strict observance of the law" (H). "Temperance" is the last refuge of brewers as patriotism of other scoundrels. According to a Treasury release, May 23, 1935, the Ebling Brewery Co. of Brooklyn was indicted for furnishing equipment to 38 retail establishments. *Brewery Age* for April 1935, p. 19, remarked that the Code by which such trade relations between brewers and sellers were forbidden, "was the occasion of grand-stand play in the line of reform. . . . We all know how little has been accomplished. *Men who should have led the industry have been among the most flagrant transgressors*" (I). The United Brewers' Industrial Foundation proposes a plan to sell beer only to respectable outlets. It is alleged to be operating in seven states, all near-dry. It does not dare, or care, to go into really wet states. By backing groups of distributors it is building up what may become a powerful protective trade machine against state prohibition.

CENSORING LEGISLATION

They are again strong enough to dictate legislation. "Constant vigilance is necessary in federal laws," writes the Secretary of the U. S. Brewers' Association (49). "About 4,500 bills affecting beer were introduced during this session of the state legislatures. If you stop to consider that some of them ran to 100 pages you will observe the enormous volume of material that we handled. A daily letter was sent to members regarding this legislation."

At the Federal Alcohol Control Hearings (50) Mr. Choate described how the larger distillers and brewers controlled thousands of saloons in the old days. "That inevitably threw them into politics, inevitably led them to seek control of state and municipal legislation, and brought about an unhealthy political ambition which, in my judgment, was one of the first causes of Prohibition." To obviate the return of such conditions a federal permit system was instituted as a warning and preventative against law violation. As Mr. Choate truly said, "The proposed revocation of permits of those selling in dry states would be more effective than criminal procedure." Section 317 also provided for the forfeiture of brewery permits in the event of flagrant or wilful removal of beer for sale without payment of tax. But the brewers will brook no control even for the protection of national revenue. "The brewers refused to agree to this provision," were the haughty words of brewer Bruckmann, former chairman of the Brewers' Code Authority. They sent members to Washington. "No committee appearing before a Congressional Committee ever represented such a large percent of the industry," said brewer Ruppert at the Los Angeles Brewers' Convention, and added dryly, "The bill enacted was without permit provision for brewers. This Association properly may claim credit for the protection of the industry from much adverse legislation" (51). Also for obtaining favorable legislation as when brewers' bonds were reduced 50% (52). Since then the Federal Alcohol Administrator, Captain Alexander, has repeatedly asked that the brewers be put under permit (*Brewers' Journal,* Jan. 1938, p. 40). A word from Mr. Roosevelt to Congress would bring this about. It remains unspoken.

PROPOSED POLITICAL MOBILIZATIONS

"Help must be given," wrote the *Brewers' Journal* (Jan. 1936, p. 25) "to the several hundred thousand . . . retailers whose aggregate contacts run into several million each year . . . several million voters to offset the balance of power that the drys held in the years before Prohibition." A gigantic national body "to organize every retailer of beer as political worker on election day" is called for. "We deem it of great importance that brewers in each locality interest themselves in the attitude of candidates for Congress and state legislature" (*Brewers' Journal,* Sept. 15, 1936, pp. 26, 29). The *American Brewer* (October 1938, p. 12) agrees: "Every unit of the brewing industry should know the attitude of every man standing for public office in the coming election and in every other election. . . . And having obtained the information every unit should use all legitimate means to help those who hold liberal views. . . . Investigation will uncover avowed enemies of the industry. . . . The first step in doing so is the job of checking up (so) as to reduce it to a system. . . . If brewers will inaugurate a candidate checkup system and keep it up from year to year, it should follow, as a matter of course, that the major political parties will be quick to give additional consideration to the power and influence of the industry."

The Yale law professor, Mr. Sturges, as head of the Distillers' Institute, outlined a program of reform. Article 2: "Companies would be required to discontinue most of their present public relations and political activities" (*Business Week*, Oct. 28, 1939). So they were in politics after all! When these distillers were brought before the Temporary National Economic Committee in Room 318, Senate Building, it came out that their operations were financed by a levy of $2 per thousand for all sales by distilleries, a sizable fund amounting to $1,246,610.60 in five years (T. N. E. C. Hearings Pt. 6,2651). Their technical adviser denied lobbying. "They conveyed information to legislators only to urge that such legislation be passed as was strictly in the public interest . . . they advised wise legislation" (pp. 2640, 2633). Yet one cannot but believe that they, as well as the brewers, were working, while President Roosevelt held his hand, to liquidate remaining state prohibition laws and to prevent higher taxation.

. . . .

The old organizations of allied trades are being revived in the National Institute of Manufacturers and Distributors (Nat'l Press Bldg., Washington) to help finance political fights. The *Brewers' Journal* of May 1936 gives names of some members: "Owens-Illinois Glass, Kelvinator Sales, Atlas Copper and Brass, Crown, Cork and Seal, Johns-Manville" and other important firms besides cooperage, malt, beer-machinery, and similar firms.

"If the National (Brewers) Association has to go into politics so be it," chimed in *The Brewery Age* (Aug. 1935, p. 35). Into politics have they gone according to their own confession. *The Brewers' Journal* for July 1935 (p. 24) described their activities in a Georgia campaign. Four advertisements were put weekly in the

258 country newspapers of the state; outdoor posters put in 225 locations; 50,000 auto-bumper strips with the words, "Vote for free school books May 15, 1933," distributed. They are putting money into local option fights (53). Congressman Berlin describes how he was defeated in the Pennsylvania primaries: "W. P. A. workers, a bunch of howling hyenas, were loaded onto trucks and carted to the polls to vote against me, and 500 barrels of free beer from Guffey-controlled breweries were distributed at my opponents' rallies" (54). In California, according to Mr. Seldes (*Freedom of the Press*, p. 120), the brewers were found to be campaigning alongside of big business against Upton Sinclair. The California Newspapers' Publishing Association is charged with taking money from the California Brewers' Association to pay for the preparation and printing of articles to this end. This propaganda came *nominally* from "Steadfast Californians Associated"!

. . . .

The result has been the reestablishment of a great centralized political power. Mr. Lecky, in his "History of England in the 18th Century" (Vol. 1, p. 479), declared the coming of gin-drinking "the most momentous fact of the 18th century, incomparably more so than any event in the purely political or military annals of the country,—the main counteracting influence to the moral, intellectual, and physical benefits that might be expected from increased prosperity." If things continue along Rooseveltian pro-alcohol lines this may become sooner or later the case with the United States. The brewery octopus was near death during Prohibition. Now it claims to be the seventh largest industry in the country. It has been fed as fattening swine are fed, by relief spending, defense spending, and other indirect largess. "We are beginning to feel the effect of defense spending. . . . We should take advantage of this opportunity to the fullest extent" (*Am. Brewer*, March 1941). . . . "Whisky is in for some mighty prosperous days. Never before since Repeal have we seen as plentiful days as we now are enjoying. Payrolls are at record peaks" (*Mida's Criterion*, July 1941, p. 7) (J).

"It is quite clear that the government is anxious not to interfere with the brewery industry," continues the *American Brewer* (July '40:15). "In the White House and at the Capitol there is a keen recognition of the fact that the brewers . . . pay into the Treasury each year approximately a half billion dollars." When, however, the proposal was made that they share with the government their defense-spending prosperity by submitting to an extra dollar per barrel beer tax, their political friends in the Roosevelt administration rallied in protest. Messrs. Henderson and Eccles, presumably representing the President, appeared before the Ways and Means Committee in opposition. They were supported by the Secretary of War (in civil life law partner of Elihu Root, brewers' attorney) and by the Secretary of the Navy. Yet the matter lay altogether outside the official province of these gentlemen.

Of this action the President of the United States Brewers' Association said: "This is one of the most important developments of the brewery industry since the relegalization of beer. It is a recognition by the Ways and Means Committee of the partnership that exists between the brewery industry and the government and the economic necessity of maintaining this partnership on a sound business basis" (i.e. low taxation) (*Am. Brewer,* July 1941). (American beer tax $6 a barrel: English, 165 shillings per standard bbl. as against 80 sh. before the present war and 7 sh. 9d. in 1914 [*American Brewer,* April 1941, p. 39]).

The Wet House is seemingly doing all in its power to build up this mighty parasitic enemy of good government, clean politics, and social welfare. "Since Sept. 9th," says the *American Brewer* (Sept. 1941), "the brewing industry has been enabled to *a preference rating A-10 as a food-processing industry. It is now one of the essential industries. . . . The brewers have now a strong voice in matters that concern them,"* and on p. 44, *"the position (has) been taken by the Administration that beer is essential to maintaining the morale of the army."*

KEEP KEGS ROLLING, KEEP STEINS FLYING
KEEP BEEROCRACY FROM DYING

Pearl Harbor illustrated the indispensability of beer for "morale." One hour after the Japanese planes appeared, all Honolulu drink shops were closed by martial law (K).

Beer attacks the kidneys and preeminently the heart, making men short-breathed and corpulent. It is the pace-maker for venereal diseases. The first selective draft threw out 57,000 men, or 4% of all, because of these infections. Parran and Vandelehr have told us what has happened since to our clean citizen army. We may be sure that the obscene flood of beer, which has drenched that army, has played its part in sending multitudes of soldiers, poisoned with syphilis, to hospitals. Yet President Roosevelt, when he drew the first draft number at the fish bowl in Washington, had said, and it went over the great radio networks, "They must return to civilian life strong and healthy and self-respecting and decent and free." The *Brewers' Digest*, May 1941, brags of the prospect of fastening the beer habit on "millions" of army boys. Mr. Roosevelt talks of the importance of saving food, "an essential war material" (Jan. 7, 1942), but the brewers are assured that brewing of grain will not be interfered with. Same story from England. According to Churchill, workers in British heavy industries are in dire need of protein food,—meat, cheese, eggs. But pork, beef, and poultry raisers cannot get grain enough and are killing off stock. Six hundred thousand tons of barley go into British brewery hoppers yearly, besides sugar, rice, and other foods, a large portion being brought across the ocean in endangered ships. Shipping space is used to send beer to troops in Iceland and hundreds of thousands of cases of American beer to British soldiers in Egypt, this last being paid for in lend-lease (*Am. Brewer*, Nov. 1941, p. 33).

It is even reported of a landing-field in New Guinea, "Everything—machinery, cows, guns, supplies, *and beer in thousands of cases*—had to be flown in by air-plane" (The *Spotlight*, June 1942).

The Canadian correspondent of the *Christian Century* wrote, July 29, 1942, "The reverse in Libya is giving emphasis to previous protests against the priorities granted to train-loads of Canadian beer which, through all the winter months, have been tying up cargo space for 18,000 sea miles from the Atlantic coast to the Suez Canal . . . cargo space that through the precious months of last winter could have been given to guns and tanks and planes sufficient to fill a train of box cars fifty miles long."

Britain buys and destroys her colonial banana crop since the more precious meats require the refrigerator-ship space (*Sat. Ev. Post*, May 16, 1942, p. 28). Yet there is a constant flow to America of whisky made in Britain from American lend-lease grain. How shipping-space in war-time is turned over to the drink-interest is stated boastingly in a full page advertisement in the *N. Y. Times* for Nov. 28, 1940, p. 48, "The British navy is mistress of the seas and the malt whiskies in King's Ransom Scotch are still being . . . *sent 30,000 miles around the world to mellow*. The rolling of the casks in the ship's hold (is) a mixing such as no human hands or machinery could make."

Meanwhile Lord Woolton, English food administrator, warns his countrymen against feeding birds!

Three thousand lives were lost in Pearl Harbor. But in 1941 alone there were 20,000 accidents, chiefly in war industrial plants, which were fatal, and 75,000 which permanently disabled. Also 1,750,000 cases of other injuries (*Life*, April 6, 1942). Careful German factory studies have established a close nexus between drink and factory accident. "It is at the bars and pubs that the enemy gets most of his information," reports Lieut. Clairmonte of the British Naval Intelligence. "A word of warning from a bartender and a ship might be saved, or a whole convoy sail unmolested."

Housewives are asked to surrender aluminum utensils, but the brewers retain their aluminum beer barrels. Honest distributors cannot get tires but brewery trucks were able to secure them long after others, indeed, until public protest forced the Administration's hand. In every direction national defense is hampered by these German-American *Herrenvolk*. In President Wilson's war they were liquidated; in President Roosevelt's they are given all kinds of privileges and priorities. Thus after 60,000 tons of virgin metal had been allocated for their use, the War Production Board, by Order M-72-A, allowed them to help themselves to 100,000 additional tons of scarce steel and tin scrap salvaged in the nation-wide collection campaign. When the Tin-scrap Section Chief protested, he was demoted and both press and radio have been silent about the matter. His successor appealed (Oct. 18 radio comment) to housewives to use one less can of can-goods per week in order to help out the tin famine!

How can one explain these idiocies, these military, hygienic, economic paradoxes?

They are presumably the ultimate out-workings of brewery political power based on campaign contributions, political organization, deliverable vote, secret deals. Henry George once said that there was as little "democracy" in New York city, because of brewery control, as in Constantinople. Lord Randolph Churchill, father of the present beer-friendly Churchill, compared the ominous liquor power of England to a Prussian army in the heart of Britain (Life, Vol. 2, p. 398). Marshal Petain, desperately trying by partial prohibitions to save France from alcoholic death, is blocked by *"electoral considerations"* according to a *N. Y. Times* correspondent, *"for the liquor lobby is counted among the most powerful in France"* (*N. Y. Times*, Aug. 7, 1940, p. 10).

For the first time in American history the alcohol-political underworld appears to have reached the top in a Washington administration. (Cf. quotation from a liquor news-letter in *In Fact*, June 29, 1942, "In Georgia and Louisiana the vice and booze rings had a political pay-off *that worked right up to Washington*.") As a symbol of this triumph we can perhaps point to Secretary Ickes' plan to make of the site of one of the earliest breweries in America (on Tinicum Island) a National Park reservation, like those at Valley Forge and Gettysburg. The old brewery is to be reproduced (*Am. Brewer*, May 1940). "It is time for the brewing industry to have done with the idea that it is a business by sufferance. . . . It is a beverage of national respectability served to royal visitors at the White House" (*Am. Brewer*, Jan. 1941).

ROOSEVELT AND REPEAL
(Section Two)

"No one can recall a President whose words are so completely quotable against himself, whose pre-election speeches so sharply contrast with his post-election performances" (Frank Kent, "Without Grease," p. 175).

THE ROOSEVELTIAN PROGRAM, NO. V

Mr. Roosevelt's Repeal proclamation continued, *"The objective we seek through a national policy is the education of every citizen toward a greater temperance throughout the nation."*

We were told to "educate rather than to legislate," as if legislation could not be made the most effective form of education (L). The promised education has been mis-education *to* drinking, mass suggestion on an unparalleled scale. Beer signs and beer sale broke out in 1933 with the universality of a visitation of locusts and the plague continues and grows. *The Brewers' Journal* of Feb. 1935, p. 33, announced: "Beer goes on the radio in a

big way with the aid of Batten, Barton, Durstine and Osborn,
Adv. Agents (Bruce Barton). Six million radio listeners tuned
in to the eight New York stations. For three days preceding the
broadcasts, generous-sized newspaper advertisements announced
the show. These papers included every important English-speaking daily and as many foreign language newspapers. Total circulation fifteen millions." Mr. Durstine, who has charge of this
beer advertising, appeared at the conference on advertising called
by the Federal Alcohol Control, to oppose limitations on alcohol
advertising: Mr. Barton visited the 1939 Brewers' Convention and
chided them on their backwardness in advertising: "Soap men
spend twice, the cigarette industry 500 times, as much" (*Brewers'
Journal*, June 15, 1939, p. 90). The education is a deceptive one
as when Anheuser-Busch discussed "Health themes in beer" (55),
or when Schlitz in his "vitamin D advertising campaign" explained
that Schlitz beer "will prevent colds and ills" (56).

"Visualize a family group," wrote the *American Brewer*
(Feb. 1938, p. 26), "about the radio receiving-set, listening to a
program. This is the advertiser's ideal, the family group in its
moments of relaxation, awaiting a message. Nothing is equal to
this in any form of advertising. That is why radio offers such outstanding opportunity for the brewer. . . ." A display of wine
propaganda photos was placed in the lobby of the San Francisco
Public Library and the distillers' organ *Mida's Criterion* (Dec.
1937, p. 15) described it as "a subtle bit of educational work because some 15,000 men, women, and children enter the main
public library every day. *We should take advantage of every opportunity like this to inform the younger generation.*"

The Expositions of 1939 were exploited. "Twenty million
will come to Treasure Island. Instead of hunting up wine-drinkers
in the different states they will drop in at their very doors" (*Mida's
Criterion*, 1938). One great bar at the New York Exposition was
announced as "205 feet of mahogany over which beer will be dispensed, the longest in the world." Two hundred and five feet of
bar-flies, a Rooseveltian Repeal exhibit at the Exposition.

Ten liquor companies spent, in 1936, $3,523,560 in magazine
advertising (*Mida's Criterion*, Feb. 1937). In *Mida's Criterion*
(Nov. 1937) an advertisement declared:

"Think! During the year 1917, 1,715,500,000 Seagram advertisements were printed in newspapers alone.

"Think! Seagram's Christmas promotion will reach over seventy million in large size newspaper advertisements and twelve million in national magazine readers.

"Think! The public during the past three years has bought over 110,000,000 bottles of one Seagram brand."

Seagram's is controlled by ex-bootleggers, the Bronfman brothers. They have had planes towing banners 200 feet long, trailing through the New York skies, "500 miles of visibility," flashing by day and by night, "Say Seagram's and be sure." Same operations in Chicago heavens (*Mida's Criterion,* Sept. 1937, p. 105).

DESTROYING AND FALSIFYING ANTI-ALCOHOL INSTRUCTION

The only power that can counteract this mis-education is the national government. But Mr. Roosevelt's words, "The objective we seek through *a national* policy is the education of every citizen toward a greater temperance," meant nothing and were meant to mean nothing. Thus when an anti-alcohol film of strictly scientific character was offered for use in C. C. C. camps it was rejected with scorn.

The wets are seeking to eliminate what little anti-alcohol education is now given to children in the schools. Repeal Associates, the old Stayton-Du Pont outfit, announce that "their work in 1939 will be to break the strangle-hold which the drys have on our public schools." They would base their agitation on the ancient report (beloved of the brewers) of the Committee of Fifty. They are establishing "listening posts" over the country for the furtherance of this and other schemes. To secure the right kind of alcohol science for the school children, a Commission of Scientific Investigation of the Effects of Alcohol has been formed. By the brewers? Oh no! By the National Institute of Manufacturers and Dealers, manufacturers of bottles, corks, cooperage, beer machinery, etc. (One member, Owens-Illinois Glass, recently filled an order of fifty million beer bottles from brewer Bohannon of Cleveland.) So the Institute is not really as neutral as its name would imply. It proposes to enlist scientists, physicians, educators, and clergymen "for the guidance of the young, so that as they approach manhood and womanhood they will understand the place and use of alcoholic beverages." They too would correct "the unwholesome effect on our general national well-being of what is taught in our public schools" (57).

Apparently in line with these programs, the United Industrial Brewers' Foundation has secured from the Director of Applied Physiology at Yale a definition of intoxicity: "One can drink on an empty stomach a quart and a half of ordinary beer without being intoxicated" (58). The Yale discovery is characterized by the *American Brewer* (Nov. 1938) as "the greatest forward step we have made."

Only safe beer science is to be countenanced. When it was learned that the American Association for the Advancement of Science had set a committee for the study of all phases of the alcohol problem, the *American Brewer* wrote indignantly:

"Let the brewery industry investigate this project for which there has been no spontaneous public demand, and which may or may not do good. If the industry finds that the proposed investigation is not necessary, then it is very important to oppose it and lend every effort to prevent this waste of time and money."

"Beer needs no defense," is the device which appears on the cover of every issue of the *Brewer's Journal*. It appears to mean, "Beer allows no criticism."

By legislation specifically allotting liquor taxes to the support of public schools and state universities, educators are put into an embarrassing position in the matter of anti-alcohol instruction. That is the gold muzzle. But the brewers would clamp on an iron one, too. "The Brewers' Association, on its official letter-head, sent an individual personal letter to every member of the New York State Legislature, practically demanding that they support a bill which, to a large extent, would have suppressed free speech on the liquor question, and would therefore have violated the First Amendment to the Federal Constitution" (American Business Men's Research circular).

They are aiming at the suppression of anti-alcohol education over the radio. The *American Brewer* writes (July 1939): "From Washington comes a report that the Communications Commission is considering the propriety of exercising restraint over those who use the air to combat the sale of beverages having an alcoholic content. The information is like the first signs of dawn after a long night. . . . Why should not the malt beverage industry have the same protection against injustice over the air that is accorded other industries? Breweries came into operation only with the seal of government approval."

.   .   .   .

"It is through the boys of today that we hope to see a sound and everlasting Prohibition worked out in this country," said Dr. Charles Mayo, the great surgeon. The drink men would forestall him by capturing the boys. Thus the Seagram distillery, Louisville, in 1939 awarded ten scholarships to graduates from Louisville High Schools, each of $250 and running through four years of college study, "that the (recipients) may be better qualified to accept positions in the company." The liquor press urges other corporations to do the same in order to build up liquor defense. Announcement also comes that a director of the American Distilling Company has been made one of the directing heads of the 39,526 Boy Scouts of New York City. That ought to check anti-alcohol instruction among them.

THE ROOSEVELTIAN PROGRAM, NO. VI

"We have undertaken new methods. It is our task to perfect, to improve, to alter when necessary" (President Roosevelt before the Federal Council of Churches).

The masks began falling even before Repeal was accomplished. In a hearing before the Federal Bar Association, Nov. 20, 1933, Mr. Pierre S. Du Pont proposed removal of restrictions at drinking bars and on sale of liquor on Sundays, the opening of drink-shops until midnight and lowest possible taxation (60). About the only restriction left would be the Du Pont cellophane winding bands on whisky bottles. Yet in September 1930 Mr. Du Pont's published plan "for distribution and control of intoxicating liquors" called for no saloon "by any subterfuge"; local option; sales by private monopoly, the state controlling and fixing prices, and dividends limited to 6%; purchasers licensed, their licenses being revokable on complaint of relatives; no sale by glass, only in sealed packages; sales to individuals limited; number of sales-places fixed at one in 5,000 of population; no advertising.

Mr. Choate wanted no "systems," Swedish or other. "His arguments against the politics-breeding state liquor monopolies and annoying state regulations as to where, how, and when, and how much, people can drink," said the *N. Y. Times,* "are full of the seeds of wisdom" (61). *Ochs locutus est!* But the *Times* did not speak that way before Repeal. "Strict control" was then our only hope. Mr. E. L. Martin of Harper's had written: "A large proportion of existing wets are hardly less concerned to lessen the evils of alcohol than the drys are" (62). They forgot their concern after they had destroyed the Great Amendment. The A. A. P. A. and its sister organization dissolved immediately. Yet it had told us that "the Association hopes to aid the states to set up good systems of control which will promote temperance." This is the more regrettable in that one of its leaders, banker Grayson M. P. Murphy, had explained that "much really earnest consideration had been given to the subject. The state plans that would be adopted would be intelligently and really prayerfully thought out" (63).

Mayor LaGuardia would seem to be in a position to initiate some of the paper reforms which he thought so much better than Prohibition when he was Congressman LaGuardia (limited dividend drink corporations, damages paid by drink-shops where the last drink was taken, etc.) (64). He is silent. President N. M. Butler shows the same Mussulman indifference. He had told us that "there is no difficulty with the social problems which arise from the liquor traffic" (65) and proposed for New York "sale of liquor under government control in limited quantities and in sealed packages for private and domestic use. In the state of New York we could accept, obey, and enforce that law." It is safe to say that he will never lift a finger to realize his program.

"Control" has long since been given trial under the best auspices and has ignominiously failed. Secretary Daniels described (1930 Prohibition Amendment Hearings, p. 922) the Dispensary at Raleigh "honestly conducted and supervised by men of the highest character who accepted the control from sense of public duty. Never open at night, hours of sale short, no sale to minors, no advertising, large sums turned into the public treasury. Yet it grew to a monster and was closed by the very men who had started it." At the same hearings Secretary Roper gave a shattering and detailed account of the breakdown of control in South Carolina dispensaries. Control is indeed "a good horse in the stable but an arrant jade on a journey."

PRESIDENT ROOSEVELT'S CONTRIBUTION TO CONTROL

It was the national government which should have taken the lead in control and it was expected so to do. The Federal Alcohol Control Administration was established under provisions of the National Industrial Recovery Act *before Repeal,* as if to reassure voters regarding conditions after Repeal, if enacted. When Repeal came the F. A. C. A. was succeeded by the Federal Alcohol Administration (June 26, 1936), the word "Control" being dropped as the thing itself was. Congress meant it to be an independent agency composed of three members. Mr. Roosevelt never appointed more than one. "Since his commissioners were never chosen the actual administration of the Commission never came into existence" (*American Brewer,* Aug. 1940, p. 13). Retailers and state stores were exempted from required permit: also brewers who, because of their congenital lawlessness, should, before all others, have been bridled. According to Senate document 186 (76th Congress) *only seven cases of annulment occurred in its entire history and suspension cases tapered off to a total of 31 in 1938,* "a surprisingly sparse number," indeed, as the investigating committee states (p. 16). How indulgent it has been appears from the fact that, "as a matter of policy, it has accepted a nominal offer in compromise, *usually $10,* in charges that an individual operated without a permit" (14). This is all but licensing law-breakers. Hearings conducted by the Administration were marked by an easy informality. "The representatives of the Administration, and the parties generally, appeared to be extremely friendly, often addressing each other by their given names when off the record, and frequently indulging in bits of facetious aside" (p. 21). Worse still, "the Federal Alcohol Administration was not immune to pressure of lobbying. Attempts to affect the agency's judgments were made *sub rosa,* not only directly by the lobbies maintained by the industry which are *among the most potent in the country,* but also indirectly through the legislative *and executive branches* of the government" (p. 32).

The chief activities of the F. A. A. were hortatory, sad pleadings with the liquor men to obey law. The hands of the Administrator, Captain Alexander, seem to have been tied, for he would have put brewers on permit, stopped radio advertising, made the provisions of the 21st Amendment effective, and ended all references to alleged tonic, food, and medicinal qualities of beer. The

F. A. A. might have been made an ugly engine of discipline as the brewers well knew. On the 4th of April, 1940, Mr. Roosevelt abolished it "in the interest of *economy*," ever Mr. Roosevelt's outstanding interest. The comment of the brewers is significant (*American Brewer*, Aug. 1940, p. 13 and Sept., p. 30):

"The Federal Alcohol Administration has been absorbed by the Alcohol Tax Unit. It is really ended. The immediate result will be that the principles on which the F. A. A. was set up independently, to supervise the social and commercial aspects of the industry, may be forgotten. . . . The alcoholic beverage industries are now to be viewed from the revenue-producing angle. . . . With the disappearance of the F. A. A. the brewers look for a relaxation of strictness in advertising control, as in case of therapeutic value claims, noted athletes, etc."

The same publication (Jan. 1940) reported that President Roosevelt hesitated to take this action "because of the social welfare considerations he stressed in his Repeal proclamation" but "over the course of several years undercover opposition to the F. A. A. increased."

THE ROOSEVELTIAN PROGRAM, NO. VII

"It is unfair to our neighbors if we maintain a pigsty on Main Street" (Mr. Roosevelt at Poughkeepsie).

In general the only place where Control has any chance is in states which are naturally dry and at the expense of Prohibition. This Mr. Harrison confesses in "After Repeal," a book sponsored by Mr. Rockefeller. In New Hampshire, Vermont, Virginia, and Washington he considers the state monopolies successful; elsewhere, "mediocre and poor." They are "tainted with party politics. . . . There is no margin of general sobriety favoring the monopoly states, no less illegal sales. Greed for revenue is threaded through the whole political system from the national government to the municipalities." The hungry newspapers attack the monopolies in the hope of advertisements from a reinstated private sale.

Where control is most needed, as in New York City, there is indeed an Alcohol Control Board. A picture of its workings was given on New Year's Eve, 1939. Instead of 4 A. M. legal closing, all-night licenses were granted to all and sundry in the saloon business at the uncontrolling price of $10. As a consequence a thousand extra police with a hundred sergeants were needed at Times Square alone, and practically all plate-glass windows on Broadway from 42nd Street north were boarded up. A pigsty on Main Street of astronomical proportions!

REPEAL AS A PREFACE TO MORALS

Ingenious Mr. Lippmann told us before the *debâcle* that "the essence of Repeal is not the restoration of liquor but the restoration of a suppressed power to regulate liquor" (66). A feeble "power" has it proved itself. The policy of surrender to law-breaking saloon-keepers prevails. In New Jersey an attempt was made to stop selling drink on credit. After three months it was dropped. "It diverted business from dealers who observed the restriction to those who did not," explained Commissioner Burnett (67). So the husband can not only booze his pay-check but run up an account payable from next month's. What chance has the housewife?

The bar was prohibited in New York but "flagrant violation" led to repeal of the prohibition. The condition for the change was that food should be the predominant feature of the establishment. But the present pseudo-restaurants are usually little more than saloons.

The *Brewers' Journal* under the title of "Rationalizing the Regulations" announced (July 15, 1939) a ruling of the Board of License Commissioners for Baltimore that restaurants no longer have to sell more food than alcoholic beverage. "The law was plain but the fingers of restaurant owners, every time they sold a drink, wandered to the food sale key of the cash register. Not more than ten percent of those holding restaurant licenses sold more food than drink." So the Maryland legislature "very wisely" allowed the change.

Prohibition of hard liquors in drinking places was adopted in California, Colorado, Connecticut, and Indiana. But everywhere the beer-shops sold whisky contrary to law. So they repealed it. Beer was to be our salvation, "the temperance drink." "If there is one complaint more universal than any other it is that against the beer tavern," "an evil influence," "a rendezvous for criminals," says Mr. Harrison.

Prohibition of advertising is "impracticable." Severe restrictions on hours of sale have failed. If enforcement of early closing is effective the bootleg evil crops up after hours.

Licensing boards issue for revenue ends far more licenses than are desired by communities. "Every conceivable method of limitation is now being tried out and not without attendant difficulties. . . . Investigations of the transactions of brewing companies in several states disclosed such facts as the receipt of financial assistance by beer-parlor proprietors from brewers in the form of direct loans, chattel mortgages, over-due credits, etc." "Of all the regulatory tasks in connection with liquor control the prevention of tied-house practices are the most difficult."

"If restrictions are not well-rooted in public acceptance they cannot be enforced even by specially competent officials," we are told. Where this is lacking we must put up with "minimum legal control." But where half the liquor sold is illegal there can be no effective control.

Now comes an important statement from Mr. Rockefeller's investigator.

A POST-REPEAL CONFESSION

"Legalization is a great boon to the bootlegger. He was exposed at many points and he had to pay large sums for the protection of his outlawed business. Now the business in which he is engaged is not outlawed. Only his participation in it is illegal. Formerly all alcoholic beverages, except a negligible quantity of medicinal liquor, was seizable as contrabrand goods. Now untaxed liquor alone is contraband and when it gets into the serving bottles of an on-sale licensee or when it reaches the shelf of a package-store dealer with its counterfeit strip stamp and label, it is lost amidst legal supplies. After repeal the bootlegger was quick to take advantage of the legal screens behind which he could hide while carrying on his business. In many instances former bootleggers obtained liquor licenses." Who believes they sell legal liquor only?

The local police cannot always be relied on to enforce the law against political friends, we are told. Hence the need of state inspectors. But Gov. Lehman (banker for Schenley's) is quoted in opposition to such "state government snoopers."

True, indeed, Mr. Harrison, "licensing of the liquor traffic is a formidable task." The difficulties not only "seem" but are "insurmountable." As Mr. Choate has discovered, "the problems of this industry are endless."

THE ROOSEVELTIAN PROGRAM, NO. VIII

"Our greatest primary task is to put people to work" (President Roosevelt's inaugural address, 1933).

But not to anti-social work. Two British Chancellors of the Exchequer, the Right Hon. David Lloyd-George and the Viscount Snowden, have recently declared alcohol waste to be a major cause of unemployment in that it diminishes consumption and hence demand for food and manufactured products. "Drink," says Mr. Lloyd-George, "sends our manhood to swell the hopeless shuffle of the unemployment queue and herds mothers and children, sickly with under-nourishment, into the miasma of the slum."

And Lord Snowden adds: "If the money spent on drink were spent on clothing and other useful and necessary goods, six times more employment would be provided. The only hope of materially reducing unemployment is to expand the home market. No greater contribution to the object could be made than by diverting the vast sums of money now wasted on drink to more useful channels of trade. By this diversion every other trade would be stimulated *and the back of the unemployment problem would be broken"* (68).

Mr. Roosevelt took the opposite course. As a consequence in 1935 the American public, according to President Cutten of Colgate's figures based on reports of the Department of Internal Revenue, made the worthless expenditure of some three and a half billions on liquor (Cutten, *"Meet a Prohibitionist"*). Mr. Roger Babson's estimate is five billions. The entire bill for recovery and relief expenditure for the year 1935—A. A. A. A., Commodity Credit Corporations, Federal Emergency Relief, Emergency Conservation, W. P. A., Grants to States, Public Highways, River and Harbor work, Resettlement, T. V. A., Emergency Housing and everything else—amounted to $3,657,000,000, approximately the Rooseveltian alcohol bill. Yet Mr. Roosevelt now talks of increasing the purchasing power of the poorer half of the nation (M).

"BUT FOR YOUR WORDS, THEY ROB THE HYBLA BEES AND LEAVE THEM HONEYLESS"

When one compares pro-Repeal economic prediction with the gray reality of 1942 one is simply amazed at the enormities of wet hokum. Listen to Senator Barbour introducing a Repeal resolution. "We could take this fast accruing revenue and dedicate it to the cause of rehabilitation. We would employ half of it for balancing the national budget. We might allocate the other billion on agriculture and thus pave the way for lifting more than nine billions of mortgages on farm properties. We could reduce our taxes on industry and real property and by so doing we would restore bond values to a more normal investment basis and facilitate the return of solvency to many closed banks. The timid would begin to buy. Millions would provide new buying power. The demand for raw materials of every kind would lift the burden of poverty from millions of persons throughout the land" (69). So another enthusiastic wet declared (Repeal), "like Aladdin's lamp of old can change immediately crime, corruption and crippled business into law-observance, order, and prosperity" (70).

More fiscal pipe-dreams! Congressman McLeod of Michigan declared that Repeal "would start a great chain of activity that would rejuvenate our entire business structure;" Senator Bingham that it was "the one thing that would save the country" (71). He had introduced his Repeal resolution as a rider to the Home Loan Bank Bill. "It will give the workingman a chance to buy a home" (72). As if it were not just this which had happened during Prohibition as indicated by the statistics of Building and Loan assets (73).

1910	$ 945,569,000
1920	$2,534,320,000
1930	$8,828,612,000

As a matter of fact Repeal, while reestablishing this criminal industry, has worked immense detriment to legitimate ones. The market for milk has been seriously injured: also the movie industry where the drop in attendance is estimated to be about twenty-five percent. This was foreseen by Carl Laemmle who, in a broadcast Dec. 24, 1932, said: "We have got to fight the return of the saloon as a pestilence. The movie business never took such a spurt as when the saloons were closed." The *Brewers' Journal* remarked:

"Coffee sales have dropped heavily. Coffee people are planning to popularize coffee to combat the inroads of beer. There is danger, too, from the large dairy corporations" (74). So brewer Ruppert: "The milk, ice cream, tea, and coffee industries are all competing with us and the dollar is after all only so big round" (75). There's nothing very abstruse in this parable of the dollar's rim. Feeding the bull is a poor way to fatten the herd!

Lord Snowden expressed his amazement that business men and unemployment theoreticians never attacked the unemployment tragedy from the drink angle.

THE ROOSEVELTIAN PROGRAM, NO. IX

"To provide a proper and much-needed revenue to the Government" (from Mr. Roosevelt's message to Congress, March 13, 1933, asking for a beer tax).

More needed by those from whom it is taken than by the government! Lord Snowden quotes Mr. William Graham, a former Financial Secretary to the Treasury and President of the Board of Trade:

"Let it be urged as a simple economic truth that no amount of subsequent revenue which is derived from the liquor traffic will ever compensate for the original mis-direction of the outlay. . . . There is not the slightest validity in the argument that the revenue derived is for one moment important. We could abandon every copper of it and earn a substantial financial profit."

"NOTHING IS EATEN AS HOT AS IT'S COOKED"
German Proverb

Dr. N. M. Butler prophesied a beverage revenue of $1,500,-000,000 *from 17 states alone,* after Repeal (76). Revenue from this uneconomic form of taxation from the entire forty-eight states is far below this estimate and the outlook is that the Treasury will have to fight to retain it. Congressman O'Connor tells us that before Repeal the understanding in Congress was "that the tax on whisky was to be about $6 a gallon. . . . Every committee of the wet group had that definitely in mind. . . . We went to the country arguing that revenue from liquor would balance the budget. Without that argument we would not have had Repeal in ten years" (abridged). "Now the distillers with their cry 'high taxes mean the continuance of the bootlegger' are the greatest obstacle to getting fair revenue out of whisky." "They have flooded this capitol with agents to keep repeating it. They have engaged the boys from the press galleries in their publicity bureaus. But current monopoly prices are far more likely than taxes to stimulate illegal operations." "Long before Repeal, the whisky trust sat down in the Kuhn, Loeb Bldg. at 52 William Street, New York, and agreed that they would maintain a price of about $40 a case. And Mr. Weiskopf and Mr. Jacobi and the others who used to sell whisky to the bootleggers during Prohibition, and who are now in the legitimate distilling business, proceeded to consider what the traffic would bear. If there were no tax at all you would still be paying the same price" (77). The brewers, too, beat the proposed barrelage tax of $7.50 down to $5 which meant a loss of $100,000,000 to the Treasury, these brewers who, as O'Connor says, "were so patriotic during the World War that most of them were interned or under government surveillance."

Yet they are not satisfied. The first convention of the U. S. Brewers' Association after Repeal called for a reduction of federal taxes and abolition of state taxes (78). In the *Brewer and Maltster* (pp. 38, 19, 1935) one reads, "The effort to reduce taxes on beer is under way in Washington and throughout the nation. . . . Rep. Mead of New York is going to ask a $1 slash off the present $5 (i.e., tax per bbl.). *Every little helps but we still favor a $4 slash off the present $5.*"

"We have the lowest tax rate (on spirits) in the world," says Commissioner Mellot, "only one eleventh of the English $14 per gallon, one third of the Canadian $7, and one half of most of the European countries." Yet the former leader in the Congressional wet *bloc*, Mr. Hull, now Peoria distiller, asks for "at least 50% reduction" (79) (N).

"I LEAP ON BOARD, NO HELMSMAN STEERS,
I FLOAT TILL ALL IS DARK"

THE ROOSEVELTIAN PROGRAM, NO. X

"The adoption of the 21st Amendment should give material aid to the elimination of those new forms of crime which come from the illegal traffic in liquor."

So quoth President Roosevelt in his message to Congress, January 3, 1934. Congress applauded. Repeal was hardly a month old.

Mr. Choate was made Federal Alcohol Control Administrator and given offices in the Department of Justice, done in silvery gray as a Whistler nocturne. He soon found that he had no silvery problem to deal with. Frightened at the uncontrolled deluge he went to Mackinac Island and appealed to the governors in session for help. The only plan against bootlegging he could think of was to reduce all license fees and taxes.

In April 1934 he was quoted as finding illicit output colossal. "This quantity is being consumed in addition to the entire sales of legal goods which, ever since Repeal, have not run far below pre-Prohibition figures" (80). He asked for greatly enlarged appropriations for enforcement. In order to cut the price of liquor and thus confound the bootlegger, he obtained Rooseveltian sanction for a scheme chimerical *par excellence* among the chimeras of the Roosevelt administration. Unrestricted importation of whisky was allowed for thirty days and unlimited manufacture of ethyl alcohol from sources other than grain. "F. A. C. A. officials said there were about 40,000,000 gallons of American type Bourbon and rye whisky in Canada. Another considerable volume was believed to be in St. Pierre and Miquelon, in the Bahamas, and in some foreign countries, manufactured for the American smuggling trade. It was understood that all smuggling vessels on the American coast could immediately bring their stocks of liquor to customs collectors and on payment of duties, enter them" (81).

This great whisky price-lowering drive took place at the time cotton was being plowed under and hogs killed in order to raise prices. A true brain-trust move! High-priced meat, wheat, and clothes, but cheap whisky! What good did it do? Eight months later, in September 1934, Mr. Gaston of the Treasury declared that illegal sale probably exceeded legal (82) and Mr. Morgenthau, Secretary of the Treasury, was reported as saying:

"I am giving half of all my time to this job of trying to suppress liquor lawlessness. . . . If we are to continue to progress we will have to call the churches in to back this program up. There will have to be a public conscience behind it and it is time for the pulpits of the land to sound a call to that conscience. . . . We bring the bootleggers into court and these judges let them go or impose utterly inadequate sentences. . . . What are the churches going to do about it?" (83)

An interesting commentary, indeed, on Mr. E. S. Martin's talk about "clericalism" and on Congressman Tinkham's excited charges against the Methodist Building in Washington! Mr. Choate touched "the very bass string of humility" in a similar appeal to "all honest drys" (84). He needed help. A hundred or more wet Congressmen, after "special favor in behalf of their constituents either in the liquor business or wanting to get into it," blocked his legislative requests and sought to force him out of office (85). His face, long as a horse's, grew steadily longer as the months passed. Finally in despair he threw up his position and the Augean stables were turned over to another amateur Hercules, Franklin C. Hoyt, winner of the $25,000 Hearst anti-Prohibition prize. He, too, shortly disappeared (O).

THE ADMINISTRATION'S FRANKENSTEIN

"And turns no more his head
Because he knows a frightful fiend
Doth close behind him tread."

The Choate regime issued a stamp strip for the top of liquor bottles. Violation of the regulation means $1,000 fine *and* imprisonment for five years (86), a drastic punishment which might well excite the indignation of the Choate "Voluntary Lawyers" who were so wrathy against the Increased Penalties Act of 1929. These stamps are counterfeited on a gigantic scale (in Kansas City recently a million dollar business in bogus liquor stamps was uncovered) and the blown-in bottles, in spite of the fact that both manufacturer and purchaser must keep a record of them, are constantly refilled in saloons by peddling bootleggers (87). The Treasury spent $851,959 to pay 850 men to go about 91 American cities checking up the extent of this illegal retailing. In some cities it reached 40% of the drink-sellers (88).

Mr. E. P. Flynn, studying the subject for the *N. Y. Evening Post* (Dec. 26, 1939), makes a higher estimate. "About half of the liquor poured from bottles of popular brands in New York City's 10,000 bars" is substitute liquor. "Hundreds of quarts are poured from a single bottle. . . . Extensive chemical tests are necessary to prove that a bottle has been refilled." The Alcohol

Tax Unit inspectors accept a fine of $10 when they find the liquor at variance with the label. This constitutes virtually a license to continue refilling. Mr. Berkshire of the Internal Revenue says that officials and juries are too busy to take up these cases.

We are back in the days of the old whisky trust, of President Grant's secretary, Babcock, of forged revenue stamps, refilling of tax-paid stamped barrels, bribery of revenue officers (*American Mercury,* Feb. 1935, p. 483). "The police are in cahoots with the bootleggers and the state is in the grip of the illicit industry," reports Alcohol Commissioner Burnett of New Jersey (89). The liquor commissioner of Delaware, Mr. Du Pont, acknowledges that "fifty percent of the alcohol consumed in our state is bootleg" (90). Congressman Curran says of this liquor "it cuts the membranes of the throat as it goes down. You can't drink it without losing your tonsils." It is as terrible as the legal whisky which Senator Clark calls "rotgut in beautiful bottles" (91).

On December 6, 1935, Mr. Morgenthau appeared at a press conference with a dark red carnation in his coat, saying, "That is in honor of two years of Repeal" (92). Premature bravado! Wet Senator Copeland a few months before had said: "Millions are spent for enforcement that does not enforce, for tax collection which fails to collect. Conditions are getting worse, not better" (93). "The persistence, year after year, of the immense number of seizures," said Mr. Choate, "shows that illicit distilleries are replaced as fast as they are seized" (94). As a consequence the report of the Attorney-General of the United States for the year 1936 showed that 52% of commitments to all Federal institutions were for violation of the liquor laws, while 69.7% of those offenders placed on probation under the terms of the Federal law were guilty of liquor offenses.

Yes, Mr. Roosevelt, it will take far more than your blithe phrases "to trammel up the consequences" of the 18th Amendment's "assassination."

"THE WILD ANARCHY OF DRINK"
Ben Jonson

THE ROOSEVELTIAN PROGRAM, NO. XI

"Among our objectives I place the security of the men, women

and children of the nation" (President Roosevelt's Message, June 8, 1934).

"They are ringing joy-bells now; they will soon be wringing their hands," remarked Walpole when war was declared on Spain. The murderous statistics from the automobile highways should be set to the music of "Happy Days Are Here Again" as sung in the 1932 Rooseveltian Convention, the great Stadium organ leading. One cannot blame the general public. The press has seen to it that the truth about alcohol should not leak out and even now, for payment received, is printing such shameful stuff as the 70 inch distiller advertisement in the New York newspapers of aviators sipping gin at a bar on an aviation field. Anyone with an elementary knowledge of the matter could easily have predicted what was coming. "As a practically important result of our experiments," said Dr. Hugo Schultz (Institute of Pharmacopy, University of Greifswald), "it is to be emphasized that even relatively small quantities of alcohol bring to certain people a clear decrease in capacity to distinguish red and green lights. This peculiarity of alcohol is significant when the clear observation of red and green is important for the preservation of human life" (95). Similar evidence dealing with every aspect of alcohol's action on quickness of perception has been coming out of laboratories for a generation. William Allen White is reported as saying that radio, auto, and movie have built up a line of defense which makes Prohibition no longer necessary (96). On the contrary the auto has made it indispensable.

"THE ROLLING ENGLISH DRUNKARD MADE THE ROLLING ENGLISH ROAD"

Chesterton

Withdrawals of driving licenses for drunken driving outstrip all other cases. Chronic offenders are being finger-printed. The *N. Y. Times* for Nov. 15, 1936 speaks of the various devices to impress them with the heinousness of their offence. They are sent to morgues to see the broken bodies of traffic victims, brought to hospitals to visit people they have injured, made to study pictures of dozens of particularly gruesome cases. The chief of the great Cook County Hospital, Chicago, Dr. Karl Meyer, describes his staff as working frantically for days over these victims and protests against this new burden which the heedlessness of man has brought on the hospitals (97).

One would think that safety councils and automobile manufacturers would lead the nation in the introduction of blood tests for drunken drivers. Perhaps they agree with the Irish Attorney General of Illinois, Mr. Cassidy, who thinks enforced blood tests would be a violation of constitutional guarantees against unlawful search and against self-incrimination! In any case they seem unwilling to cross the brewers. The *Brewers' Journal*, Dec. 15, 1936, printed the following:

"Many months ago we suggested that our national associations should establish contact with the officials of the National Safety Council,—that in our large cities, where they have a Speeders' Court, *an arrangement be made to stop the testimony of those accused, who always say, 'I had only a couple of beers.'* In our November 15 issue we told of certain posters sponsored by the National Safety Council in an apparent tie-up with Yellow Taxis, which were a libel on beer. We have had correspondence regarding this with a certain group (not brewers) and we have been advised that contact has been made with the National Safety Council with the result that *beer will get the break it is entitled to from that organization.* The details as to how it was accomplished need not be recited here. It is sufficient to know that SOMETHING WAS DONE" (P).

The National Safety Council denies this. They could effectively fortify their denial by starting a campaign in every city to introduce the Widmark blood tests.

The American Business Men's Research Foundation charges the drink interest with greatly expanding their pre-Fourth of July liquor advertising from year to year. This, first, to stimulate sales on the Fourth and make it a day of national carousing: *secondly, to soft-pedal the press reports of accidents.* Result in 1936 double the number of accidents in 1935 and an 140% increase over 1934 in spite of nation-wide campaigns for safety.

THE UNREPEALED PROBLEM

The 21st Amendment has already earned the derisive name of "The Drunken Driver Amendment." And we are but at the beginning.

Certainly this Amendment was "built in the eclipse and

rigged with curses dark." Not only are the hospitals filling with victims of drunken accidents but the sanitoria with the infinitely more tragic victims of alcohol habit. The statistics of such cases are mounting with ominous rapidity and there is a growing *clientèle* of women. Then there is the constant enlistment of alcohol chronics, destined to move about our cities for a brief few years. Prof. Gravitz of the Charlottenburg Hospital calls them "wandering corpses" and adds: "The physician knows from his examination what a man drinks. If the liver is sick, spirits; if the kidneys and heart, beer." Family drunkards and "the long drip of human tears"! One thinks of the children of this parent- age, "misery's yet unkindled fuel," in the light of such studies as Prof. Dr. Fetscher's "Criminality in Drinkers' Families" from the ten year catalogue of all the criminal families in Saxony (*Forschungen zur Alkoholfrage,* March, 1934, p. 24). He quotes Lenz on Bertholet's obductions of alcoholized testicles: "It would be a real miracle if a poison which can completely destroy the *Keimgewebe* would not also occasion modification of the *Erbmasse.*"

The millionaires of the Association Against the Prohibition Amendment used to rave about the "tyranny" of National Pro- hibition. Before many years the nation will be crying with Lord Byron,

> "The tyrant of the Chersonese
> Was freedom's best and bravest friend."

For, as Senator Borah predicted: "Your liquor problem (is) here (again) unsettled, undetermined, haunting the corridors of Congress and tormenting public opinion, insistent of attention and rapacious in its demands." The tide is indeed out and all the sewage and broken glass of Repeal offend eye and nose. But tides turn and, later, one will come roaring back to cover up again the unsightliness and alcohol squalor of the Rooseveltian era.

REFERENCES TO CHAPTER X NOT IN THE TEXT

1. N. Y. Times, Jan. 30, 1934.
2. N. Y. Times, Dec. 5, 1934, p. 18.
3. Cong. Record, Dec. 20, 1932, p. 793.
4. N. Y. Times, Dec. 27, 1934, p. 1.
5. Digest of the Women's National Democratic Club, March 1934.
6. N. Y. Times, March 8, 1934 and The New Dealers, p. 235.
7. Am. Brewer, Sept. 1939, p. 48.

8.   N. Y. Times, Oct. 17, 1933, p. 31.
9.   N. Y. Times, May 15, 1939, p. 17.
10. Cong. Record, July 23, 1935, pp. 12,183 and 12,194.
11. Tax on Intox. Liquors Hearings, Dec. 11, 1933, pp. 28, 33, 58, 244, 258.
12. N. Y. World Almanac 1936 and Administration of Liquor Tax Laws Hearings, May 13, 1935, p. 126.
13. Private letter to Dr. C. T. Wilson.
14. Brewers' Journal, Sept. 1935, p. 25.
15. Mida's Criterion, Nov. 1935.
16. Brewers' Journal, April 1935, p. 48.
17. Administration of Liquor Tax Laws Hearings, May 13, 1935, p. 154.
18. N. Y. Times, Dec. 6, 1935, p. 1.
19. Brewers' Journal, Sept. 1935, p. 67.
20. Brewers' Journal, May 1935, p. 23.
21. F. A. C. A. Release, No. 153, Dec. 15, 1934.
22. Brewery Age, Feb. 1936, p. 32.
23. Mida's Criterion, April 1935.
24. Brewers' Journal, May 1935, p. 29.
25. N. Y. Tribune, May 21, 1934.
26. Harper's Magazine, April 1936.
27. Cong. Record, July 24, 1935, pp. 12,264 and 12,265.
28. Cong. Record, July 23, 1935, p. 12,181.
29. Survey, Sept. 27, 1913, p. 751 and Overman Report, p. 363.
30. Annals of the Am. Acad. of Polit. and Social Sciences, Sept. 1923, p. 125.
31. Fisher, The Noble Experiment, p. 380.
32. Nat'l Prohibition Hearings, April 1926, p. 32.
33. Cong. Record, July 16, 1932, p. 15,663.
34. Wickersham Report, p. 90.
35. Hearings on Nat'l Prohibition, April 1926, p. 649.
36. Borah-Butler Debate, p. 17.
37. N. Y. Times, June 6, 1932.
38. Cong. Record, Feb. 16, 1933, p. 4219.
39. Cong. Record, Jan. 17, 1934, p. 790.
40. Cong. Record, March 16, 1933.
41. Law vs. Lawlessness, p. 115.
42. Hearst's Temperance or Prohibition, p. 351, & Mirror of 1932, p. 276.
43. Cong. Record, Feb. 27, 1934, p. 3403.
44. Tax on Intoxicating Liquor Hearings, p. 297.
45. Cong. Record, July 25, 1935, p. 12,202.
46. Cong. Record, Aug. 13, 1935, p. 13,409.
47. N. Y. Times, Dec. 21, 1934: Brewery Age, Jan. 1933, p. 83.
48. Modification of Volstead Act Hearings 1932, p. 36.
49. Brewers' Journal, Nov. 1935, p. 33.
50. F. A. C. A. Hearings, June 19, 1935, p. 10.
51. Brewers' Journal, Nov. 1935, p. 31.
52. Brewers' Journal, Sept. 1935, p. 64.
53. Brewers' Journal, Jan. 1935, p. 22.
54. Philadelphia Record, May 1, 1936.
55. Brewers' Journal, Dec. 1933, p. 92.
56. Brewers' Journal, March 1936, p. 25.
57. Brewers' Journal, Nov. 1938, p. 56.
58. Am. Brewer, Nov. 1938, p. 41.
59. Prohibition Amendment Hearings, Feb. 1930, p. 337.
60. N. Y. Times, Nov. 21, 1933, p. 15.
61. Editorial in N. Y. Times.
62. Harper's Magazine, 1929, p. 260.
63. Prohibition Amendment Hearings, Feb. 1930, p. 145.
64. Modification of Volstead Act Hearings, Dec. 7, 1932, pp. 232, 233.

65. Prohibition Amendment Hearings, Feb. 1930, p. 347 and Borah-Butler debate p. 17.
66. N. Y. Herald Tribune, June 8, 1932, p. 19.
67. N. Y. Times, Dec. 9, 1936, p. 11.
68. Lord Snowden's "Stop That Waste."
69. Cong. Record, July 8, 1932, p. 14,842.
70. Committee on Manufactures Hearings, Jan. 1932, p. 91.
71. Cong. Record, Feb. 20, 1933, p. 4517 and July 16, 1932, p. 1650.
72. Cong. Record, July 8, 1932, p. 14,848.
73. U. S. Statistical Abstract 1931, p. 279.
74. Brewers' Journal, Aug. 1933, p. 28.
75. Brewers' Journal, Nov. 1935, p. 31.
76. N. Y. Times, June 19, 1932, p. 19.
77. Cong. Record, Jan. 4, 1934, p. 92 seq.
78. The American Brewer, Feb. 1934, p. 18.
79. Mida's Criterion, March 1935, p. 28.
80. N. Y. Times, April 29, 1934, p. 1.
81. N. Y. Times, Jan. 11, 1934, p. 2.
82. N. Y. Times, Sept. 2, 1934, p. 1 (Sec. II).
83. Release of Methodist Board of Temperance, March 4, 1935.
84. N. Y. Times, April 20, 1934, p. 29.
85. Boston Herald, June 18, 1936.
86. Treasury Release, March 3, 1934.
87. Administration of Liquor Taxing Laws, May 13, 1935, p. 65.
88. Cong. Record, July 23, 1935, pp. 12,184 and 12,199.
89. Syracuse Journal, April 1, 1935 (quoted in Cong. Record Nov. 30, 1934).
90. Cong. Record, Aug. 13, 1935, p. 13,417.
91. Tax on Intoxicating Liquor Hearings, Dec. 11, 1933, p. 255 and Cong. Record, Aug. 13, 1935, p. 13,404.
92. N. Y. Times, Dec. 6, 1935, p. 28.
93. Cong. Record, Aug. 13, 1935, p. 13,418.
94. Administration of Liquor Taxing Laws, May 13, 1935, p. 68.
95. Pflueger's Archiv No. 164, pp. 274–294, 1916.
96. N. Y. Times, Nov. 12, 1933, p. (IV) 6.
97. Christian Century, Nov. 25, 1936, p. 1548.

NOTES TO CHAPTER X

A.   Repeal brought back saloons and Mr. Farley knows what drink means as well as Mrs. Roosevelt. He writes of the family saloon (*Behind the Ballots,* p. 13): "It was a saloon in every sense of the word, a constant source of worry to my mother. Like all women who came from poor circumstances she had seen a great deal of poverty and wretchedness caused by men's addiction to drink. She never lost an opportunity to advise me against the use of liquor in any way."

B.   This silence appears to be calculated. *The New York Times,* on the occasion of Senator Borah's death, devoted an editorial column and a full news page to an account of his career. Now Senator Borah was known to millions above all else as the champion of the dry cause in the Senate. His reply to Senator Reed of Missouri, Feb. 18, 1929, and his great address before the Presbyterian Assembly in Baltimore, May 30, 1926, were historic utterances. His debates on Prohibition with President Butler also attracted national attention. Yet the *Times* did not once mention this outstanding activity of his life in its editorial, Jan. 20, 1940. In the full page biography it found room for just thirteen words, "He took a prominent part in the submission by Congress of the Prohibition amendment."

Pressmen and President! Mr. Roosevelt has mentioned Prohibition *at least once* since Repeal (at the National Parole Conference, 1939). Of the drink question as a whole and of "Control" he says nothing.

C.   To break down the defences of the dry states has ever been the first line of brewer political strategy.   An illustration occurs in the *American Issue* for March 8, 1913, in a statement by Mr. P. A. Baker, General Superintendent of the Anti-Saloon League, which as far as is known has never been denied.   Four weeks before the presidential election of 1912, Baker called on Wm. H. Taft, to ask him concerning inter-state liquor shipment legislation.   The interview was satisfactory.   "Mr. Taft confessed the necessity of such legislation and expressed his belief in the constitutional right of Congress to remedy the conditions we were seeking to correct."   A year later President Taft saw Baker again and said to him, "You go ahead and have a measure prepared and presented that will in the judgment of your people remedy the difficulties you are trying to reach, and you will have no trouble at this end of the line" (meaning himself).

Mr. Baker continued:

"About a year after Mr. Taft's election, in conversation with one of the prominent Democrats of the country in which we urged him to greater activity in the interests of our interstate liquor shipment legislation, he replied: 'I am in favor of that legislation and shall do what I can to advance it, but you cannot have that measure enacted into law while Taft is President!'

"With some surprise I asked why he made that statement.   Whereupon he said (I quote from memory): 'A deal was entered into at the Chicago Convention at which Mr. Taft was nominated, that in consideration for the support of the Milwaukee breweries, which doubtless included others, no interstate liquor shipment legislation should be passed while he was President.'

"Though this man is a man of high standing and is not given to reckless statements, we nevertheless felt that his information was colored by partisan prejudice and were not ready to accept it.   Later prominent Republican politicians who were active in the Chicago Convention confirmed the statements made by this Democrat, some of them going so far as to say that the consideration carried with it a partial reimbursement of the President's brother who had furnished large sums of money to secure his nomination.   We have no way of personally knowing the truth of these statements but the sources from which they came justify us (in the light of the conduct of the President in vetoing the measure after the overwhelming opinion of leading attorneys as to its constitutionality) in making these facts known to our friends.   In the light of these facts the public must judge whether he vetoed this measure because he really felt it was unconstitutional, or to carry out a deal made for him by others."

It should be recalled that Mr. Taft *held back his veto until the last hour of the last day of the session of Congress,* apparently to head off passage of the bill over his veto. But Congress countered the manoeuvre by passing the legislation at the very last minute.

That Mr. Taft was not unwilling to play ball with brewerdom is suggested by his appointment of Mr. Nagel to his cabinet. Nagel was on the directorate of Anheuser-Busch,—a political nonentity, and without special qualification for cabinet position.

D. Women's fear of pathological fat is their defence against the brewers. The N. Y. State Department of Agriculture and Markets listed beer among fattening goods. "Alcohol is fattening. Avoid it in any form if you want to reduce." This was distributed by the Bureau of Milk Publicity. The brewers immediately succeeded in having it suppressed (*Brewers' Journal*, March 1936, p. 40).

E. District Attorney Thomas E. Dewey illustrated this on the air, October 25, 1939. The O'Connell machine, Albany, N. Y., as other corrupt liquor machines in Boston, New York, Chicago, Kansas City, and Jersey City, supports Mr. Roosevelt politically. Its head, ex-convict Dan O'Connell, operates it with the aid of brothers Ed and John. Its powerhouse is the Hedrick brewery. In Albany barrooms must sell Hedrick beer. If they refuse the city police and (mark it!) *inspectors of the Alcohol Board of Control* visit their places, "snooping, prying, and slamming their way about on the slightest pretext." They trump up all kinds of charges and delay renewal of licenses. But to those handling Hedrick's product the sky is the limit,—slot machines, "hostesses," all night sale. Hedrick tax assessment is half that of other brewers. This machine engages in ballot-stuffing and raises tax assessments of Republican voters.

It goes back to the beginning. Jefferson insisted that "nothing had corrupted the legislation of the country or the administration of the country more than the use of intoxicating drink" and that "if he were to commence again his presidential career he would make it one of the conditions on which he would nominate anyone to office that, at least as long as a man continued in office, he should abstain from intoxicating liquor wholly." Quoted by S. J. May, Address at Dryden, N. Y., July 4, 1855.

F. *N. Y. Times,* July 29, 1933, p. 1. Standard Brands, anticipating Repeal, will erect a building in Brooklyn for rectifying gin.

G. Congressman O'Malley says he was unable to get a permit for a cooperative distillery in Wisconsin for Wisconsin farmers wishing to distil their grain into whisky. "They have not the necessary business experience" (F. A. C. A. Hearings, June 19, 1935, p. 96).

H. Senator Goff read at the Hearings on Senate Campaign Expenditures, June 1926, p. 1496, "The brewers, as represented in the board of trustees of the U. S. Brewing Assn., submit the following proposal for consideration of civic bodies concerned with Prohibition enforcement. In case Congress will authorize the increase of alcoholic content in cereal beverages to 2.70% alcohol by weight, the manufacturers will themselves undertake, as a matter of trade organization, to see that all individual manufacturers comply with the limitation, and will furnish to the government all evidence, which their own trade activity will develop, showing violation by manufacturers." We have seen what a brewer's promise is worth.

How short-lived their penitence ever is came out in evidence by the Hon. Thomas B. Love before the Ways and Means Committee in 1932. The state of Texas had convicted its leading brewers in a sensational trial in 1915–16. Only a year after this utterly crushing exposure occurred the following:

"It is a matter of record both in the Texas legislature and Federal court, wholly undisputed, that in 1917 six brewers paid to the governor of Texas in currency in his office at Austin $25,000 each, as a loan, which each brewer charged off to expense, on his books, for income taxes. They testified in court that this payment was made because the governor 'had been perfectly fair with the brewery business.' One brewer said, '*In my opinion such an expense is an ordinary expense of the brewers' business.*' Another justified the payment of this large sum to the governor because 'The brewers made a good deal of money during the Ferguson administration' " (Ways and Means Hearings, Dec. 7, '32, p. 671).

I.   Schlitz and Co. was charged with 2,100 different violations affecting signs under the F. A. C. A. (Cong. Record, August 13, 1935, p. 12, 268).

"Does anyone believe that the liquor industry will ever police itself?" asks Mr. Alexander, Federal Alcohol Commissioner. In the near-dry state North Dakota where they are on their good behavior they have come as far as this,—retail dealers attached to the Wine and Spirits Institute agree to attack drunken driving with announcements over their bars offering "to accept patron's car keys and see the patron home and his car garaged" (*Mida's Criterion*, April 1938, p. 15).

J.   The government might well examine the extent to which poor-relief has become rich brewer relief. The Connecticut Citizens' Committee, Donald G. North, chairman, has inquired of selectmen throughout the state. It discovers in certain cases "an alarmingly high portion of the daily receipt of retail liquor and beer outlets to be made up of town relief checks" (*N. Y. Times*, Jan. 23, 1939). The county welfare board of Noble County, Minn., has ordered those receiving old age pensions and W. P. A. benefits, not to purchase beer with their money and has furnished to every beer parlor a list of such persons (*Am. Brewer*, May 1, 1938, p. 24). The New Deal has, in a way, and because of Rooseveltian Repeal, endowed the underworld. Mr. C. R. Cooper tells us that gamblers and liquor men agree that 20% of W. P. A. payments go to them (*Designs in Scarlet*, p. 308).

K.   The Roberts' investigation affirmed, "Except for a negligible number, the use of intoxicating liquor on the preceding evening did not affect their efficiency." But the *Chicago Sun* of Dec. 26, 1941, p. 4 quotes Mrs. Offield, wife of a navy patrolman, "*Most of the naval people* had been out the night before to parties and *we were all sleeping late.*" Federal

Housing Commissioner C. J. Peitsch of Honolulu tells us that booze debauchery was *customary* in Honolulu Saturday nights, and that service men were largely represented in it.

When the 428 drink-shops were closed it was clear again what Prohibition can do when it is not Mellonized. General Emmons is quoted in the *Honolulu Advertiser* of Jan. 9, 1942, "The labor leaders don't want liquor, the ministers don't want it, the workingmen don't want it. *All the army admits the present rule is good.* Nobody really wants liquor sold again." And Police Chief Gabrielson reports "not one case of sabotage, stickup, or murder since Dec. 7th."

But the liquor men wanted liquor again and sold it now is, after nearly three months of successful enforcement. Mr. Stimson, Sec'y of War, is a Wall St. wet. Behind Mr. Roosevelt are the corrupt political machines of the cities and the now powerful drink interest. What chance have the people's wishes? Yet we are fighting "to save democracy"!

L.   Dr. Panunzio reported that Prohibition seemed to have had the most significant effect upon the children of the foreign-born. These young people, being under the influence of the public schools, seem not only to be universally total abstainers but also stanch carriers of Prohibition sentiment into the home. Cases are reported of children who, with their mothers, strenuously opposed the manufacture and use of liquor in the homes (" Prohibition a National Experiment").

M.   National Prohibition was effecting amazing social improvements under Mr. Roosevelt's very eyes if he had but opened them. In "Dry Dutchess County" by Paul Hasbrouck (*Christian Herald,* Oct. 1932) one learns what incontrovertible blessing it brought to the President's own home county. Alcohol psychoses fell one half. The Associated Charities which assigned intemperance as the cause in 20 out of 70 cases in its first report (1911) listed it only in 3 out of 487 applications in 1931. Prohibition was relief without billion borrowing! After five years of Rooseveltian Repeal the *N. Y. Times* for Oct. 20, 1938, reported indictment of thirty-one members of a Dutchess county liquor ring which included two federal reserve agents, a former justice of the peace and the county jailer of Hyde Park. They operated eleven wildcat stills, produced 320,000 gallons of 190 proof illicit liquor and defrauded the government of at least $2,500,000 in taxes.

N.   Congressman Berlin reckons that the whisky trust produces whisky at $3.50 a gallon, all taxes paid, and sells it for $20. So they have money wherewith to advertise and incidentally to control the press.

"Here's Schenley's advertisement," says Congressman Fuller. "This appeared in the press all over the country *and every time you see one of these advertisements you see an editorial or news item running along with it.* Why? Because these trust distillers are big newspaper advertisers" (Cong. Record, Feb. 27, 1932, p. 3,404 and July 23, 1935, p. 12,184).

O.   Judge Hoyt, like Professor Yandell Henderson, differentiates between beer and distilled liquor. "Distillation," he wrote, in his prize
essay, "is the work of man. Fermentation is the act of nature and that
to many must mean the act of God." Gambrinized theology to match
Gambrinized physiology! He probably knows now much more about the
godly brewers.

P.   At a meeting of the United Brewers' Industrial Foundation "an-
nouncement was made that the American Medical Association, with a
membership of more than 100,000 physicians, has approved recommendations for scientific standards of intoxication and 'under-the-influence
drunken driving cases' which will greatly help to free beer from the
threadbare alibi of guilty motorists that they drank 'only one or two
beers' " (*American Brewer,* June 1939, p. 21).

The Travellers' Insurance Company issues a booklet of 38 pages, its
1940 study of motor accidents. Now the Medical Examiner of the City of
New York has pointed out as a result of careful studies, that, in at least
40% of all fatal accidents on the highway in 1937, the drinking of alcoholic beverage by the deceased person was a factor (P. 5 Statistical
Report). (In passing we note, p. 30, that of 1,434 cases of toxic injuries,
21 were from lead poisoning, 2 from phosphorus, 1,026 from alcohol.)

In 1939, 32,000 persons were killed by auto accidents, and 1,210,200
injured. "The Travellers' Insurance Company assigns 13.5% to 'without
right of way,' 14.6% to wrong side of the road, 14.7% to reckless driving, 11.6% to off roadway. There is further great detail given concerning ages of those killed, direction cars were travelling, types of cars involved, days when accident occurred, etc., but *next to nothing about the
relation of liquor to this slaughter.* Except for two brief notices there is
no indication in this entire report that drink has any relation to the homi-
cidal motor car. Are our safety experts afraid to face the facts?" (Sum-
marized from *Christian Century,* March 20, 1940.)

APPENDIX I

THE 1917 MEMORIAL FOR NATIONAL PROHIBITION

The tactics of the wets have all along been to depict Prohibition as the policy of rustics and its supporters as uncouth, ill-clad, and fanatical. Thus Mr. H. L. Mencken writes: "No man born or reared as what is called a gentleman has ever been numbered among them. In the South they emerged unanimously from the poor white trash and in the Middle West they came from the bleaker farms full of grasshoppers and fleas" (*American Mercury*, Jan. 1931, p. 33). In 1917 Prof. Irving Fisher and ex-Gov. E. N. Foss of Massachusetts sought to disprove such ideas and drew up a Memorial for National Prohibition to be signed by persons hitherto unassociated with the movement. The text of the Memorial with representative signatures,—there were a thousand in all,—follows:

In view of the scientifically proved unfavorable effects of the use of alcoholic beverages even in small quantities,

And in view of the colossal evils which the manufacture and sale of alcoholic liquor entails,

And in view of the inadequateness of all methods hitherto employed to check or regulate these evils,

And in view of the great growth of public sentiment on this subject as shown by antialcohol legislation through most of our national area,

The undersigned believe the time has come for the federal government to take steps looking to the prohibition in the United States of the manufacture, sale, import, export, and transport of alcoholic liquors.

Signed:

James Brown Scott, Sec'y of the Carnegie Endowment for International Peace
Darwin P. Kingsley, President of the N. Y. Life Insurance Co.
Dr. Theodore C. Janeway, Physician-in-Chief, Johns Hopkins Hospital
Dr. F. W. Taussig, Professor of Economics, Harvard University.
Henry F. Osborn, LL.D., President of the American Museum of Natural History
F. A. Vanderlip, President of the National City Bank
Judge E. H. Gary, Chairman of the U. S. Steel Corporation
Professor George H. Palmer, Harvard University
Winston Churchill, Novelist

Judge C. C. Kohlsaat, U. S. Circuit Court

George W. Stevens, President of the Chesapeake and Ohio R. R.

Francis Carter Wood, M.D., Director of Cancer Research, Columbia University

James G. White, President of J. G. White and Co., Inc., Engineers

Julian Kennedy, General Superintendent Carnegie, Phipps and Co.

W. G. Bierd, President of the Chicago and Alton R. R.

H. Coulby of Pickands, Mather and Co., President of the Pittsburgh S. S. Co.

Howard Elliott, President of the N. Y., New Haven and Hartford R. R.

M. E. Brumbaugh, Governor of Pennsylvania

George W. Cable, Novelist

David R. Forgan, President of the National City Bank, Chicago

Orville Wright, Aeronaut and inventor

Dr. Emmett Holt, Professor in Children's Diseases, Columbia University

A. R. Erskine, President of the Studebaker Corporation

H. T. Herr, General Manager and Vice President of Westinghouse Machine Co.

W. J. Harahan, President of the Seaboard Air Line Railway

James Long, President of A. B. Farquhar Co., Ltd., Steel Manufacturers

Eben B. Clarke, Vice-President, Firth-Sterling Steel Co.

Dr. Charles H. Brent, Bishop of the Philippines

William Z. Ripley, Professor of Economics, Harvard University

John S. Pillsbury, President of the Pillsbury Flour Mills

L. M. Bowers, President of the Cleveland Steel Co.

W. A. May, President of the Pennsylvania Coal Co.

Harland B. Howe, Judge of U. S. District Court, St. Johnsbury, Vt.

Alston G. Dayton, Judge U. S. District Court, West Virginia

Mark Sullivan, Editor of Collier's

Simon Lake, inventor and President of Lake Submarine Co.

Clark Howell, Editor of the Atlanta Constitution

Victor C. Wright, Dean of Medical School, University of Michigan

Warren S. Stone, Chief of Brotherhood of Locomotive Engineers

Dr. Henry S. Drinker, President of Lehigh University

J. J. Eagan, President of the American Cast Iron Pipe Co., Birmingham

Senator George Wharton Pepper of Pennsylvania

David Starr Jordan, Chancellor of Leland Stanford University

Nelson A. Miles, Lieut.-General U. S. Army

Ray Stannard Baker, Editor of the American Magazine

Ellen F. Pendleton, President of Wellesley College

Dr. Ludvig Hektoen, Director Institute for Infectious Diseases, Chicago

M. T. Pickles, General Manager American Bridge Co., Ambridge, Pa.

Wallace H. Rowe, President of Pittsburgh Steel Co.

Henry D. Walbridge, President of Pennsylvania Electric Co., etc.

Albert J. Stone, Vice President of the Erie R. R.

J. M. Gruber, Vice-President of the Great Northern R. R.

E. H. Hopkins, President of Dartmouth College

William Fellowes Morgan, President of Brooklyn Bridge Cold Storage Co.

Woodbridge N. Ferris, Governor of Michigan
Booth Tarkington, Novelist
J. F. Welborn, President of Colorado Fuel and Iron Co.
Upton Sinclair, Novelist
E. W. Kemmerer, Professor of Economics, Princeton University
Wm. R. Newbold, Professor of Philosophy, University of Pennsylvania
S. S. McClure, Editor of McClure's Magazine
Francis E. Baker, Presiding Judge U. S. Circuit Court of Appeals
John Laing, President Wyatt Coal Co., West Virginia (12 mines)
J. A. Campbell, President Youngstown Sheet and Tube Co.
James Schermerhorn, Editor Detroit Times
Wm. A. Harris, Genl. Manager, American Sheet & Tinplate Co., Canton,
    Ohio
James Bowron, President Gulf State Steel Co.
John Crosby, Washburn-Crosby Flour Mills, Minneapolis
W. DeL. Walbridge, President American Coal Co.
Robert Dollar, President Dollar Steamship Lines, San Francisco
Robert Garrett of Robert Garrett and Sons, Bankers, Baltimore
Charles Thaddeus Terry, Professor of Law, Columbia University
Dr. M. J. Rosenau, Professor of Preventive Medicine, Harvard University
Frederick Frelinghuysen, President of Mutual Benefit Life Insurance Co.
Dr. Chas. B. Davenport, Dept. of Experimental Evolution, Cold Spring
    Harbor
John D. Rockefeller, Jr., Chairman of the Rockefeller Foundation
Luther Burbank, plant breeder
Robert Treat Paine, trustee
C. C. Chesney, General Manager General Electric Co., Pittsfield, Mass.
Dr. W. W. Keen, president of the American Surgical Association
Hon. John Wanamaker, merchant
Jack London, Author of "The Call of the Wild"
Dr. Richard C. Cabot, Harvard Medical School
and 915 more signers.

This Memorial was sent to the Associated Press and to all
the leading newspapers of the country at the time when the 18th
Amendment was under consideration in Congress. As far as was
observed it was neither printed nor referred to by any newspaper
in the land.

APPENDIX II

VARSITY NOTES

Prof. Y. Henderson of Yale stated before that one-time stalk-
ing-horse of the brewers, the National Municipal League, that "almost the only successful experiment that has ever been conducted

in the United States on the subject of control of alcoholic beverages was the 3.2% beer experiment. . . . I was the principal witness *and I got most of the others.*" Now he has published a book in defense of beer entitled, "A New Deal in Liquor." The brewers approve: the scientists scoff.

German-American Brewers

As far as the brewing industry is concerned . . . this book is beyond doubt the greatest argument ever advanced in its defense (*Am. Brewer,* Feb. 1933, p. 82).

The U. S. Brewers' Ass'n has purchased a sufficient number of copies to supply its entire membership. It is also sponsoring the circulation of Dr. Henderson's book to members of state control commissions, state legislatures, as well as to certain prominent wets and drys (The *American Brewer,* Jan. 1935, p. 6: *Brewers' News,* Jan. 31, 1935).

German Physiologists

Among the critics of Prof. Henderson are Prof. Dr. Otto Graf of the *Kaiser Wilhelm Institut fuer Arbeitsphysiologie* and Dr. Ernst Gabriel of the Steinhof Sanatorium, Vienna. Supporting himself on the experimentation of Gylys, Rosemann, and Widmark described, Prof. Graf stated that:

"Psychologically no confirmation of an essentially different effect of light drinks, either quantitative or qualitative, may be found. . . . This has been confirmed repeatedly by very thorough experiments."

Dr. Gabriel declares Prof. Henderson "completely ignorant of facts which should be known to every authority on the alcohol problem" and then quotes specialists in alcohol treatment such as Dr. Georgi of Darmstadt who affirms that:

"Without beer alcoholism we would have no alcohol problem in Germany." The Municipal Alcohol Commission of Augsburg reported that in 1931–32 the cases of alcoholism due to beer were 87% of the total. Another, reporting that at least 75% of addicts under his treatment were beer-drinkers, added, "Henderson must be interpreting life from his laboratory and be quite oblivious to reality." But there is no indication that Prof. Henderson ever made any laboratory experiments on this subject.

In 1917 he memorialized Congress for the prohibition of *all* alcoholic liquors. Now he would refuse us even local option and advocates reducing beer taxation from $5 to $3 per barrel (Tax on Intox. Liquors Hearings, pp. 104 and 108). After 1917 and up to the time of his appearance before Congress, he seems to have taken no interest in the subject. Yet he is described as "an internationally known expert on the alcohol question," on what grounds it would be difficult to discover.

This is but one more illustration of how extensively American universities are in arrears in the study of this life and death question. In going through the books on this subject in the Yale Library I have noticed that various reports did not even have their leaves cut, *Une famille des degenérés heredo-alcooliques dans l'oeuvre de Dostoievsky,* in which the brothers Karamazov are shown to be "a museum of alcoholic heredity": also a *Compte rendu du Congrès contre alcoolisme et la tuberculose* of the Universities of Montauban, Bordeaux, and Toulouse. These uncut leaves are a symbol.

Prof. Raymond Pearl also has the commendation of those whose intimacies are with the wets, as for example M. Yves Guyot. In the *Journal des Economistes,* p. 299, Jan. 15, 1925, Pearl's conclusions are trumpeted as from "one of America's greatest universities." But Dr. H. Westergaard of Copenhagen describes Pearl's "Alcohol and Longevity" as "one of the most confused books I have ever read," and insists that his methods are obsolete, that he is ignorant of statistical literature. Frets, pathologist of the Hospital for Mental Diseases, Rotterdam, contrasts Pearl's results with those of Ceni, Van der Hoeven, Mairet, Laitenen, Combemale, Pfoerringer, Kern and Bluhm, and criticises "his many and serious methodological errors."

And Columbia University! Congressman Sirovitch is an alcohol scientist whose testimony caused as much hilarity in Congress as that of Henderson of Yale. When he mentioned to President Butler that courses in biology and chemistry had formed the basis of his wet speeches, Butler suggested that these speeches be submitted as a thesis. He did so and is now Master of Science! Of "Alcohol in Moderation and Excess," by two Virginia professors, equally inexpert regarding the alcohol question, the *American Brewer* says: "It should have a place in the library of every brewery executive" (Dec. 1938, p. 19). Perhaps! But nowhere else!

His and Ruetimeyer long ago exposed Prof. Haeckel's falsification of plates in the interest of advocated theories. A case of the same sort is reported among the alcoholic experimenters. One indignant assistant made formal affidavit to that effect. Let us hope that in time it will be made public. An illustration of a widespread academic misapprehension is found in "Brandeis and the Modern State" by A. T. Mason, Professor of Politics in Princeton. Prof. Mason thinks Justice Brandeis' decisions favoring the 18th Amendment were a departure from his usual liberal course "with pacifists, socialists and other radicals when restrained by regulatory legislation" (p. 219). He is apparently oblivious to the fact that the alcohol capital is a mighty buttress of reaction and a dangerous menace to democratic government.

*   *   *   *   *

But the blue ribbon goes to Harvard.

The State St. Investment Corporation of Boston is an affair of Harvard men, Cabots, Saltonstalls, Sedgwicks, with two Harvard Treasurers, Messrs. Shattuck and C. F. Adams (of the Morgan preferred list). The University holds 20,000 shares. I examined the investments of this Corporation in 1935 (Poor's Manual for Executives, p. 2481) and lo! 60,000 shares of Schenley's Distillers Corp., worth $3,090,000, "led all the rest." Keane's Institutional Holdings of Securities, 1936, p. 1331 revealed a similar investment of 14,000 shares in National Distillers' Products Corp., and Poor's Fiscal Volume, p. 1694, showed a holding of 21,000 shares of Commercial Solvents which distills Bourbon whisky. The State St. Investment Corporation's investment in U. S. Industrial Alcohol, tied up with Penn-Maryland and other distilleries, is given as 18,500 shares: in Distillers' Corporation Seagram in 1936, 18,400 shares, worth $1,496,000.

> What of the night, Harvard?
> An auto up-rears, crushed ribs and white faces.
> What of smashed head-light, Harvard,
> The booze you voted for, championed, sell at a profit?
> Once more, Harvard, cars on a staggering road.
> Once more, drivers with hip-flasks, bottles proclaiming
> Once more, once more, the ineluctable Schenley.
> Once more the smash-up and a drunk world.
>   From the 1936 State St. Ter-Monetary Ode.

Schenley's Distillers' Corporation is charged with addressing to the retail trade a confidential circular entitled, "A Plan for Pulling in Non-Drinkers. An Effective Assault on the Market of Non-Drinkers or Very Infrequent Drinkers. A Plan by Which at Least

Four Drinks Will Be Ordered Where There Have Been None Before." Mr. Adams of the Harvard Board of Overseers is more conservative. Addressing a thousand newly entered Freshman lambs he told them "to train their minds as they would their bodies, and to shun the sort of popularity which went with an easy 'yes' for the second drink" (*N. Y. Times,* Sept. 23, 1933).

IN DARKEST HARVARD

Harvard's record in the alcohol matter is as its evil record of anti-slavery days.

It was the Harvard professors Jackson, Bigelow, Bowen, Horsford, *et al.,* who led in breaking down the Massachusetts Prohibition Law of the seventies.

It was Eliot '53, Bowditch, '61, and their Harvard associates, who attempted to sterilize anti-alcohol instruction in the Massachusetts schools.

(President Eliot's father, Congressman Samuel A. Eliot, voted for the Fugitive Slave Law of 1850. But the hounds on the heels of slaves were woolly lambs compared with the hounds of alcohol habit and alcohol mania which, decade after decade, make life a hell for hundreds of thousands. Attempts to limit the run of these psychic blood-hounds by instructing school-children and by preventative legislation met, during many years, Charles W. Eliot's constant opposition.)

Francis G. Peabody '69 was primarily responsible for the Committee of Fifty Report which has done perhaps more than any one thing to slow down the movement against alcohol.

In *The Liquor Problem,* Peabody's summary of the five volume report, he declared that his committee did not represent missions (that is relief of the alcohol-sick) but hard-boiled science (p. 8). *Yet this summary did not once mention the only important scientific studies made by the Committee,* those on Prof. Hodge's dogs for reaction time and those by Prof. Abbott relating to alcohol and infection. These experiments disproved the general pre-suppositions of the Committee and mention of them was therefore suppressed in his work for the lay public. As a further illustration of Harvard alcohol VERITAS we may add that the disconcerting experiments were abandoned on the ground that the Committee did not have money enough to pay for whisky and animals (Physiolog. Aspects, Vol. 1, p. 395)! But the Committee's unspeakable nonsense to the effect that "the term poison belongs with equal propriety . . . to coffee, pepper, ginger, and common salt" as to alcohol, was here reprinted (p. 23).

I never hear the little Peabody bird's plaintive note in my upper field but I think of this Harvard theologian's pro-alcohol science, "Food value of alcohol, alcohol, alcohol."

In the very heart of Harvard's architectural disarray stands the Adolphus Busch Building. This king brewer was manipulator of legislatures and promoter of villainous dives. His building was given to Harvard after the publication of Peabody's Committee of Fifty Report and may pass as a piece of grateful recognition, *Pour le Mérite!* This building symbolized the *entente cordiale* which Fox and Koren were seeking to establish between "the thoughtful" and brewerdom.

Penrose '85 was the worst exemplar of beer politics that this nation has ever known. Barnes '88, wet Republican boss of New York state, was of the same garden variety.

Tinkham '94 was an uncouth and violent Congressional wet. Piatt Andrew '93 voted along with him: also Gallivan '88.

Stone '94, son of the President of the Associated Press, had full secret charge of the publicity of the U. S. Brewers Assn. Oppenheim '88 was also a clandestine hireling of the brewers.

Sedgwick '94 published in the *Atlantic,* as unbiased science, the swindle articles of brewers' man Koren.

Greene '96 was author of an article (*Atlantic,* Oct. 1926) advocating "acquiescence in and encouragement of nullification" of the National Prohibition law.

Codman '92 was wet leader in Massachusetts, hand in glove with the brewers. Close behind him were Rackemann '81, Lincoln '95, Austen Fox '69.

Hearst ran truthless wet newspapers. Ogden Mills '04 and his lieutenant Lippmann '09 also misled the public with wet journalism.

Choate '97 headed the Voluntary Committee of Lawyers to spike the Increased Penalties Act.

Tuckerman '94 sought legal expedients to make void the 18th Amendment. Judge Clark '11 declared it unconstitutional.

Prof. Persons of the Department of Economics was hired writer for the United Brewers' Industrial Foundation (*American Brewer,* May 1938, p. 27).

The Harvard plebiscite of March 1930 was carried by the wets 25 to 1. The frouziest slum of New York or Chicago would not have voted wetter.

Finally it was Roosevelt '03 who, with every doubtful device at his disposal, drove through ratification of Repeal.

And after Wall St. had broken down the Amendment, the graduates of this class-conscious university, at their 1934 Commencement, celebrated the event with derisive clothing and horseplay. The Class of 1924 was accompanied by a beer-truck with a bar at the tail, serving to all and sundry: and the Class of '31, all wearing bartenders' white jackets and aprons, operated another. The Olympian J. Pierpont Morgan '86 could be seen consecrating the demonstration by quaffing ale in public.

Now mark the difference between a university of rich men, enmeshed in tradition, and an objectively scientific one.

Prof. Dr. Hans Horst Meyer, of University of Vienna, was at his death probably the most distinguished figure in the world of modern medicine. About the time the Jerome D. Greenes and Julian Codmans were railing at prohibition, he retired from his professorship, and on this occasion, as a parting dissertation, read an essay on alcohol poisoning. After a critical and detailed statement of all the injuries which the use of alcohol brings to the human organism, he went on to declare, *as the only satisfactory remedy, its absolute prohibition.*

* * * * *

It can never be too often emphasized that pro-alcohol action is essentially a class move. At Harvard it is in line with the thumbs-down Sacco-Vanzetti finding and with the crowding of char-women's wages below the legal Massachusetts minimum requirement, when the university budget topped ten million. Harvard financiers who are selling these prodigious amounts of whisky securities know that purchase by large numbers of people will tend to intrench the alcohol capital and therewith general capital and their own class position. Harvard physiologists engage in the cruelest types of vivisection. The torture of stolen household pets in the name of science is an evil and futile thing. Whisky traders are responsible for other types of torture,—deliriums, wrecked nervous systems, family anxieties and shame. The press for Oct. 6th, 1937 gives a pertinent illustration:

"Mrs. Adams of Wareham, Mass., was granted a divorce today . . . after she had testified that John Quincy Adams, descendant of an illustrious namesake, was so fond of gin that he carried a bottle with him when he took a bath."

"I have been a citizen of Cambridge for many years," said Prof. William James at the University of Chicago, "and in my time there has been in Eastern Massachusetts no form of public iniquity that has not had at its head some graduate of Harvard" (Religious Education, 1906, p. 88). Certainly this is true enough in the field of alcohol study and alcohol politics.

APPENDIX III

"TOWARD LIQUOR CONTROL"

There was something of the Eastern monarch, of Darius or Shalmanesar, in the post-Prohibition decree which went forth from 26 Broadway: "Some months ago I came to the conclusion that a study of the practise and experience of other countries would be a genuine service. . . . I therefore asked Mr. Raymond B. Fosdick and Mr. Albert L. Scott to organize such a study."

Neither of these two friends of Mr. Rockefeller had any acquaintance with the technical literature of the alcohol problem. They sent Mr. L. V. Harrison (later serving the Distillers' Institute as writer of anti-Prohibition literature) to Northern Europe to examine the Bratt System and the monopolies of Russia and Finland. "More than any one person," we are told (*Toward Liquor Control,* p. 14), "Mr. Harrison is responsible for the chapter on systems of control." Mr. Rockefeller says of this book, "It represents a careful and conscientious investigation." I happened to be in Sweden at the time and made inquiry at the hotels as to the length of Mr. Harrison's stay. It was two days in Leningrad, four days in Helsingfors, eight days in Stockholm! Mr. Axel Axelman, of the state-subsidised bureau for alcohol study in Stockholm, got in touch with him at my suggestion and gave him an afternoon of help. His report to me was, "Mr. Harrison seems ready to learn!"

One hears, "Of course Mr. Rockefeller has all the resources for getting at the truth." Certainly the treasures of oil are at his disposal, but the treasures of wisdom are another thing. Mr. W.

H. Allen, in his book, "Rockefeller,—Giant, Dwarf, Symbol," has devoted page after page to exposition of the worthlessness of Rockefeller surveys and studies. But nothing more trivial and misleading has been sponsored by him than the Fosdick-Scott book, "Toward Liquor Control," offered to the American public as a serious study of alcohol legislation.

How different it might have been! "The Rockefeller Foundation is *not yet* ready to take hold of the question," wrote John Koren to Herbert Stone (Overman Report, p. 778). Stone was son of the head of the Associated Press; Koren, President of the American Statistical Association. Both were in the secret pay of the U. S. Brewers' Association. Koren was after the Rockefellers to finance a pseudo-scientific organization which he had formed for the international alcohol interests and the Rockefeller Foundation was so naive, and so badly informed, as to be giving the proposal serious consideration.

Now it happened that, at this very time, the medical science of Europe had, by formal petition, asked the Rockefeller Foundation to establish an Institute for Alcohol Research to settle once and for all the various theoretical and practical questions related to this subject. This Memorial was signed by one hundred and twenty-five leading figures in Continental medicine, including Dr. Roux of the Pasteur Institute, Prof. Paul Ehrlich, the great blood investigator, most of the medical faculty of the University of Vienna (Prof. Anton Weichselbaum, the greatest anatomist of the time, Dr. Kassovitz, Hans Horst Meyer, Carl von Noorden) and by such personages as Dr. Lannelongue, the eminent French surgeon, Prof. Charles Richet of the University of Paris, M. Salomon Reinach, M. Alfred Fouillée the philosopher, M. Jules Clarétie of the Comédie Française, and so on. But Mr. Rockefeller's judgment of opportunity is so imperfect that he let slip this rare one of giving the world the unbiased truth on this question through the research of its most competent students. Indeed he seems never even to have answered the Appeal. At least so Dr. Scharffenberg of Oslo, Secretary of the Committee, told me some years ago.

A CHRONOLOGY FOR THE 18TH AMENDMENT

(Introductory)

1851 Maine enacts statutory Prohibition.

1880 Kansas adopts constitutional Prohibition.

1884 Maine's Law made constitutional.

1887 Dec. 5—Decision of Supreme Court in case of Mugler v. Kansas. Compensation denied to drink sellers and manufacturers. "A state law, enacted as a police regulation looking to the preservation of public morals, prohibiting the manufacture and sale of intoxicating liquors, is not repugnant to any clause of the Constitution of the United States."

1888 Supreme Court decision Bowman v. Chicago and Northwestern Railroad. Brooks High License Law enacted in Pennsylvania.

1889 North and South Dakota adopt Constitutional Prohibition.

1890 (April 25) Original Package decision in case of Leisy v. Hardin (State has no power to prohibit importation of liquor for individual use).

1890 August 8, Wilson Act passes Congress. "Intoxicating liquors transported into a state are subject to the laws of state and not exempt therefrom by reason of being introduced therein in original packages."

1893 South Carolina Dispensary law passed.
      Anti-Saloon League founded by H. H. Russell in Ohio.

1894 Committee of Fifty organized by F. G. Peabody of Harvard Divinity School.

1896 South Dakota repeals Constitutional Prohibition.

1901 Congress passes the Anti-Canteen Law.

1903 State Prohibition repealed in New Hampshire and Vermont.
      March 3, 1903, the sale of intoxicants prohibited in the Capitol—Washington.

1906 Attorney-General Trickett enforces Prohibition in Kansas.

1907 Georgia and Oklahoma adopt statutory Prohibition.

1909 Mississippi and North Carolina adopt statutory Prohibition.

1911 Attempt to repeal Constitutional Prohibition in Maine defeated.

1912 West Virginia adopts Constitutional Prohibition.

1913 March 1, Congress passes the Webb-Kenyon bill over President Taft's veto —Dec. 10, Committee of One Thousand presents to Congress proposed Amendment for National Prohibition.

1914 Dec. 22, House votes for National Prohibition, 197 to 189.

1915–1917 Prohibition adopted in Alabama, Arkansas, Idaho, Iowa, South Carolina, Michigan, Nebraska, South Dakota, Montana, Alaska, the District of Columbia, New Mexico, Indiana, Utah, New Hampshire, Wyoming and Porto Rico.

1917

Jan. 8, 1917 Supreme Court upholds constitutionality of the Webb-Kenyon Act prohibiting transport of liquors in interstate commerce from wet to dry states

Mar. 3, 1917 Reed Bone-Dry Amendment to the Post Office Appropriation Bill forbidding personal importation into dry territory and alcohol advertisement in dry territory.

(276)

May 18, 1917   Sale of drink to soldiers prohibited; Oct. 6 this prohibition extended to men in the navy.

Aug. 1, 1917   The 18th Amendment adopted by the Senate 65 to 20.

Aug. 10, 1917   Food Control Bill signed by President Wilson with an amendment providing that the production of distilled spirits for beverage purposes must cease Sept. 8, 1917. Also gave President discretion to limit or prohibit use of food materials in manufacture of beer and wine.

Sept. 8, 1917   Manufacture of distilled spirits ceases.

1917   American Medical Association states that alcohol has no medicinal value.

Dec. 11, 1917   Use of food materials for beer reduced 30% by presidential proclamation: alcohol content reduced to 2¾% by weight.

Dec. 18, 1917   The 18th Amendment adopted by Congress and sent to the states for ratification.

1918

Mar. 6, 1918   Sale of liquor within five miles of naval training stations prohibited by Navy Department.

Sept. 6, 1918   Agricultural Appropriation Bill passed with amendment prohibiting manufacture of beer and wine after May 1, 1919 and forbidding sale of distilled, malt and vinous intoxicants after June 30, 1919. Approved by President Nov. 21, 1918.

Sept. 16, 1918   Proclamation of President Wilson prohibiting the use of foodstuffs in production of malt liquors and closing breweries.

Sept. 18, 1918   Joint resolution authorized the President to establish dry zones around coal mines, shipyards, and munition plants.

Sept. 27, 1918   Overman Committee of Senate begins investigation of brewers.

Dec. 1, 1918   The use of food material in manufacture of beer ceases.

Dec. 10, 1918   Decision of Supreme Court in Idaho Prohibition Case. (A citizen has no constitutional right to possess liquor for personal use if the state wishes to forbid it.)

In 1918   Florida, Ohio, Nevada, Texas, Vermont adopted state prohibition.

1919

Jan. 13, 1919   Supreme Court decision upheld the constitutionality of the Reed Bone-dry amendment prohibiting importation for personal use.

Jan. 20, 1919   The Secretary of State announced that on Jan. 16, 1919, thirty-six states had ratified the 18th Amendment to take effect Jan. 16, 1920.

June 14, 1919   Demonstration of A. F. L. in Washington against prohibition of sale of beer.

July 1, 1919   War Prohibition went into effect.

Oct. 27, 1919   President Wilson vetoes the National Prohibition Enforcement Act (Volstead Act). On the same day the House passes it over his veto and on Oct. 28, the Senate does the same.

Nov. 4, 1919   Kentucky adopts Constitutional Prohibition.

Nov. 12, 1919   J. F. Kramer appointed National Prohibition Commissioner.

Dec. 15, 1919   Supreme Court upholds constitutionality of the War Prohibition Act of Nov. 21, 1918.

Dec. 17, 1919   Rhode Island brought suit in Supreme Court to declare the 18th Amendment void.

1920

Jan.	5, 1920	Supreme Court decision Ruppert v. Caffey. One half of one percent definition of intoxicity held to be valid.
Jan.	16, 1920	National Prohibition goes into effect.
Jan.	30, 1920	Bureau of Internal Revenue issued regulations as to medical use of wine and liquor, limiting prescription to one pint in ten days.
Feb.	25, 1920	Motion in House to repeal Volstead Act defeated by 80 to 34; again March 4, 254 to 84.
Mar.	2, 1920	Governor of New Jersey signed bill permitting manufacture and sale of 3.5% beer.
Mar.	4, 1920	New Jersey files suit with U. S. Supreme Court to render void the 18th Amendment.
Mar.	24, 1920	Gov. Smith of New York approves Walker Act for 2.75% beer in New York state.
June	1, 1920	Supreme Court decision Hawke v. Smith. Referenda provisions of state constitutions inapplicable to U. S. Constitution.
June	7, 1920	Supreme Court decision Rhode Island v. Palmer. 18th Amendment valid: binds all legislative bodies, courts and public officers.
Aug.	18, 1920	Adoption of the 19th Amendment granting suffrage to women by ratification by Tennessee, 36th state.

1921

Mar.	3, 1921	Decision of Attorney General. Limit of permits for medicinal liquor not authorized.
Mar.	8, 1921	Attorney General A. Mitchell Palmer rules permission of sale of beer for medicine.
May	16, 1921	Supreme Court decision Dillon v. Gloss. Seven years limitation upon ratification did not invalidate the 18th Amendment.
May	1921	Mrs. Willebrandt appointed Assistant Attorney-General.
June	1, 1921	Supreme Court decision U. S. v. Yuginovitch. Prohibition tax sustained. Former internal revenue laws superseded by Volstead Act.
June	10, 1921	Roy A. Haynes appointed National Prohibition Commissioner.
July	11, 1921	Ships forbidden to bring liquor within three miles of shores of the United States.
July	1921	Supervising Federal Prohibition agents abolished and enforcement put under 48 state directors.
Aug.	1921	Wm. C. McConnell appointed Prohibition Director in Pennsylvania.
Nov.	23, 1921	Wills-Campbell Supplemental Act prohibiting medicinal beer and creating the Bureau of Prohibition.
Dec.	31, 1921	Death of Senator Penrose.

1922

Feb.	17, 1922	Congress empowered Commissioner of Internal Revenue to concentrate distilled spirits in a few government warehouses.
Mar.	9, 1922	New Jersey ratified the 18th Amendment.
May	15, 1922	Supreme Court decision that the transportation of liquors from foreign countries through an American port to another foreign port is prohibited by the Volstead Act.
Oct.	6, 1922	Decision of Attorney General that American ships on the high seas are under Prohibition laws; also foreign ships within the three mile limit: They may not bring liquors even under seal into American ports.

Oct. 16, 1922   Britain government protests seizure by United States of vessels engaged in illegal liquor traffic outside the three mile limit. Declines to adopt proposed extension to twelve mile limit.

Nov. 7, 1922   Wright Enforcement Bill carried in California referendum by 33,934 majority: Initiated beer amendment defeated in Ohio by 189,472 majority.

Dec. 11, 1922   Supreme Court decision U. S. v. Lanza et al. Prosecution by a state not a bar to prosecution by Federal Courts.

1923

Feb. 9, 1923   LaMontagne brothers sentenced to jail for bootlegging.

Mar. 27, 1923   Armstrong-Snyder enforcement Act passed by Pennsylvania legislature.

Mar. 31, 1923   Sentence given in Gary conspiracy case.

Apr. 30, 1923   Supreme Court decision Cunard S. S. Co. v. Mellon. The 18th Amendment applied to both United States and foreign shipping within three mile limit: inapplicable beyond.

June 1, 1923   Repeal of the Mullan-Gage Enforcement law in New York.

June 20, 1923   Chief Justice Taft's speech at the Yale Commencement luncheon.

Aug. 2, 1923   Death of President Harding.

Oct. 18, 1923   Conference of governors at West Baden, Ind., for effective enforcement.

Oct. 26, 1923   British government accepts in principle the 12 mile limit for search of vessels.

Nov. 1923   Prohibition enforcement law in Nevada repealed.

1924

Jan. 8, 1924   Major General S. D. Butler assumes office as Director of Public Safety in Philadelphia, Pa.

Jan. 23, 1924   Liquor smuggling treaty with Great Britain signed. Proclaimed May 22nd.

Feb. 8, 1924   Wm. H. Anderson sentenced for forgery.

Feb. 16, 1924   Hearings before the Committee on Alcoholic Liquor Traffic. 68th Congress, Survey of Alcoholic Liquor Traffic.

Mar. 10 to May 5, 1924   Hearings before House Committee on the District of Columbia, 68th Congress, Firearms and Intoxicants.

Mar. 12, 1924 to May 15   Hearings before Select Committee of Senate to investigate Attorney-General Daugherty.

Mar. 28, 1924   Attorney General Daugherty resigns at request of President Coolidge.

Apr. 17, 1924   Harlan F. Stone appointed Attorney General.

Apr. 21, 1924 to May 21   Hearings before the House Committee on the Judiciary, 68th Congress on Proposed Modification of the Prohibition Law (2.75% beer).

Apr. 29, 1924   N. M. Butler speaks before the Missouri Society.

May 19, 1924 to June 30   Liquor smuggling treaties with Germany, Sweden, Norway, Denmark, Italy, Canada and France.

June 9, 1924   Supreme Court upholds the Willis-Campbell Act of Nov. 1921 forbidding sale of beer as medicine.

Nov. 1924   Massachusetts sustains its enforcement (Baby Volstead) law by a referendum majority of 8,183.

Nov. 1924   Investigation of the Internal Revenue Department of the Treasury.

Dec. 18, 1924 Hearings before Senate Committee on the Judiciary 68th Congress, on Bureau of Prohibition (Crampton Bill).

Dec. 18, 1924 Senator Reed attacks "legal poisoning of industrial alcohol" in Congressional hearing on Crampton bill. Dec. 28, 1924, forty deaths in N. Y. City attributed to poison in alcohol.

1925

Jan. 30, 1925 Means and Felder convicted of conspiracy.

Mar. 2, 1925 Supreme Court decision Carroll v. U. S. Right to search automobiles without a U. S. Warrant where probable cause exists, sustained.

Mar. 3, 1925 Act passed for confiscation of vessels and vehicles used in violation of National Prohibition law.

Mar. 5, 1925 Federal District Attorney Buckner opens campaign with padlock injunctions.

Mar. 17, 1925 John G. Sargent made Attorney-General.

Apr. 1, 1925 General L. C. Andrews placed in charge of Federal Prohibition enforcement.

Apr. 1, 1925 State Federal Prohibition Directors supplemented by 24 Federal administrators corresponding to the Federal judicial districts. Effective Sept. 1.

May 3, 1925 Great mobilization of Coast Guard craft to wipe out rum runners between Fire Island and Barnegat.

1926

Feb. 2, 1926 Hearings on Civil Service and Prohibition. House Committee.

Feb. 5, 1926 Church Temperance Society's anti-Prohibition demonstration.

Feb. 8, 1926 Cardinal O'Connell attacks Prohibition.

Mar. 2, 1926 Poll of 452 newspapers on Prohibition.

Apr. 5, 1926 to 24th Hearings before the Sub-committee on the Judiciary, 69th Congress on The National Prohibition Law.

Apr. 27, 1926 Mellon-Andrews bill separating Prohibition Unit from Bureau of Internal Revenue and placing enforcement under immediate authority of the Secretary of the Treasury passed, House 195 to 6.

May 8, 1926 President Coolidge issues executive order making state, county and municipal officers federal officials for law enforcement.

Nov. 1, 1926 Supreme Court decision that an offender against Prohibition law may be prosecuted in both state and federal courts for the same offense.

Nov. 2, 1926 Montana votes for repeal of the State enforcement law by 10,249 majority. In referenda for repeal of state enforcement laws drys won in Colorado by 46,923, in California by 63,617 and in Missouri by 255,543 majorities.

Nov. 26, 1926 Supreme Court upheld limitation of whisky prescription medicine.

1927

Feb. 2, 1927 The Mellon-Andrews plan for a government-controlled corporation to manufacture and distribute medicinal whisky defeated by House Committee on Ways and Means.

Mar. 3, 1927 Reorganization Bill of 1927. Creation of Bureau of Prohibition in Department of Treasury and extension of Civil Service Act to positions in the field service.

Apr. 8, 1927 Borah-Butler debate in Boston.

May 16, 1927 Supreme Court decision, U. S. v. Sullivan. Profits derived from illicit liquor traffic not exempt from federal income tax.

May 21, 1927 Hon. Seymour Lowman appointed Assistant Secretary of Treasury in charge of Prohibition enforcement to succeed General L. C. Andrews. Dr. James M. Doran appointed Commissioner of Prohibition.

Mar. 25, 1927 Second anti-Prohibition Demonstration of the Church Temperance Society.

June 27, 1927 Major Chester P. Mills resigns from Federal Prohibition Administration of the New York District. Effective July 1. Succeeded by Mr. Maurice Campbell.

Sept. 5, 1927 Death of Wayne B. Wheeler.

Nov. 21, 1927 Supreme Court decision, Marron v. U. S. Seizure of books and papers of an evidential character justifiable even if not described on the search warrant.

Dec. 12, 1927 Treasury decision fixing the amount of industrial alcohol to be manufactured during the coming year.

1928

Jan. 3, 1928 *Osservatore Romano* anti-Prohibition article in N. Y. Tribune.

Jan. 13, 1928 In Civil Service examination more than 1500 out of 2000 Prohibition agents fail to pass.

Apr. 9, 1928 Supreme Court decision Donnelley v. U. S. Failure of Federal Prohibition director to report for prosecution violations coming to his knowledge an indictable offence.

June 4, 1928 Supreme Court decision, Olmstead v. U. S. Evidence of conspiracy obtained by tapping telephone wires into dwelling houses held admissable in criminal trials.

June 27, 1928 N. Dakota sustains its Constitutional Prohibition, 103,696 to 96,837.

July 19, 1928 Asheville, N. C. Conference of Dry Anti-Smith Democrats.

Aug. 11, 1928 Hoover's Palo Alto speech of acceptance, speaks of Prohibition as "a great social and economic experiment, noble in motive, and far-reaching in purpose."

Aug. 22, 1928 Gov. Alfred E. Smith's acceptance speech asks for a referendum of National Prohibition and state determination in the matter.

Nov. 6, 1928 Herbert C. Hoover elected President (444 to 87 electoral votes). Dry governors elected in 43 of the 48 states. Massachusetts votes to request Congress to repeal by 283,223 majority.

Dec. 25, 1928 Durant Prize of $25,000 on best methods of enforcement awarded to Major Chester P. Mills.

1929

Jan. 2, 1929 W. R. Hearst offers $25,000 Prize on Prohibition and Temperance. Awarded June 1, to Franklin C. Hoyt.

Jan. 23, 1929 Voluntary Committee of Lawyers, Inc., organized.

Mar. 2, 1929 Increased Penalties Act (Jones-Stalker bill) approved by President Coolidge. (Fines not to exceed $10,000 or imprisonment for more than five years.)

Mar. 13, 1929 Jenks Enforcement bill killed in the N. Y. Assembly 74 to 72.

Mar. 22, 1929 Sinking of the Canadian rum-runner "I'm Alone" beyond 12 mile limit. Arbitration agreed on April 25th.

Mar. 25, 1929 Shooting of Mrs. de King, wife of bootlegger in Aurora, Ill.

Apr. 2, 1929 Wisconsin in advisory referendum votes to repeal the Severson Enforcement Act. Repealed May 29, 1929.

Apr. 22, 1929   President Hoover speaks at dinner of Associated Press, New York.

May 20, 1929   Wickersham Committee appointed. National Committee on Law Observance and Enforcement.

May 26, 1929   Mrs. Mabel Willebrandt resigns as Asst. Attorney General.

June 6, 1929   President Hoover sends a special message to Congress asking for a joint commission of Congress to study Prohibition reorganization.

June 8, 1929   H. Virkula shot by customs patrol.

July 16, 1929   Mr. Wickersham appeals to conference of governors at Groton, Vt., for cooperation in enforcement.

Oct. 1, 1929   President Hoover appoints John McNab to draft a project for better enforcement of Prohibition.

Oct. 16, 1929   Attorney General Mitchell asked by Senator Sheppard to give ruling on guilt of liquor purchaser.

Nov. 1, 1929   G. Aaron Youngquist succeeds Mrs. Willebrandt as Assistant Attorney-General in charge of Prohibition Enforcement.

Dec. 3, 1929   In message to Congress President Hoover recommends transfer of investigation functions from Treasury to Department of Justice.

Dec. 5, 1929   Alabama State Court declared purchaser of liquor guilty under the state law.

Dec. 27, 1929   Senator Norris demands resignation of Secretary Mellon as first step in program for better enforcement.

1930

Jan. 13, 1930   President Hoover in message to Congress urges speeding up and strengthening of Prohibition enforcement.

Jan. 14, 1930   Grand Jury absolves Coast Guard in Black Duck affair.

Jan. 20, 1930   Secretary of War Hurley extended Prohibition to U. S. Military forces throughout the world as a military law.

Jan. 23, 1930   Col. A. W. W. Woodcock appointed director of Bureau of Prohibition under Department of Justice.

Jan. 27, 1930   Attorney General Mitchell announces his purpose to appoint as U. S. attorneys and marshals only those in sympathy with the law and abstainers.

Feb. 10, 1930   Senator Wheeler introduces resolution to investigate Bureau of Prohibition.

Feb.-April, 1930   Hearings before the House Committee on the Judiciary, 71st Congress. To Amend the Prohibition Amendment.

Mar. 17, 1930   Hearings before the Senate Committee on the Judiciary, 71st Congress, "Investigation of Prohibition Enforcement."

Mar. 31, 1930   The N. Y. World's bootlegger poll.

Apr. 8, 1930   Hearings before Senate Committee on District of Columbia on Prohibition Enforcement in the District (Howell bill).

April-May, 1930   Lobby Investigation Hearings. Senate Sub-committee on the Judiciary, 71st Congress. Testimony of the A. A. P. A.

Apr. 28, 1930   President Hoover in special message to Congress asks for legislative cooperation to hasten law enforcement.

May 5, 1930   Supreme Court decision Danovitz v. U. S. Barrels and containers forfeitable when offered for sale in a mode to disclose intention to sell for use in the unlawful manufacture of liquors.

May 15, 1930   Dwight W. Morrow's anti-Prohibition speech in Newark, N. J.

May 23, 1930   Literary Digest's 1920 Poll on Prohibition closed.

May 26, 1930   Supreme Court decision U. S. v. James E. Farrar. The purchaser of intoxicating liquor for beverage purpose not guilty of an offense under the Volstead Act.

May 27, 1930   Act to transfer to Attorney General certain functions in the administration of the National Prohibition Act, to create a Bureau of Prohibition in the Department of Justice, etc. Supervision of Industrial alcohol entrusted to Treasury's Bureau of Industrial Alcohol.

July   1, 1930   Prohibition Reorganization Act of 1930 became effective. A. W. W. Woodcock, Director of Bureau of Prohibition; Dr. Doran, Commissioner of Industrial Alcohol.

Sept. 10, 1930   Governor Roosevelt of New York states: "Repeal would cure a lot of public delinquency."

Nov. 4, 1930   Massachusetts repeals enforcement code by a majority of 284,877. Illinois and Rhode Island vote for Repeal of the 18th Amendment.

Nov. 18, 1930   American Bar Association votes for Repeal: 13,779 to 6,340.

Nov. 24, 1930   Supreme Court decision. Jury trials can be dispensed with in petty cases.

Dec. 16, 1930   Judge William Clark's decision against the constitutionality of the 18th Amendment.

1931

Jan. 15, 1931   President Hoover signs the Stobbs Act mitigating the Increased Penalties Act.

Jan. 20, 1931   Report of the Wickersham Commission sent to Congress by President Hoover. House Document 722, 71st Congress.

Feb. 24, 1931   Supreme Court decision (unanimous) U. S. v. Sprague. The 18th Amendment not void because ratified by legislatures instead of by Conventions. This reversed Judge William Clark of Dec. 16, 1930.

Mar. 13, 1931   Massachusetts legislature requested Congress to call a Repeal-Convention. In 1931 legislatures of New York, R. I., Ct., Wyoming, and New Jersey pass similar resolutions.

Apr. 13, 1931   Gov. Emmerson of Illinois vetoes the O'Grady-McDermott Enforcement Repeal bill.

Sept. 24, 1931   American Legion votes for a referendum on National Prohibition by a vote of 1008 to 394.

Oct. 17, 1931   Al Capone sentenced.

1932

Jan.   8, 1932   Hearings begin before Senate Committee on Manufacturers, 72nd Congress, On Amendment of Prohibition Act. (The Bingham Beer Resolution, rider to the Home Loan Bank bill.)

Jan. 13–19, 1932 Hearings before House Committee on the Judiciary, 72nd Congress, Mellon Impeachment Proceedings.

Feb.   5, 1932   Senate confirms Hon. A. W. Mellon as Ambassador to Great Britain.

Feb.   9, 1932   Hearings before the Committee of the District of Columbia, 72nd Congress "Supplementing the National Prohibition Act in the District of Columbia."

Mar. 14, 1932   The Beck-Linthicum resolution defeated 227 to 187. It would have returned control to the states.

Apr. 19, 1932   Hearings before the Senate Sub-Committee on the Judiciary on Modification or Repeal of National Prohibition.

May 14, 1932   The Beer Parade in New York.

May 18, 1932   The Senate votes against the Tydings Amendment to the Revenue Bill which would have legalized 4% beer by volume. Vote 61 to 24.

May 23, 1932   Hull-O'Connor bill legalizing 2.75% beer by weight defeated in the House, 228 to 169.

June 6, 1932   John D. Rockefeller, Jr.'s anti-Prohibition letter to President N. M. Butler.

July   2, 1932   Governor F. D. Roosevelt announces to the Democratic National Convention in Chicago the "doom" of the 18th Amendment.

Aug. 11, 1932   Mr. Hoover in his acceptance speech abandons National Prohibition.

Nov. 8, 1932   Twelve states in one or another way vote for Repeal.

Dec.   5, 1932   Garner Resolution for Repeal introduced. Defeated 272 to 144.

Dec.   7–14, 1932   Hearings before House Com. on Ways and Means, 72nd Congress on Modification of the Volstead Act.

Dec. 23, 1932   House passes Collier 3.2% beer bill, 230 to 165.

Dec. 23, 1932   Senate votes 48 to 23 against motion to take up Bingham Beer Resolution.

1933

Feb. 20, 1933   Congress submits 21st Amendment to Conventions of States.

Mar. 3, 1933   Legislation in Congress regarding wiretapping and payment of informers.

Mar. 13, 1933   President Roosevelt's message advocating immediate modification of the Volstead Act to allow the sale of beer.

Mar. 20, 1933   Congress legalizes manufacture and sale of 3.2% beer by weight (the Cullen bill). In effect April 7.

Mar. 31, 1933   President Roosevelt signs Copeland-Celler Medicinal Liquor Bill. Effective April 7, 1933.

Apr. 5, 1933   Congress passes legislation for sale of 3.2% beer in the District of Columbia.

Apr. 10, 1933   Michigan holds first convention for ratification of 21st Amendment.

June 16, 1933   Congress passes the N. I. R. A. Act under which the Federal Control Administration was established Nov. 22, 1933, to regulate liquor traffic after Repeal.

Dec.   5, 1933   Utah Convention approved the 21st Amendment making Repeal of the 18th Amendment effective.

Dec. 11, 1933   Hearings before the Ways and Means Committee of the 73rd Congress on Tax on Intoxicating Liquor.

1934

Jan.   8, 1934   National Municipal League makes public draft of a bill to establish state control in 48 states.

Jan. 11, 1934   Liquor Taxing Act of 1934. This also repealed the advertising clause of the Reed Amendment of 1917.

Mar. 2, 1934   Repeal of the Federal Prohibition laws in Porto Rico and the Virgin Islands: on March 26 in Hawaii: April 12 in Alaska.

May 13, 1934   Governor Lehman signs Klenfeld bill legalizing bars in New York.

June 18, 1934   Legislation passed to protect the revenue by requiring information concerning the disposition of substances used in the manufacture of distilled spirits.

1935

Feb. 26, 1935   Alabama voted against Repeal.

May 15, 1935   Georgia votes against Repeal but allows sale of beer.

May   1935   North Carolina made provision for state liquor stores.

May   1935   Hearings before the Committee on Ways and Means, 74th Congress, on Administration of Liquor Tax Laws.

June   1935   Hearings before the Committee on Ways and Means, 74th Congress on Federal Alcohol Control Administration.

Aug. 5, 1935   Anti-smuggling Act empowering the President to establish customs enforcement areas not more than 50 nautical miles outward from the outer limits of customs waters.

Aug. 24, 1935   Texas repeals constitutional Prohibition.

Aug. 29, 1935   Federal Alcohol Administration Act passed.

Aug. 30, 1935   The Revenue Act of 1935 repealed the special $1,000 excise tax first imposed by the Revenue Act of 1918 upon persons manufacturing or selling liquors in states in violation of state or local law.

Sept. 16, 1935   F. C. Hoyt succeeds J. H. Choate, Jr., as F. A. C. Administrator.

Nov. 5, 1935   Kentucky repeals Constitutional Prohibition.

1936

June 23, 1936   Congress enacted the Liquor Enforcement Act of 1936 to enforce the 21st Amendment. Effective July 25, 1936. This also repealed the Reed Bone-Dry Amendment.

June 26, 1936   Act to insure collection of Revenue and to amend Federal Alcohol Administration Act.

Nov. 3, 1936   Initiative measure for local option defeated in California. North Dakota repeals Prohibition by 19,266 majority. Oklahoma retains Prohibition by a majority of 123,798.

Nov. 9, 1936   U. S. Supreme Court in case of State Board of Equalization of California v. Young's Market Co. upheld the right of the States to fix the conditions and limitations upon which intoxicating liquors may be imported or transported into a State.

INDEX

CHAPTER IX

THE DEBACLE

The House of Representatives is, even in the best of times, hardly a pleasant place to a patriot. The hall is dark; the heavy coffered ceiling gives one a feeling of claustrophobia. The galleries are filled with the riff-raff of Washington. On the right of the Speaker is a portrait of Washington. In his day he put down a whisky rebellion with a strong arm. The semicircle of politicians facing this portrait capitulated to our modern whisky rebellion in a way to stir his indignant soul. The political editor of the *Baltimore Sun,* Mr. Kent, has said of this 73rd (Repeal) Congress: "It touched the lowest level in ability, integrity, and intelligence of any Congress in our memory" (1).

LIQUOR'S HOUSE OF RUBBER-STAMPATIVES

"Each month's delay means a loss of $80,000,000 revenue," shouted Mr. Celler, a Jewish representative from Brooklyn in the House discussions of Dec. 5th, 1932 (2). Directly after Repeal Mr. Celler appeared, with bootlegger Sam Ungerleider, on the roster of the National Organization of the Wine and Liquor Industry (3) (A). "Shall a miserable financier," cried Chatham, speaking on the Stamp Act, "come with the boast that he can fetch a peppercorn into the exchequer by the loss of millions to the nation?" Mr. Celler's Russian Jewish colleague, Mr. Dickstein, was in equal haste. Mr. Rainey, the Democratic floor-leader, had moved suspension of rules for a naked Repeal resolution: "The 18th Article of Amendment is hereby repealed." Forty minutes were to be allowed for debate. Had not both Republican and Democratic platforms said that the Repeal Amendment should be "immediately" proposed and "promptly" submitted? They did not wait even to notify the President that the House was in session. Mr. Sumners of Texas suggested a three hours debate instead of forty minutes.

"I object," said Mr. Dickstein. "I object," said Mr. Dick-

shops, and 119 night-clubs. Yet in 1929 the Police Commissioner of New York stated that there were 32,000 open saloons in New York City.

I.   The sponsors of this parade included Mr. Phelps Phelps of the A. A. P. A., President Ryan of the Central Trades and Labor Council, and E. E. Spofford, Nat'l Commander of the American Legion. The old combination! Also Swope of the *World* and Mrs. W. R. Hearst.

J.   Brewer Andrae: "A compilation of the population of the U. S. of foreign extraction or origin by state or cities with their actual voting strength and the location of the foreign language newspapers has been prepared and is ready to be placed in the hands of campaign managers whenever elections may be called. . . . The foreign vote is eight millions, more than a third of the voting strength of the country. *It is more susceptible to the guidance of leaders than any other element in the country*" (Overman Report, pp. 1253 and 1187).

The rector of Trinity Church, facing Wall Street, Dr. Stetson, was out touting for "Beer and Taxation." While young society women in New York were organized into The Service League "to fight Prohibition," (NYT, Oct. 10, 1931, p. 3) working girls under the lead of the A. F. L. were mobilized into the "Working Girls Ass'n Against Prohibition" (NYT, July 25, 1932, p. 17).

K.   Mrs. Raymond Robins: "No one can live in such a community as the old 17th Ward in Chicago without learning to know the hideousness of the whisky story. If there is drinking in the tenement home the wife and mother knows its terror, for there is no escape from those four narrow walls. I think with reverence of that great army of silent women whose courage never failed them amid suffering of which they never spake. . . . Daily the tragedy of the dance halls entered the homes. The liquor interests steadily moved towards political control of every organized effort for pleasure. There are no words with which to speak with adequate censure of these forces of evil which never hesitated to traffic in the lives and souls of the boys and girls" ("Law vs. Lawlessness," pp. 47–48).

L.   Mr. Roosevelt in "On Our Way," p. 262, says: ". . . a very warm friendship and a very high respect for Mayor Cermak's ability, friendship, and loyalty to his friends, would have made his loss a heavy one to me under any circumstances."